# GLOBALISMS

# GLOBALIZATION

*Series Editors*
**Manfred B. Steger**
*Royal Melbourne Institute of Technology and University of Hawai'i–Manoa*
and
**Terrell Carver**
*University of Bristol*

"Globalization" has become *the* buzzword of our time. But what does it mean? Rather than forcing a complicated social phenomenon into a single analytical framework, this series seeks to present globalization as a multidimensional process constituted by complex, often contradictory interactions of global, regional, and local aspects of social life. Since conventional disciplinary borders and lines of demarcation are losing their old rationales in a globalizing world, authors in this series apply an interdisciplinary framework to the study of globalization. In short, the main purpose and objective of this series is to support subject-specific inquiries into the dynamics and effects of contemporary globalization and its varying impacts across, between, and within societies.

*Globalization and War*
Tarak Barkawi

*Globalization and Human Security*
Paul Battersby and Joseph Siracusa

*Globalization and American Popular Culture*
Lane Crothers

*Globalization and Militarism*
Cynthia Enloe

*Globalization and Law*
Adam Gearey

*Globalization and Feminist Activism*
Mary E. Hawkesworth

*Globalization and Postcolonialism*
Sankaran Krishna

*Globalization and Social Movements*
Valentine Moghadam

*Globalization and Terrorism*
Jamal R. Nassar

*Globalization and Culture*
Jan Nederveen Pieterse

*Globalization and International Political Economy*
Mark Rupert and M. Scott Solomon

*Globalisms, Third Edition*
Manfred B. Steger

*Rethinking Globalism*
Edited by Manfred B. Steger

*Globalization and Labor*
Dimitris Stevis and Terry Boswell

*Globaloney*
Michael Veseth

 Supported by the Globalization Research Center at the University of Hawai'i, Mānoa

# GLOBALISMS

## THE GREAT IDEOLOGICAL STRUGGLE
## OF THE TWENTY-FIRST CENTURY

## THIRD EDITION

## MANFRED B. STEGER

ROWMAN & LITTLEFIELD PUBLISHERS, INC.
*Lanham • Boulder • New York • Toronto • Plymouth, UK*

ROWMAN & LITTLEFIELD PUBLISHERS, INC.

Published in the United States of America
by Rowman & Littlefield Publishers, Inc.
A wholly owned subsidiary of The Rowman & Littlefield Publishing Group, Inc.
4501 Forbes Boulevard, Suite 200, Lanham, Maryland 20706
www.rowmanlittlefield.com

Estover Road, Plymouth PL6 7PY, United Kingdom

British Library Cataloguing in Publication Information Available

Library of Congress Cataloging-in-Publication Data

Steger, Manfred B., 1961–
    Globalisms : the great ideological struggle of the twenty-first century / Manfred B.
Steger.—3rd ed.
        p.   cm.—(Globalization)
    Rev. ed. of: Globalism. 2nd ed. c2005.
    Includes bibliographical references and index.
    ISBN-13: 978-0-7425-5587-7 (pbk. : alk. paper)
    ISBN-10: 0-7425-5587-9 (pbk. : alk. paper)
    ISBN-13: 978-0-7425-5791-8 (electronic)
    ISBN-10: 0-7425-5791-X (electronic)
    1. Globalization.   I. Steger, Manfred B., 1961—Globalism.   II. Title.
HF1379.S738 2009
303.48'2—dc22                                                  2008036421

Printed in the United States of America

∞ ™ The paper used in this publication meets the minimum requirements of
American National Standard for Information Sciences—Permanence of Paper for
Printed Library Materials, ANSI/NISO Z39.48-1992.

integration of markets: rising living standards, reduction of global poverty, economic efficiency, individual freedom and democracy, and unprecedented technological progress.[18] Ideally, the state should only provide the legal framework for contracts, defense, and law and order. Public-policy initiatives should be confined to those measures that liberate the economy from social constraints: privatization of public enterprises, deregulation instead of state control, liberalization of trade and industry, massive tax cuts, strict control of organized labor, and the reduction of public expenditures. Other models of economic organization were discredited as being "protectionist" or "socialist." Indeed, the stunning collapse of Soviet-style communism in 1989–1991 proved to be a particularly useful trump card in the rhetorical arsenal of these market globalists.

Seeking to enshrine their neoliberal paradigm as the self-evident and universal order of our global era, they translated into ideological claims an overarching global rather than national imaginary. As I have pointed out elsewhere, by "global imaginary" I mean people's deep-seated, almost pre-reflexive consciousness of belonging to a community that transcends national boundaries.[19] Articulating this global imaginary as concrete political programs and agendas, market globalists in the 1990s suggested that all peoples and states were equally subject to the logic of globalization, which was, in the long run, beneficial and inevitable, and that societies had no choice but to adapt to this world-shaping force.[20] This interpretation of globalization as driven by the irresistible forces of the market and technology was frequently expressed in quasi-religious language that bestowed almost divine wisdom on the market.[21]

## SELLING "GLOBALIZATION" IN THE 1990s

Let us take a concrete example to illustrate the selling of market globalism in the 1990s. In 2000, the American magazine *BusinessWeek* featured a cover story on globalization that contained the following statement: "For nearly a decade, political and business leaders have struggled to persuade the American public of the virtues of globalization." Citing the results of a national poll on globalization conducted in April 2000, the article goes on to report that most Americans were of two minds on the subject. On the one hand, about 65 percent of the respondents thought that globalization was a "good thing" for consumers and businesses in both the United States and the rest of the world. On the other hand, they were afraid that globalization might lead to a significant loss of American jobs. In addition, nearly 70 percent of those polled believed that free-trade agreements with low-wage countries were responsible for driving down wages in the United States. The article ends on a rather combative note by issuing a stern warning to American politicians and business leaders not to be "caught off guard" by the arguments of "antiglobalist" forces. In order to assuage people's increasing anxiety on the subject, American "decision makers" ought to be more effective in highlighting the benefits of globalization. After all, the article concludes, the persistence of public fears over globalization might result in a significant backlash, jeopardizing the health of the international economy and "the cause of free trade."[22]

This cover story contained two important pieces of information with regard to the ideological dimensions of globalization. First, there was the author's open admission that political and business leaders were actively engaged in selling their preferred market version of globalization to the public. In fact, he saw the construction of arguments and images that portray globalization in a positive light as an indispensable tool for the realization of a global order based on free-market principles. No doubt, such favorable visions of globalization pervaded public opinion and political choices at the time. Since language and ideas mattered in the ongoing struggle to persuade the global public of the virtues of globalization, neoliberal decision makers had to become expert designers of an attractive ideological container for their market-friendly political agenda. Given that the exchange of commodities constitutes the core activity of all market societies, the discourse on globalization itself turned into an extremely important commodity destined for public consumption.

Second, the polling data presented in the *BusinessWeek* cover story revealed the existence of a remarkable cognitive dissonance between the American people's normative orientation toward globalization and their personal experiences in the globalizing world. How else can one explain that a sizable majority of respondents were afraid of the negative economic impact of globalization on their lives while at the same time deeming globalization to be a "good thing"? One obvious answer is ideology. Promarket visions of globalization shaped a large part of public opinion, even if people's daily experiences reflected a less favorable picture. For example, the same *BusinessWeek* article also told the harrowing story of a factory worker employed by the Goodyear Tire & Rubber Company in Gadsden, Alabama. Having lost his job after Goodyear shifted most of its tire production to low-wage jobs in Mexico and Brazil, the worker had been only recently rehired by the same company for much less money. Still, the article concluded this disturbing story by reaffirming the overall positive impact of economic globalization: "Polls have shown for years that a solid majority of Americans believe that open borders and free trade are good for the economy."[23]

*BusinessWeek* is only one among dozens of magazines, journals, newspapers, and electronic media that, over two decades, have been feeding their global audiences a steady diet of market-globalist claims serving a concrete political purpose. They present globalization in such a way as to advance the material and ideal interests of those groups in society who benefit the most from the liberalization of the economy, the privatization of ownership, a minimal regulatory role for government, efficient returns on capital, and the devolution of power to the private sector. Like all ideologists, market globalists engage continuously in acts of simplification, distortion, legitimation, and integration in order to cultivate in the public mind the conviction that the globalization of markets is a "good thing." When people accept the claims of market globalism, they simultaneously accept as authority large parts of the comprehensive political, economic, and intellectual framework of neoliberalism. Thus, the ideological reach of market globalism goes far beyond the task of providing the public with a narrow explanation of the meaning of globalization. Most importantly, it is a compelling story that sells an overarching worldview, thereby creating collective meanings and shaping personal and collective identities.

## THE ORIGINS OF THE GREAT IDEOLOGICAL STRUGGLE OF THE TWENTY-FIRST CENTURY

By the end of the 1990s, market globalism had managed to spread to all parts of the world by employing its dominant codes and hegemonic meanings through its powerful arsenal of ideological representation, co-option of local elites, political coercion, and economic power.[24] Despite their formidable efforts, however, the dominant vision of neoliberal globalization became increasingly tarred by the reality of growing social inequalities and rising cultural tensions. "Global justice" networks sprang up, and justice-globalist demonstrations erupted in Seattle, Washington, D.C., Davos, Salzburg, Bangkok, Melbourne, Prague, Quebec City, Gothenburg, and many other cities around the world. The massive protests at the August 2001 G-8 Summit in Genoa, Italy, were the most powerful sign yet that the reigning ideology had come under severe attack from people around the world who rejected the neoliberal dream of a single global economy driven by unimpeded market forces and anchored in consumerist culture. Increasingly viewing globalization as the Americanization of the world order—the global imposition of a particular economic and cultural model in the name of universality—global justice movements had intensified their counteroffensive.

As we will discuss in chapter 3 in more detail, the reaction from market globalists was swift and unambiguous in its shift from what political scientist Joseph Nye calls "soft power"—the capacity to shape opinion, interests, and identities in favor of the globalist model—to "hard power"—the massive use of military and economic force to compel compliance.[25] Claiming to act in defense of democracy and freedom, market globalists began to rely more heavily on the coercive powers of the state to keep dissidents in check. Mainstream media fueled public fears by pushing the stereotype of chaotic, Molotov cocktail–throwing "antiglobalizers" on ill-informed television audiences around the world. These attempts to stabilize the neoliberal model by means of generating fear were increasingly reflected in public discourse. Globalizing markets were now portrayed as requiring ample protection against irrational forces. In other words, the allegedly "inevitable" evolution of the market-globalist project suddenly needed to be helped along by strong law enforcement measures and military mechanisms that would "beat back" the "enemies of democracy and the free market."

By the time al Qaeda launched its devastating attacks on the world's most recognized symbols of a U.S.-dominated global economy and military power, the link between political violence and justice globalism was already so firmly anchored in the public mind that a number of commentators in the global North immediately named "radical elements in the antiglobalization crowd" as prime suspects. When it became clear that a jihadist-globalist network led by Osama bin Laden and Ayman al-Zawahiri was behind the attacks, the negative stereotype of the chaotic justice globalist was joined by that of the monstrous Islamist terrorist organized in clandestine cells around the world. As market globalism clashed head-on with jihadist globalism, dominant power elites turned the security crisis afflicting their paradigm into a golden opportunity for extending their hegemony on new terms. As we shall discuss in chapter 3, the remarkable merger of neoliberal market language and a neoconservative security agenda marked the birth of imperial globalism. Countries are told in no uncertain terms to stand with the leader of market globalism—the United States of America—on the side of "civilization" against the forces of "terrorism" or face the consequences of their bad choice. To be "civilized" means not only to embrace American-style democracy and free markets but also to refrain from criticizing American foreign policy. Countries like France, Germany, and Russia, which opposed the Iraq War, paid a high price for their insubordination. Incessantly subjected to ridicule and slander in the American-dominated global media, they found themselves cut out of lucrative contracts for rebuilding Iraq by a vengeful Bush administration.

Initially confined to Afghanistan and Iraq, the Global War on Terror soon expanded to other parts of the world, like Somalia and Indonesia. It opened up the terrifying prospect of a war without end, eerily reminiscent of George Orwell's nightmare vision of a world based on "doublethink" and "newspeak": Oceania has always been at war with either Eurasia or Eastasia—depending on the Party's whims. As the first decade of the twenty-first century draws to a close, it appears that the new century has, indeed, turned into a battlefield of clashing ideologies over the meaning and direction of globalization. Market globalism and its two main challengers appear to be locked in a protracted ideological struggle.

## CONCLUDING REMARKS

This study follows a suggestion made by several prominent social researchers who have called for a more extensive analysis of the production and global circulation of globalist ideologies.[26] This necessary exploration can be facilitated by the analytic distinction between *globalization*—a set of social processes of increasing interdependence defined and described by various commentators in different, often contradictory ways, and *globalisms*—political ideologies like market globalism, justice globalism, and jihadist globalism that endow globalization with their preferred norms, values, and meanings.[27] I do not mean to suggest, however, that globalism (the rhetorical package) exists in isolation from globalization (the material process). Ideologies are never idle constructs without foundations in material phenomena. Social institutions, concrete political and economic processes, and the selective ideological interpretation of these processes form an interconnected whole. I employ the distinction between globalization and globalism because I do not want to lose sight of the considerable role played by ideas, beliefs, language, and symbols in shaping the conditions of the social world.

Following Max Weber's suggestion to broaden Karl Marx's materialist account of social formation, I refuse to bestow on economic "materiality" the unquestioned causal primacy it has received from the pens of orthodox Marxists. Rather, I suggest that a society and an epoch must be understood as being as much the product of ideas as the outcome of material forces. This book's focus on the ideational and normative dimensions of globalization is important for a variety of reasons. Although there has been a "cultural turn" in the fledgling transdisciplinary field of global studies, most academic treatments of globalization still tend to concentrate on its economic aspects. While helpful in explaining the intricacies of international trade policy, global financial markets, and worldwide flows of goods, services, and labor as well as transnational corporations, offshore financial centers, foreign direct investment, and the new international economic organizations, such narrow accounts leave the reader with the fallacious impression that globalization is primarily an economic phenomenon.

To be sure, the discussion of economic matters must be a significant part of any comprehensive account of globalization, but the latter should not be conflated with the former. It is equally necessary to explore the role of ideas in these processes. Conventional books on globalization often take one aspect of global dissemination, such as trade or investment, and talk about the ways in which the phenomenon is causing changes elsewhere. That globalization is a material process is taken for granted. This book, however, suggests that globalization is also a linguistic and ideological practice—a persuasive story embedded in a neoliberal political project that most of us are being asked to embrace. For this reason, my analysis of globalism adopts a less conventional approach, one that critically analyzes the ideological dynamics of globalization unfolding in the 1990s (market globalism versus justice globalism) and after 9/11 (imperial globalism versus jihadist globalism and justice globalism).

My focus on the ideas and metaphors behind these three main globalisms allows me to explore the discursive strategies and historical context of social forces as they attempted to spin their preferred stories of globalization.[28] It is my intention to spell out clearly and with as many instructive examples as possible 1) how various claims and assumptions of globalists legitimize, reinforce, and defend particular political agendas with global implications; 2) how these ideologies have clashed with each other; and 3) how their core ideological claims have been modified as a result of these confrontations. Situating itself squarely within the intellectual tradition of critical theory, this book seeks to provide readers with an understanding of how dominant beliefs about globalization fashion their realities and to show that these beliefs can be changed. Pointing to concrete instances of human suffering and environmental degradation and showing how particular social forces justify these developments, critical theorists of globalization have consistently challenged the claims of market globalism and jihadist globalism.[29] Although critical theorists of globalization like this author are sympathetic to the ideological posture of justice globalism, they have not been reluctant to offer constructive criticisms of the existing shortcomings of this ideology.[30] Indeed, new perspectives on globalization have proliferated in the past decade as a result of critical intellectual interventions. Rather than heralding the end of ideology, the conflicting articulations of the global imaginary remind us that different forms of globality are possible. History has no predetermined outcomes or premature endings.

# Chapter 2

# The Academic Debate over Globalization

## THE BLIND SCHOLARS AND THE ELEPHANT

The ancient Buddhist parable of six blind scholars and their encounter with an elephant illustrates the nature of the ongoing academic debate on globalization. Since the blind scholars did not know what the elephant looked like and had never even heard its name, they resolved to obtain a mental picture and thus the knowledge they desired by touching the animal. Feeling its trunk, one blind man argued that the elephant was like a lively snake. Another man, rubbing along its enormous leg, likened the animal to a rough column of massive proportions. The third person took hold of its tail and insisted that the elephant resembled a large, flexible brush. The fourth man felt its sharp tusks and declared it to be like a great spear. The fifth man examined its waving ear and was convinced that the animal was some sort of fan. Occupying the space between the elephant's front and hind legs, the sixth blind scholar groped in vain for a part of the elephant. Consequently, he accused his colleagues of making up fantastic stories about nonexistent things, asserting that there were no such beasts as "elephants" at all. Each of the six blind scholars held firmly to his story of what he knew an elephant to be. Since their scholarly reputation was riding on the veracity of their respective findings, the blind men eventually ended up arguing and fighting about which story contained the correct definition of the elephant. As a result, their entire community was riven asunder. Suspicion and general distrust became the order of the day.[1]

The parable of the blind scholars and the elephant contains many valuable lessons. First, one might conclude that reality is too complex to be fully grasped by imperfect human beings. Second, although each observer correctly identified one aspect of reality, the collective mistake of the blind men lay in their attempts to reduce the entire phenomenon to their own partial experience. Third, the maintenance of communal peace and harmony might be worth much more than the individual sense of superiority that comes with stubbornly clinging to one's—often one-sided—understanding of the world. Fourth, it would be wise for the blind scholars to return to the elephant and exchange their positions to better appreciate the whole of the elephant as well as the previous insight of each man.

Representing a contemporary version of this ancient parable, the debate over globalization has been taking place over the past two decades in two separate but related arenas. One battle has been fought mostly within the narrow walls of academia, while the other has been unfolding in the popular arena of public discourse. Although there are some common themes and overlapping observations, the academic debate differs from the more general discussion in that its participants tend to focus on the analytical rather than the normative or ideological dimension of globalization. Certainly, there has been an explosion in the number of books and articles on the subject published by both academic and trade outlets. Consulting the electronic database Factiva, which holds some 8,000 newspapers, magazines, and reports worldwide, the global studies scholar Nayan Chanda showed that the number of items mentioning globalization grew from a mere two in 1981 to a high of 57,235 in 2001. Since then, it has stabilized at an annual average of about 45,000.[2]

Many of the principal participants in the academic debate reside and teach in the wealthy countries of the Northern Hemisphere, particularly the United States and the United Kingdom. Their disproportionate intellectual influence reflects not only existing power relations in the world but also the global dominance of Anglo-American ideas. Although they share a common intellectual framework, these scholars hold radically different views regarding the definition of globalization and its scale, chronology, impact, and policy outcomes. Part of the reason why there is so much disagreement has to do with the fact that globalization itself is a fragmented, incomplete, uneven, and contradictory set of social processes. James N. Rosenau, for example, has defined globalization in terms of what he calls "fragmegrative dynamics" to "underscore the contradictions, ambiguities, complexities, and uncertainties that have replaced the regularities of prior epochs."[3]

As the parable of the blind scholars and the elephant suggests, academics often respond to the analytical challenge by trying to take conceptual possession of globalization—as though it were something "out there" to be captured by the "correct" analytical framework. Indeed, as Stephen J. Rosow points out, many researchers approach globalization as if they were dealing with a process or an object without a meaning of its own prior to its constitution as a conceptual "territory."[4] Moreover, since it falls outside the boundaries of established academic disciplines, the study of globalization has invited armies of social scientists, scholars in the humanities, and even natural scientists to leave their mark on an intellectual terra incognita.

As a result, various scholars have invoked the concept of globalization to describe a variety of changing economic, political, and cultural processes that are alleged to have accelerated since the 1970s. No generally accepted definition of globalization has emerged, except for such broad descriptions as "increasing global interconnectedness," "the rapid intensification of worldwide social relations," "the compression of time and space," "distant proximities," "a complex range of processes, driven by a mixture of political and economic influences," and "the swift and relatively unimpeded flow of capital, people, and ideas across national borders."[5] A number of researchers object to those characterizations, some going so far as to deny the existence of globalization altogether. And yet the past few years have also seen some emerging areas of consensus as well as the rise of the new transdisciplinary field of "global studies."

It is the purpose of this chapter to introduce the reader to the principal academic approaches to the subject proposed by leading scholars during the past ten to fifteen years. These range from the suggestion that globalization is little more than "globaloney" to interpretations of globalization as an economic, political, or cultural process. Although such examinations are necessary for gaining a better understanding of globalization, I argue that these social-scientific approaches to the subject ought to be complemented by interpretive explorations of the ideational and normative dimensions of globalization.

## GLOBALIZATION IS "GLOBALONEY"

A small number of scholars contend that existing accounts of globalization are incorrect, imprecise, or exaggerated. They note that just about everything that can be linked to some transnational process is cited as evidence for globalization and its growing influence. Hence, they suspect that such general observations often amount to little more than "globaloney."[6] The arguments of these globalization critics fall into three broad categories. Representatives of the first group dispute the usefulness of globalization as a sufficiently precise analytical concept. Members of the second group point to the limited nature of globalizing processes, emphasizing that the world is not nearly as integrated as many globalization proponents believe. In their view, the term "globalization" does not constitute an accurate label for the actual state of affairs. The third group of critics disputes the novelty of the process while acknowledging the existence of moderate globalizing tendencies. They argue that those who refer to globalization as a recent process miss the bigger picture and fall prey to their narrow historical framework. Let us examine the respective arguments of these three groups in more detail.

### REJECTIONISTS

Scholars who dismiss the utility of globalization as an analytical concept typically advance their arguments from within a larger criticism of similarly vague words employed in academic discourse. Besides globalization, another often-cited example for such analytically impoverished concepts is the complex and ambiguous phenomenon of nationalism. Craig Calhoun, for example, argues that nationalism and its corollary terms "have proved notoriously hard concepts to define" because "nationalisms are extremely varied phenomena," and "any definition will legitimate some claims and delegitimate others."[7] Writing in the same critical vein, Susan Strange considers globalization a prime example of such a vacuous term, suggesting that it has been used in academic discourse to refer to "anything from the Internet to a hamburger."[8] Similarly, Linda Weiss objects to the term as "a big idea resting on slim foundations."[9]

Scholarly suggestions for improvement point in two different directions. The first is to challenge the academic community to provide additional examples of how the term "globalization" obscures more than it enlightens. Such empirically based accounts would serve as a warning to extreme globalization proponents. Ultimately, the task of more careful researchers should be to break the concept of globalization into smaller, more manageable parts that contain a higher analytical value because they can be more easily associated with empirical processes. This rationale underlies Robert Holton's suggestion to abandon all general theoretical analyses in favor of middle-range approaches that seek to provide specific explanations of particulars.[10]

The second avenue for improvement involves my own suggestion to complement the social-scientific enterprise of exploring globalization as an objective process with more interpretive studies of the ideological project of globalism. Following this argument, the central task for scholars working in the emerging field of globalization studies would be to identify and evaluate the ideological maneuvers of prominent proponents and opponents who have filled the term with values and meanings that bolster their respective political agendas.

## SKEPTICS

The second group emphasizes the limited nature of current globalizing processes. This perspective is perhaps best reflected in the writings of Robert Wade and Paul Hirst and Graham Thompson.[11] In their detailed historical analysis of economic globalization, Hirst and Thompson claim that the world economy is not a truly global phenomenon but one centered on Europe, eastern Asia, and North America. The authors emphasize that the majority of economic activity around the world still remains primarily national in origin and scope. Presenting recent data on trade, foreign direct investment, and financial flows, the authors warn against drawing global conclusions from increased levels of economic interaction in advanced industrial countries. Hirst and Thompson advance an argument against the existence of economic globalization based on empirical data in order to attack the general misuse of the concept. Without a truly global economic system, they insist, there can be no such thing as globalization: "as we proceeded [with our economic research] our skepticism deepened until we became convinced that globalization, as conceived by the more extreme globalizers, is largely a myth."[12]

Buried under an avalanche of relevant data, one can nonetheless detect a critical-normative message in the Hirst–Thompson thesis: it is to show that exaggerated accounts of an "iron logic of economic globalization" tend to produce disempowering political effects. For example, the authors convincingly demonstrate that certain political forces have used the thesis of economic globalization to propose national economic deregulation and the reduction of welfare programs. The implementation of such policies stands to benefit neoliberal interests.

But there also remain a number of problems with the Hirst–Thompson thesis. For example, as several critics have pointed out, the authors set overly high standards for the economy in order to be counted as "fully globalized."[13] Moreover, their efforts to construct an abstract model of a perfectly globalized economy unnecessarily polarizes the topic by pressuring the reader to either completely embrace or entirely reject the concept of globalization. Perhaps the most serious shortcoming of the Hirst–Thompson thesis lies in its attempt to counteract neoliberal economic determinism with a good dose of Marxist economic determinism. Their argument implicitly assumes that globalization is primarily an economic phenomenon. As a result, they portray all other dimensions of globalization—culture, politics, and ideology—as reflections of deeper economic processes. While paying lip service to the multidimensional character of globalization, their own analysis ignores the logical implications of this assertion. After all, if globalization is truly a complex, multilevel phenomenon, then economic relations constitute only one among many globalizing tendencies. It would therefore be entirely possible to argue for the significance of globalization even if it can be shown that increased transnational economic activity appears to be limited to advanced industrial countries.

## MODIFIERS

The third and final group of globalization critics disputes the novelty of the process, implying that the label "globalization" has often been applied in a historically imprecise manner. Robert Gilpin, for example, confirms the existence of globalizing tendencies, but he also insists that many important aspects of globalization are not novel developments. Citing relevant data collected by the prominent American economist Paul Krugman, Gilpin notes that the world economy in the late 1990s appeared to be even less integrated in a number of important respects than it was prior to the outbreak of World War I. Even if one were to accept the most optimistic assessment of the actual volume of transnational economic activity, the most one could say is that the postwar international economy has simply restored globalization to approximately the same level that existed in 1913. Gilpin also points to two additional factors that seem to support his position: the globalization of labor was actually much greater prior to World War I and international migration declined considerably after 1918. Hence,

Gilpin warns his readers against accepting the arguments of "hyper-global-izers."[14]

Similar criticisms come from the proponents of world-system theory. Pioneered by neo-Marxist scholars such as Immanuel Wallerstein and Andre Gunder Frank, world-system theorists argue that the modern capitalist economy in which we live today has been global since its inception five centuries ago.[15] Driven by the exploitative logic of capital accumulation, the capitalist world system has created global inequalities based on the domination of modernizing Western "core" countries over non-Western "peripheral" areas. These forms of exploitation were inscribed in nineteenth-century systems of colonialism and imperialism and have persisted in the twentieth century in different forms. World-system theorists reject, therefore, the use of the term "globalization" as referring exclusively to relatively recent phenomena. Instead, they emphasize that globalizing tendencies have been proceeding along the continuum of modernization for a long time.

The greatest virtue of the world-system critique of globalization lies in its historical sensitivity. Any general discussion of globalization should include the caution that cross-regional transfers of resources, technology, and culture did not start only in the past few decades. Indeed, the origins of globalizing tendencies can be traced back to the political and cultural interactions that sustained the ancient empires of Persia, China, and Rome. On the downside, however, a world-system approach to globalization suffers from the same weaknesses as the Marxist economic-determinist view pointed out previously in my discussion of the Hirst–Thompson thesis. Wallerstein leaves little doubt that he considers global integration to be a process driven largely by economic forces whose essence can be captured by economistic analytical models. Accordingly, he assigns to culture and ideology merely a subordinate role as "idea systems" dependent on the "real" movements of the capitalist world economy.[16]

However, more recent studies produced by world-system scholars acknowledge that the pace of globalization has significantly quickened in the last few decades of the twentieth century.[17] Ash Amin, for example, has suggested that much of the criticism of globalization as a new phenomenon has been based on quantitative analyses of trade and output that neglect the qualitative shift in social and political relations. This qualitative difference in the globalizing process, he argues, has resulted in the world capitalist system's new configuration as a complex network of international corporations, banks, and financial flows. Hence, these global developments may indeed warrant a new label.[18] In their efforts to gauge the nature of this qualitative difference, world-system theorists like Barry K. Gills have begun to focus more closely on the interaction between dominant-class interests and cultural transnational practices.[19] In so doing, they have begun to raise important normative questions, suggesting that the elements of the "ideological superstructure"—politics, ideas, values, and beliefs—may, at times, neutralize or supersede economic forces. Leslie Sklair, for example, highlights the importance of what he calls "the culture-ideology of global consumerism."[20]

Overall, then, all three groups of globalization critics make an important contribution to the academic debate on the subject. Their insistence on a more careful and precise usage of the term forces the participants in the debate to hone their analytical skills. Moreover, their intervention serves as an important reminder that some aspects of globalization may neither constitute new developments nor reach to all corners of the earth. However, by focusing too narrowly on abstract issues of terminology, the globalization critics tend to dismiss too easily the significance and extent of today's globalizing tendencies. Finally, the representatives of these three groups show a clear inclination to conceptualize globalization mostly along economic lines, thereby often losing sight of its multidimensional character.

## GLOBALIZATION IS AN ECONOMIC PROCESS

The widespread scholarly emphasis on the economic dimension of globalization derives partly from its historical development as a subject of academic study.[21] Some of the earliest writings on the topic explore in much detail how the evolution of international markets and corporations led to an intensified form of global interdependence. These studies point to the growth of international institutions such as the European Union, the North American Free Trade Association, and other regional trading blocs.[22] Economic accounts of globalization convey the notion that the essence of the phenomenon involves "the increasing linkage of national economies through trade, financial flows, and foreign direct investment . . . by multinational firms."[23] Thus, expanding economic activity is identified as both the primary aspect of globalization and the engine behind its rapid development.

Many scholars who share this economic perspective consider globalization a real phenomenon that signals an epochal transformation in world affairs. Their strong affirmation of globalization culminates in the suggestion that a quantum change in human affairs has taken place as the flow of large quantities of trade, investment, and technologies across national borders has expanded from a trickle to a flood.[24] They propose that the study of globalization be moved to the center of social-scientific research. According to their view, the central task of this research agenda should be the close examination of the evolving structure of global economic markets and their principal institutions.

Studies of economic globalization are usually embedded in thick historical narratives that trace the gradual emergence of the new postwar world economy to the 1944 Bretton Woods Conference.[25] Pressured by the United States, the major economic powers of the West decided to reverse the protectionist policies of the interwar period (1918–1939) by committing themselves to the expansion of international trade. The major achievements of the Bretton Woods Conference include the limited liberalization of trade and the establishment of binding rules on international economic activities. In addition, the Bretton Woods participants agreed on the creation of a stable currency exchange system in which the value of each country's currency was pegged to a fixed gold value of the U.S. dollar. Within these prescribed limits, individual nations were free to control the permeability of their borders, which allowed them to set their own economic agendas, including the implementation of extensive social welfare polices. Bretton Woods also set the institutional foundations for the establishment of three new international economic organizations. The International Monetary Fund was created to administer the international monetary system. The International Bank for Reconstruction and Development, or World Bank, was initially designed to provide loans for Europe's postwar reconstruction. Beginning in the 1950s, its purpose was expanded to fund various industrial projects in developing countries around the world. In 1947, the General Agreement on Tariffs and Trade (GATT) became the global trade organization charged with fashioning and enforcing multilateral trade agreements. Founded in 1995, the World Trade Organization emerged as the successor organization to GATT. As will be shown in later chapters of this book, both the philosophical purpose and the neoliberal policies of this new international body became the focal points of intense ideological controversies over the effects of economic globalization in the late 1990s.

During its operation for almost three decades, the Bretton Woods system contributed greatly to the establishment of what some observers have called the "golden age of controlled capitalism."[26] According to this interpretation, existing mechanisms of state control over international capital movements made possible full employment and the expansion of the welfare state. Rising wages and increased social services secured in the wealthy countries of the global North a temporary class compromise.

Most scholars of economic globalization trace the accelerating integrationist tendencies of the global economy to the collapse of the Bretton Woods system in the early 1970s. In response to profound changes in the world economy that undermined the economic competitiveness of U.S.-based industries, President Richard Nixon decided in 1971 to abandon the gold-based fixed-rate system. The combination of new political ideas and economic developments—high inflation, low economic growth, high unemployment, public-sector deficits, and two major oil crises within a decade—led to the spectacular election victories of conservative parties in the United States and the United Kingdom. These parties spearheaded the neoliberal movement toward the expansion of international markets (a dynamic supported by the deregulation of domestic financial systems), the gradual removal of capital controls, and an enormous increase in global financial transactions. Within the next three decades, neoliberal economic ideas and policies spread rapidly from the Anglo-American center to the rest of the world. These diffusionist dynamics were greatly facilitated by increasingly interdependent state behavior.[27] During the 1980s and 1990s, neoliberal efforts to establish a single global market were further strengthened through comprehensive trade-liberalization agreements that increased the flow of economic resources across national borders. The rising neoliberal paradigm received further legitimation with the 1989–1991 collapse of command-type economies in Eastern Europe.

Shattering the postwar economic consensus on Keynesian principles, free-market theories pioneered by Friedrich Hayek and Milton Friedman established themselves as the new economic orthodoxy, advocating the reduction of the welfare state, the downsizing of government, and the deregulation of the economy. A strong emphasis on "monetarist" measures to combat inflation led to the abandonment of the Keynesian goal of full employment in favor of establishing more "flexible" labor markets. In addition, the dramatic shift from a state-dominated to a market-dominated world was accompanied by technological innovations that lowered the costs of transportation and communication. The total value of world trade increased from $57 billion in 1947 to an astonishing 12.6 trillion in 2005.

In addition to the issue of free trade, perhaps the two most important aspects of economic globalization relate to the changing nature of the production process and the liberalization and internationalization of financial transactions. Indeed, many analysts consider the emergence of a transnational financial system the most fundamental economic feature of our time.

Its key components include the deregulation of interest rates, the removal of credit controls, and the privatization of government-owned banks and financial institutions. As sociologist Manuel Castells points out, the process of financial globalization accelerated dramatically in the late 1980s as capital and securities markets in Europe and the United States were deregulated. The liberalization of financial trading allowed for the increased mobility among different segments of the financial industry, with fewer restrictions and a global view of investment opportunities.[28]

Moreover, advances in data processing and information technology contributed to the explosive growth of tradable financial value. New satellite systems and fiber-optic cables provided the nervous system of Internet-based technologies that further accelerated the liberalization of financial transactions. As captured by the snazzy title of Microsoft founder Bill Gates's best-selling book, many people conducted "business at the speed of thought." Millions of individual investors utilized global electronic investment networks not only to place their orders but also to receive valuable information about relevant economic and political developments. In the first years of the twenty-first century, e-businesses, dot-com firms, and other virtual participants in the information-based economy traded nearly half a trillion dollars over the Web in the United States alone. However, a large part of the money involved in expanding markets had little to do with supplying capital for productive investment—putting together machines, raw materials, and employees to produce salable commodities and the like.

Most of the growth occurred in the purely money-dealing currency and securities markets that trade claims to draw profits from future production. Aided by new communication technologies, global rentiers and speculators earned spectacular incomes by taking advantage of weak financial and banking regulations in the emerging markets of developing countries. However, since these international capital flows can be reversed swiftly, they are capable of creating artificial boom-and-bust cycles that endanger the social welfare of entire regions. The 1997–1998 Southeast Asia crisis was one such economic disaster created by unregulated speculative money flows, followed by similar debacles in Russia (1998), Brazil (1999), and Argentina (2000–2003).

While the creation of international financial markets represents a crucial aspect of economic globalization, another important economic development of the past three decades also involves the changing nature of global production. Powerful firms with subsidiaries in several countries, transnational corporations (TNCs) became the primary engines of production. Their numbers skyrocketed from 7,000 in 1970 to 78,000 in 2006. Consolidating their global operations in an increasingly deregulated global labor market, enterprises like Wal-Mart, General Motors, Exxon-Mobil, Mitsubishi, and Siemens belong to the two hundred largest TNCs, which account for over half the world's industrial output. A comparison of gross domestic product (GDP) and corporate sales in 2005 reveals that forty-two of the world's one hundred largest economies were corporations; fifty-eight were countries. The availability of cheap labor, resources, and favorable production conditions in the Third World enhanced both the mobility and the profitability of TNCs. Accounting for over 70 percent of world trade, these gigantic enterprises expanded their global reach as their direct foreign investments rose approximately 15 percent annually during the 1990s.[29]

Their ability to "outsource" manufacturing jobs—that is, to cut labor costs by dispersing economic production processes into many discrete phases carried out by low-wage workers in the global South—is often cited as one of the hallmarks of economic globalization. In recent years, outsourcing has begun to threaten white-collar jobs in the global North as well. For example, transnational law firms based in the United States have outsourced low-level office work, such as the drafting of research memos and the surveying of laws under different jurisdictions, to lawyers and paralegals in India who are paid between $6 and $8 per hour—about one-third of what their American counterparts are paid.[30]

In manufacturing, the formation of such "global commodity chains" allows huge corporations like Nike and General Motors to produce, distribute, and market their products on a global scale. Nike, for example, subcontracts 100 percent of its goods production to 75,000 workers in China, South Korea, Malaysia, Taiwan, and Thailand.[31]

Transnational production systems augment the power of global capitalism by enhancing the ability of TNCs to bypass the nationally based political influence of trade unions and other workers' organizations in collective wage-bargaining processes. While rejecting extreme accounts of economic globalization, Gilpin nonetheless concedes that the growing power of TNCs has profoundly altered the structure and functioning of the global economy:

> These giant firms and their global strategies have become major determinants of trade flows and of the location of industries and other economic activities around the world. Most investment is in capital-intensive and technology-intensive sectors. These firms have become central in the expansion of technology flows to both industrialized and industrializing

economies. As a consequence, multinational firms have become extremely important in determining the economic, political, and social welfare of many nations. Controlling much of the world's investment capital, technology, and access to global markets, such firms have become major players not only in determining international economic policies, but political affairs as well.[32]

Nokia Corporation is one such example. Named after a small town in southwest Finland, Nokia rose from modest beginnings a little more than a decade ago to become a large TNC that manufactures thirty-seven of every one hundred cell phones sold worldwide. Today, its products connect over 1 billion people in an invisible web around the globe. However, Nokia's gift to Finland—the distinction of being the most interconnected nation in the world—came at the price of economic dependency. Nokia is the engine of Finland's economy, representing two-thirds of the stock market's value and one-fifth of the nation's total export. It employs 22,000 Finns, not counting the estimated 20,000 domestic employees who work for companies that depend on Nokia contracts. The corporation produces a large part of Finland's tax revenue, and its $30 billion in annual sales almost equals the entire national budget. Yet, when Nokia's growth rate slowed in recent years, company executives let it be known that they were dissatisfied with the country's relatively steep business taxes. After Nokia's 2007 merger with Siemens, many Finnish citizens fear that decisions made by this gigantic corporation might pressure the government to lower corporate taxes and, as a direct consequence of the lost revenues, cut the country's generous and egalitarian welfare system.[33]

## GLOBALIZATION IS A POLITICAL PROCESS

As the Nokia example of TNCs shows, economic perspectives on globalization can hardly be discussed apart from an analysis of political processes and institutions. Most of the debate on political globalization involves the weighing of conflicting evidence with regard to the fate of the modern nation-state. In particular, two questions have moved to the top of the research agenda. First, what are the political causes for the massive flows of capital, money, and technology across territorial boundaries? Second, do these flows constitute a serious challenge to the power of the nation-state? These questions imply that economic globalization might be leading to the reduced control of national governments over economic policy. The latter question, in particular, involves an important subset of issues pertaining to the principle of state sovereignty, the growing impact of intergovernmental organizations, and the prospects for global governance.

An influential group of scholars considers political globalization as a process intrinsically connected to the expansion of markets. In particular, steady advances in computer technology and communication systems such as the World Wide Web are seen as the primary forces responsible for the creation of a single global market.[34] As Richard Langhorne puts it, "Globalization has happened because technological advances have broken down many physical barriers to worldwide communication which used to limit how much connected or cooperative activity of any kind could happen over long distances."[35] According to even more extreme technological-determinist explanations, politics is rendered powerless in the face of an unstoppable and irreversible technoeconomic juggernaut that will crush all governmental attempts to reintroduce restrictive policies and regulations. Economics is portrayed as possessing an inner logic apart from and superior to politics. According to this view, it is this combination of economic self-interest and technological innovation that is responsible for ushering in a new phase in world history in which the role of government will be reduced to that of a handmaiden to free-market forces. As Lowell Bryan and Diana Farrell assert, the role of government will ultimately be reduced to serving as "a superconductor for global capitalism."[36]

Perhaps the most influential representative of this view in the 1990s was Kenichi Ohmae. Projecting the rise of a "borderless world" brought on by the irresistible forces of capitalism, the Japanese business strategist argues that, seen from the perspective of real flows of economic activity, the nation-state has already lost its role as a meaningful unit of participation in the global economy. As territorial divisions are becoming increasingly irrelevant to human society, states are less able to determine the direction of social life within their borders. Since the workings of genuinely global capital markets dwarf their ability to control exchange rates or protect their currency, nation-states have become vulnerable to the discipline imposed by economic choices made elsewhere over which states have no practical control. In the long run, the process of political globalization will lead to the decline of territory as a meaningful framework for understanding political and social change. No longer functioning along the lines of discrete territorial units, the political order of the future will be one of regional economies linked together in an almost seamless global web that operates according to free-market principles.[37]

It is important to note that many neo-Marxist scholars also share such an economistic interpretation of political globalization. Caroline Thomas, for example, portrays politics merely as a consequence of global processes driven by a reinvigorated capitalism that has entered the stage wherein accumulation is taking place on a global rather than a national level. Consequently, she insists that the concept of globalization "refers broadly to the process whereby power is located in global social formations and expressed through global networks rather than through territorially-based states."[38]

A second group of scholars disputes the view that large-scale economic changes simply happen to societies in the manner of natural phenomena such as earthquakes and hurricanes. Instead, they highlight the central role of politics—especially the successful mobilization of political power—in unleashing the forces of globalization.[39] This view rests on a philosophical model of active human agency. If the shape of economic globalization is politically determined, then shifting political preferences are capable of creating different social conditions. Daniel Singer, for example, argues that at the root of the rapid expansion of global economic activity lies neither a "natural law of the market" nor the development of computer technology but political decisions made by governments to lift the international restrictions on capital: "Once the decisions were implemented in the 1980s, the technology came into its own. The speed of communication and calculation helped the movement of money to reach astronomical proportions."[40] The clear implication of Singer's view is that nation and territory still do matter—even in a globalized context.

Hence, this group of scholars argues for the continued relevance of conventional political units, operating in the form of either modern nation-states or "global cities."[41] At the same time, most proponents of this view understand that the development of the past few decades has significantly constrained the set of political options open to states, particularly in developing countries. Jan Aart Scholte, for example, points out that globalization refers to gradual processes of "relative deterritorialization" that facilitate the growth of "supraterritorial" relations between people.[42] Scholte emphasizes, however, that his concession to deterritorialization does not necessarily mean that nation-states are no longer the main organizing forces in the world. Equipped with the power to regulate economic activities within their sphere of influence, states are far from being impotent bystanders to the workings of global forces. If concrete political decisions were responsible for changing the international context in the direction of deregulation, privatization, and the globalization of the world economy, then different political decisions could reverse the trend in the opposite direction.[43] To be sure, it might take a crisis of international proportions brought on by various globalization processes to provide states with the incentive to make their boundaries less permeable to transnational flows. Still, even this scenario shows that it is possible to reverse seemingly irresistible globalizing tendencies. The core message of this group of academics is loud and clear: politics is the crucial category on which rests a proper understanding of globalization.

A third group of scholars suggests that globalization is fueled by a mixture of political and technological factors. John Gray, for example, presents globalization as a long-term, technology-driven process whose contemporary shape has been politically determined by the world's most powerful nations. According to Gray, it is the ultimate objective of the neoliberal Anglo-American initiative to engineer a global free market. Regardless of the ultimate success or failure of this political project, however, the British political theorist predicts that the "swift and inexorable spawning of new technologies throughout the world" will continue, making the technology-driven modernization of the world's societies "a historical fate."[44] Still, Gray asserts that no nation has the hegemonic power to realize a universal free market. In fact, he predicts that the world economy will fragment as its imbalances become insupportable. Thus, Gray foresees a gloomy ending to the current political efforts to establish a single global market: "Trade wars will make international cooperation more difficult. . . . As global laissez-faire breaks up, a deepening international anarchy is the likely human prospect."[45]

A far less pessimistic version of a perspective that combines technology and politics to explain globalization can be found in Castells's classic three-volume study on the rise of the "network society." The Spanish sociologist separates the powerful forces fueling globalization into three independent processes: "The information technology revolution; the economic crisis of both capitalism and statism, and their subsequent restructuring; and the blooming of cultural social movements."[46] As a result of these developments, elaborate networks of capital, labor, information, and markets have linked up to create conditions favorable to the further expansion of the global economy. Castells points to the rise of a new "informational capitalism" based on information technology as the indispensable tool for the effective implementation of processes of socioeconomic restructuring. In this context, he acknowledges both the crisis of the nation-state as a sovereign entity and the devolution of power to regional and local governments as well as to various supranational institutions.

On the other hand, Castells also emphasizes the continued relevance of nation-states as crucial bargaining agencies that influence the changing world of power relationships. As new political actors emerge and new public policies are implemented, the role of culture increases: "Culture as the source of power, and power as the source of capital, underlie the new social hierarchy of the Information Age."[47] While pointing to the potential for global economic and ecological disasters brought on by globalization, Castells ends on a far more positive note than Gray: "The dream of the Enlightenment, that reason and science would solve the problems of humankind, is within reach."[48]

A fourth group of scholars approaches political globalization primarily from the perspective of global governance. Representatives of this group analyze the role of various national and multilateral responses to the fragmentation of economic and political systems and the transnational flows permeating through national borders.[49] Some researchers believe that political globalization might facilitate the emergence of democratic transnational social forces emerging from a thriving sphere of "global civil society." This topic is often connected to discussions focused on the impact of globalization on human rights and vice versa.[50] For example, Martin Shaw emphasizes the role of global political struggles in creating a "global revolution" that would give rise to an internationalized, rights-based Western state conglomerate symbolically linked to global institutions. Thus, he raises the fascinating prospect of "state formation beyond the national level."[51] Democratic theorist John Keane has put forward a similar model of what he calls "cosmocracy"—a messy and complex type of polity understood as "a conglomeration of interlocking and overlapping sub-state, state, and suprastate institutions and multi-dimensional processes that interact, and have political and social effects, on a global scale."[52] In the aftermath of 9/11, however, both Shaw's and Keane's optimistic vision of a postimperial multilateralism directed by a Western political conglomerate seems to be out of step with the reality of a unilateralist American Empire.

Political scientists such as David Held and Richard Falk articulate in their respective writings the need for effective global governance structures as a consequence of various forces of globalization. Both authors portray globalization as diminishing the sovereignty of national governance, thereby reducing the relevance of the nation-state. Much to their credit, Held and Falk are two of the most vociferous advocates for moving the academic debate on globalization in a more ideational and normative direction. Falk in particular calls for a closer analysis of the ways in which neoliberal ideology has played a major role in associating globalization with a particular set of ideas and assumptions.[53]

In Held's view, neither the old Westphalian system of sovereign nation-states nor the postwar global system centered on the United Nations offers a satisfactory solution to the enormous challenges posed by political globalization. Instead, he predicts the emergence of a multilayered form of democratic governance based on Western cosmopolitan ideals, international legal arrangements, and a web of expanding linkages between various governmental and nongovernmental institutions. Rejecting the charge of utopianism often leveled against his vision, Held provides empirical evidence for the existence of a tendency inherent in the globalization process that seems to favor the strengthening of supranational bodies and the rise of an international civil society. He predicts that democratic rights will ultimately become detached from their narrow relationship to discrete territorial units.

If Held's perspective on political globalization is correct, then its final outcome might well be the emergence of a "cosmopolitan democracy" that would constitute the "constructive basis for a plurality of identities to flourish within a structure of mutual toleration and accountability." His vision of a cosmopolitan democracy includes the following political elements: a global parliament connected to regions, states, and localities; a new charter of rights and duties locked into different domains of political, social, and economic power; the formal separation of political and economic interests; and an interconnected global legal system with mechanisms of enforcement from the local to the global.[54] In fact, even in the post-9/11 context, Held refuses to abandon his hopes for restructuring world order toward a "cosmopolitan social democracy" characterized by "strong competent governance at all levels—local, national, regional, and global."[55]

In a similarly optimistic vein, Falk argues that political globalization might facilitate the emergence of democratic transnational social forces anchored in a thriving civil society. Distinguishing his vision of a popular-democratic globalization from below from the market-driven, corporate globalization from above, Falk analyzes the capacities of political actors to challenge the prevailing dominance of neoliberal globalization in a series of key arenas. These include the role of international institutions and regimes, the influence of the media, the changing nature of citizenship, and the reorientation of state activities. Falk retains a strong thematic focus on the capacities of nation-states to implement a cosmopolitan agenda. His writings consistently raise the important question of "whether the state will function in the future mainly as an instrument useful for the promotion and protection of global trade and investment or whether, by contrast, the state can recover its sense of balance in this globalizing setting so that the success of markets will not be achieved at the expense of the wellbeing of peoples."[56] However, in his recent reevaluation of global governance in the era of the "Great Terror War," Falk concedes that "September 11 reinforces the essential structural challenge to globalization, namely, the relevance of information and networking to the exercise of power, establishing the need to incorporate non-state actors into the procedures and institutions of world order."[57]

A number of academic critics have challenged the idea that political globalization is fueling a development toward cosmopolitan democracy. Most of their criticism boils down to the charge that Held and Falk indulge in an abstract idealism that fails to engage with current political developments on the level of policy. Some critics argue that the emergence of private authority has increasingly become a factor in the post–Cold War world. In their view, global collective actors like religious terrorists and organized criminals are not merely symptoms of the weakening nation-state, but their actions also dim the prospects for the rise of cosmopolitan democracy.[58] Moreover, skeptics like Robert Holton raise the suspicion that Held and Falk do not explore in sufficient detail the cultural feasibility of global democracy. As cultural patterns become increasingly interlinked through globalization, critics argue, the possibility of resistance, opposition, and violent clashes becomes just as real as the cosmopolitan vision of mutual accommodation and tolerance of differences.[59]

## GLOBALIZATION IS A CULTURAL PROCESS

Held and Falk might respond to these criticisms by arguing that one major strength of their approach lies in viewing globalization not as a one-dimensional phenomenon but as a multidimensional process involving diverse domains of activity and interaction, including the cultural sphere. Indeed, any analytical account of globalization would be woefully inadequate without an examination of its cultural dimension. A number of prominent scholars have emphasized the centrality of culture to contemporary debates on globalization. As sociologist John Tomlinson puts it, "Globalization lies at the heart of modern culture; cultural practices lie at the heart of globalization."[60] The thematic landscape traversed by scholars of cultural globalization is vast, and the questions they raise are too numerous to be completely fleshed out in this short survey. Rather than presenting a long laundry list of relevant topics, this section focuses on two central questions raised by scholars of cultural globalization. First, does globalization increase cultural homogeneity, or does it lead to greater diversity and heterogeneity? Or, to put the matter into less academic terms, does globalization make people more alike or more different? And, second, how does the dominant culture of consumerism impact the natural environment?

Most commentators preface their response to the first question with a general analysis of the relationship between the globalization process and contemporary cultural change. Tomlinson, for example, defines cultural globalization as a "densely growing network of complex cultural interconnections and interdependencies that characterize modern social life." He emphasizes that global cultural flows are directed by powerful international media corporations that utilize new communication technologies to shape societies and identities. As images and ideas can be more easily and rapidly transmitted from one place to another, they profoundly impact the way people experience their everyday lives. Culture no longer remains tied to fixed localities such as town and nation but acquires new meanings that reflect dominant themes emerging in a global context. This interconnectivity caused by cultural globalization challenges parochial values and identities because it undermines the linkages that connect culture to fixity of location.[61]

A number of scholars argue that these processes have facilitated the rise of an increasingly homogenized global culture underwritten by an Anglo-American value system. Referring to the global diffusion of American values, consumer goods, and lifestyles as "Americanization," these authors analyze the ways in which such forms of "cultural imperialism" are overwhelming more vulnerable cultures. The American sociologist George Ritzer, for example, coined the term "McDonaldization" to describe the wide-ranging process by which the principles of the fast-food restaurant are coming to dominate more and more sectors of American society as well as the rest of the world. On the surface, these principles appear to be rational in their attempts to offer efficient and predictable ways of serving people's needs. Only toward the end of his study does Ritzer allow himself to address the normative ramifications of this process: when rational systems serve to deny the expression of human creativity and cultural difference, they contribute to the rise of irrationality in the world. In the long run, McDonaldization leads to the eclipse of cultural diversity and the dehumanization of social relations.[62]

The prominent American political theorist Benjamin R. Barber also enters the normative realm when he warns his readers against the cultural imperialism of what he calls "McWorld"—a soulless consumer capitalism that is rapidly transforming the world's diverse population into a blandly uniform market. For Barber, McWorld is a product of a superficial American popular culture assembled in the 1950s and 1960s and driven by expansionist commercial interests: "Its template is American, its form style . . . [m]usic, video, theater, books, and theme parks . . . are all constructed as image exports creating a common taste around common logos, advertising slogans, stars, songs, brand names, jingles, and trademarks."[63]

Much to its credit, Barber's analysis moves beyond offering a "value-free" account of the forces of McWorld. His insightful account of cultural globalization contains the important recognition that the colonizing tendencies of McWorld provoke cultural and political resistance in the form of "jihad"—the parochial impulse to reject and repel Western homogenization forces wherever they can be found. Fueled by the furies of ethnonationalism and/or religious fundamentalism, jihad represents the dark side of cultural particularism. Barber sees jihad as the "rabid response to colonialism and imperialism and their economic children, capitalism and modernity." Guided by opposing visions of homogeneity, jihad and McWorld are dialectically interlocked in a bitter cultural struggle for popular allegiance. Barber insists that both forces ultimately work against a participatory form of democracy, for they are equally prone to undermine civil liberties and thus thwart the possibility of a global democratic future.[64]

As might be expected, Barber's dialectical account received a lot of public attention after the events of 9/11. They also helped to resurrect Samuel Huntington's 1993 thesis of a "clash of civilizations" involving primarily the West and Islam. This rather crude argument relies on overly broad definitions and generalizations that divide the post-1990 world into nine "major contemporary civilizations."[65] Within a year of the terrorist attacks, dozens of books offered endless permutations of the arguments first presented by Barber and Huntington. For example, legal scholar Amy Chua and philosopher Roger Scruton warned their readers that "the global spread of markets and democracy is a principal, aggravating cause of group hatred and ethnic violence throughout the non-Western world" and that "globalization has plunged the Islamic world into crisis by offering the spectacle of a secular society maintained in being by man-made laws, and achieving equilibrium without the aid of God."[66] For such commentators, the lessons drawn from this clash between the "West and the rest" were obvious: "In the face of this [religious violence] we in the West must . . . do what we can to reinforce the nation-state. . . . This means that we must constrain the process of globalization, so as to neutralize its perceived image as threat from the West to the rest."[67]

Proponents of the cultural homogenization thesis offer ample empirical evidence for their interpretation. They point to Amazonian Indians wearing Nike sneakers, denizens of the southern Sahara purchasing Texaco baseball caps, and Palestinian youths proudly displaying their Chicago Bulls sweatshirts in downtown Ramallah. Documenting the spread of Anglo-American culture facilitated by the deregulation and convergence of global media and electronic communication systems, some commentators even go so far as to insist that there no longer exist any viable alternatives to the "Americanization" of the world. For example, French political economist Serge Latouche argues that the media-driven, consumerist push toward "planetary uniformity" according to Anglo-American norms and values will inevitably result in a worldwide "standardization of lifestyles."[68]

The cultural homogenization thesis also relies to some extent on arguments that point to the power of the Anglo-American culture industry to make English the global lingua franca of the twenty-first century. Today, more than 80 percent of the content posted on the Internet is in English. Almost half the world's growing population of foreign students are enrolled at Anglo-American universities.[69] And yet it would be too simplistic to conclude that the globalization of English is inevitable. As political scientist Selma Sonntag puts it, "Global English represents globalization-from-above, but it also contains the possibility of globalization-from-below, most plausibly in terms of a subaltern resistance to linguistic hegemony. Globalization pushes forward global English hegemony, but in doing so it creates its own antithesis."[70]

Hence, it is one thing to acknowledge the powerful cultural logic of global capitalism, but it is quite another to assert that the cultural diversity existing on our planet is destined to vanish. In fact, several influential academics offer contrary assessments that link globalization to new forms of cultural diversity.[71] Roland Robertson has famously argued that global cultural flows often reinvigorate local cultural niches. Contending that cultural globalization always takes place in local contexts, Robertson predicts a pluralization of the world as localities produce a variety of unique cultural responses to global forces. The result is not increasing cultural homogenization but "glocalization"—a complex interaction of the global and local characterized by cultural borrowing.[72] These interactions lead to a complex mixture of both homogenizing and heterogenizing impulses.

Often referred to as "hybridization" or "creolization," the processes of cultural mixing are reflected in music, film, fashion, language, and other forms of symbolic expression. Sociologist Jan Nederveen Pieterse, for example, argues that exploring "hybridity" amounts to "mapping no man's land." For Nederveen Pieterse, the hybridity concept "does not preclude struggle but yields a multifocus view on struggle and by showing multiple identity on both sides, transcends the 'us versus them' dualism that prevails in cultural and political arenas."[73] Ulf Hannerz, too, emphasizes the complexity of an emerging "global culture" composed of new zones of hybridization. In these regions, meanings derive from different historical sources that were originally separated from one another in space but have come to mingle extensively. Hence, rather than being obliterated by Western consumerist forces of homogenization, local difference and particularity evolve into new cultural constellations and discourses.[74]

In addition to addressing the question of whether globalization leads to cultural homogeneity or heterogeneity, scholars like Nederveen Pieterse, Hannerz, and Robertson seek to expand the concept of globalization by portraying it as a multidimensional "field." In their view, globalization is both a material and a mental condition, constituted by complex, often contradictory interactions of global, local, and individual aspects of social life. Cultural theorists such as Ulrich Beck and Arjun Appadurai have refined this argument by contrasting common interpretations of globalization as a "process" with the less mechanical concept of "globality," referring to "the experience of living and acting across borders."[75]

Appadurai identifies five conceptual dimensions or "landscapes" that are constituted by global cultural flows: ethnoscapes (shifting populations made up of tourists, immigrants, refugees, and exiles), technoscapes (development of technologies that facilitate the rise of TNCs), finanscapes (flows of global capital), mediascapes (electronic capabilities to produce and disseminate information), and ideoscapes (ideologies of states and social movements). Each of these "scapes" contains the building blocks of the new "imagined worlds" that are assembled by the historically situated imaginations of persons and groups spread around the globe.[76] Suspended in a global web of cultural multiplicity, more and more people become aware of the density of human relations. Their enhanced ability to explore and absorb new cultural symbols and meanings coexists in uneasy tension with their growing sense of "placelessness." Focusing on the changing forms of human perception and consciousness brought on by global cultural flows, Beck and Appadurai discuss subjective forms of cultural globalization that are often neglected in more common analyses of "objective" relations of interdependence.

Sociologist Martin Albrow also uses the concept of globality to describe a new condition where people and groups of all kinds refer to the globe as the framework for their beliefs and actions. Analyzing the complex web of interactions underlying this epochal shift in people's consciousness, he concludes that a dawning "global age" is slowly supplanting the old conceptual framework of modernity. A proper understanding of this new era demands that researchers revise dogmatic Enlightenment ideas of progress and science and instead embrace a more cautious and pragmatic universalism that explicitly recognizes the uncertainties and contingencies of the global age. Albrow speaks of a new condition of "globality" that is profoundly different from modernity in that there is no presumption of centrality of control. In short, the project of modernity has ended.[77]

On this issue, then, the debate on cultural globalization has linked up with the long-standing controversy in political and social theory over whether our present age should be understood as an extension of modernity or whether it constitutes a new condition of postmodernity characterized by the loss of a stable sense of identity and knowledge.[78] Indeed, scholars of cultural globalization have shown more willingness to engage in sustained investigations of the normative dimension of globalization than their colleagues in political science or economics.

The same is true for those researchers who have explored the connection between cultural globalization and the natural environment, especially in light of the escalating problem of global climate change. After all, how people view their natural environment depends to a great extent on their cultural milieu. For example, cultures steeped in Taoist, Buddhist, and various animist religions often emphasize the interdependence of all living beings—a perspective that calls for a delicate balance between human wants and ecological needs. Nature is not considered a mere "resource" to be used instrumentally to fulfill human desires. The most extreme manifestations of this anthropocentric paradigm are reflected in the dominant values and beliefs of consumerism. The U.S.-dominated culture industry seeks to convince its global audience that the meaning and chief value of life can be found in the limitless accumulation of material possessions.

The two most ominous ecological problems connected to the global spread of consumer culture are human-induced global climate change, such as global warming, and the worldwide destruction of biodiversity. The rapid buildup of gas emissions, including carbon dioxide, methane, and chlorofluorocarbons in our planet's atmosphere, has greatly enhanced Earth's capacity to trap heat. The resulting "greenhouse effect" is responsible for raising average temperatures worldwide. Indeed, the U.S. Union of Concerned Scientists has presented data suggesting that the global average temperature increased from about 53.3°F in 1880 to 57.9°F in 2000. Further increases in global temperatures could lead to partial meltdowns of the polar ice caps, causing global sea levels to rise by up to three feet by

2100—a catastrophic development that would threaten the many coastal regions of the world. Indeed, the impact of such drastic rises in temperature would be massive rises in sea levels as a result of polar ice caps melting, which in turn would lead to the extinction of species such as the polar bear and also the disappearance of many small Pacific islands. This in turn creates a host of economic, social, and political problems as displaced populations seek refuge in countries not as affected by global warming. Changes to weather patterns and temperatures would also have a significant impact on food production and availability and access to water. Those most likely to be affected are people in the global South, who are least responsible for the processes that have contributed to bringing the world to this point of environmental crisis. As we shall see, the potential economic and political ramifications of global climate change and other ecological problems are dire, particularly for people living in developing countries in the global South.

With regard to the loss of biodiversity, many biologists today believe that we are now in the midst of the fastest mass extinction of living species in the 4.5-billion-year history of the planet. Environmental sociologist Franz Broswimmer concedes that this problem is not new in natural history, but he points out that human beings in our age of globalization have managed to destroy species and their natural habitat at an alarming rate. Broswimmer fears that up to 50 percent of all plant and animal species—most of them in the global South—will disappear by the end of the twenty-first century.[79]

But it has only been in the past few years that governments, corporations, and intergovernmental organizations have begun to appreciate the significant economic effects of the ecological challenges brought about by globalization. In 2006, Sir Nicholas Stern, former chief economist for the World Bank, released one of the most comprehensive and alarming reports on the economic and ecological impacts of climate change. The *Stern Review on the Economics of Climate Change* estimates, using formal economic models, that if the global community does not take action now to address climate change, the results will be the equivalent of the loss of 5 percent of global GDP each year, now and forever. There is even potential for the damages to be more severe, resulting in the loss of up to 20 percent of global GDP. By contrast, if action is taken now to reduce and offset the most severe impacts of climate change, the total cost will be less than 1 percent of global GDP.[80] Other reports into the economic impacts of climate change include rising costs of basic foodstuffs and water supply as higher-than-usual temperatures and altered rainfall patterns impact on water sources, animals, and farming industries. Other industries such as tourism will also feel the effects of climate change as skiing resorts receive reduced snowfall and natural tourist attractions such as glaciers melt. Natural disasters such as Hurricane Katrina in the United States in 2005 and Cyclone Nargis in Myanmar in 2008 are also likely to increase in frequency, length, and intensity as a result of climate change, leading to increased expenditure for governments in preparing for and dealing with the effects of these disasters, not to mention the utter destruction these changes will wreak within individual lives and populations. The world is already experiencing many of the economic effects related to global climate change. These effects are likely to intensify in the coming years as global average temperatures continue to rise and rainfall patterns become more and more erratic.

An interesting crossover among economic, political, and ecological dimensions of globalization is the use of market-based policy instruments to manage environmental problems. Initiatives such as carbon "trading" and biodiversity "banks" are emerging in policy discussions at national and global levels about approaches to global warming, species extinction, and overpopulation. Implicit in the use of these market-based policy tools, however, is still the driving neoliberal ideological assumption that the market can self-regulate and solve all problems, that capitalist-based consumerism is a sustainable way to live, even an appropriate way to address ecological problems created by capitalist overconsumption in the first place.

Despite this litany of bad ecological news, one might find reason for cautious optimism in the bright side of globalization—the rising number of international treaties and agreements on the environment, such as the 1997 Kyoto Protocol on global warming, the 2002 Johannesburg World Summit, and the 2007 UN Bali Climate Summit that tackled such enormous issues as carbon dioxide emission standards, transboundary pollution, and ecological sustainability. Unfortunately, however, most of the ensuing agreements lack effective international enforcement mechanisms. Moreover, the governments of such major environmental polluters as the United States, Russia, and China have not yet ratified some of the key agreements.

## GLOBALIZATION AND IDEOLOGY: TOWARD A CRITICAL EXAMINATION OF GLOBALISM

This chapter has introduced some of the main analytical perspectives in the academic debate on globalization. Still, this overview does not encompass all topics of the ever-expanding discourse on the subject. In addition to exploring the economic, political, and cultural dimensions of globalization, many scholars have raised a number of additional topics, such as the structure and direction of transnational migration flows, the emergence of transnational social movements such as the women's movement, the spread of global diseases, transnational crime, and the globalization of military technology linked to a transnationalization of defense production.[81]

Indeed, the globalization of warfare and military operations has received special attention in post-9/11 debates on the Global War on Terror. While paid security experts and mercenaries are certainly not a new phenomenon, there has been an increasing global trend in the new "security industry" to provide sophisticated military services—from simple weapons training to outfitting entire armies—to mostly private corporations with ample financial resources. Take, for example, Defense System Limited, a security firm based in London. Employing former KGB agents, a former White House security adviser, and scores of former military officers from dozens of countries, this corporation sells its expertise in death and destruction to "[p]etrochemical companies, mining or mineral extraction companies and their subsidiaries, multinationals, banks, embassies, NGOs, national and international organizations. . . . [P]eople who operate in a very dodgy, hostile type of environment."[82]

But, rather than providing a full account of every conceivable aspect of the debate, the purpose of this chapter is to show that there exists no scholarly agreement on a single conceptual framework for the study of globalization. Academics remain divided on the validity of available empirical evidence for the existence and extent of globalization, not to mention its normative and ideological implications. Fredric Jameson, for example, questions the utility of forcing such a complex social phenomenon as globalization into a single analytical framework.[83] He argues that such attempts result frequently in either further disagreements or the elevation of a partial view to the unassailable truth and last word on the subject.

The persistence of academic divisions on globalization notwithstanding, it is important to acknowledge some emerging points of scholarly agreement in recent years.[84] Moreover, there is much value in the intellectual advances brought about by analytical research programs for the study of globalization. No serious scholar would wish to disavow the importance of conceptual clarity and precise formulations. But the impulse to separate the social-scientific study of globalization from ideological and normative matters often serves to further perpetuate stale disputes over definitions and methodological differences. As Ian Clark puts it, "While there can be no objection to a precise definition of globalization, definitions should not be permitted to resolve the underlying issues of substance and historical interpretation."[85]

Any overly objectivist approach to globalization is bound to overlook the insight that all social-scientific concepts are simultaneously analytical and normative. This dual status of concepts means that they never merely describe that to which they refer but are also necessarily engaged in a normative process of meaning construction.[86] Yet many scholars believe that the normative/ideological nature of the globalization debate that takes place mostly in the public arena actually interferes with and obstructs the formulation of more "objective" or "value-free" accounts of globalization. This instinctive scholarly fear of ideological "contamination" derives partly from the historic mission of academic institutions. Like their nineteenth-century predecessor, today's universities subscribe to the belief that the world is, in principle, knowable and controllable through a balanced operation of human rationality. This means that scholars are encouraged to conduct their research within established parameters of objectivity and neutrality in order to reach a clear understanding of the phenomenon in question. Matters of ideology—particularly one's own political and moral preferences—are seen as compromising the scientific integrity of the research project. Therefore, the normative dimension of ideology is often excluded from academic attempts to understand globalization.

In fact, a discussion of the normative/ideological dimension of the phenomenon is often seen as unscientific "journalism." However, this argument misses the dynamics of globalization as a public discourse. The public debate over globalization that occurs largely outside the walls of academia represents an important aspect of the phenomenon itself. As several empirical studies have shown, the term "globalization" in the press "appears to be associated with multiple ideological frames of reference, including 'financial market,' 'economic efficiency,' 'negative effect,' and 'culture.'"[87] If a researcher wants to understand the material and ideal stakes raised in the debate, then these "multiple ideological frames of reference" generating public judgments regarding the meanings and likely consequences of globalization represent an important subject of study. Thus, the researcher must enter the value-laden arena of ideology. The task can no longer be limited to an objective classification of the constitutive parts of the elephant called "globalization," but a critical assessment of the language about globalization that is constitutive of the phenomenon itself. Rather than being rejected as a confusing cacophony of subjective assertions, the exhibited normative preferences and the rhetorical and polemical maneuvers performed by the main participants in the public debate on globalization become the focus of the researcher's critical task.

In my view, it is virtually impossible for globalization scholars to interpret the public discourse on the subject apart from their own ideological and political framework. In spite of the obvious dangers inherent in this move, the inclusion of one's own beliefs and values does not necessarily invalidate one's research project. As the German philosopher Hans-Georg Gadamer has pointed out, the motivations and prejudices of the interpreter condition every act of understanding.[88] Hence, it would be a mistake to consider the researcher's values and preconceptions solely as a hindrance to a proper understanding of social processes. In fact, the interpreter's inescapable normative involvement enables the very act of understanding. Thus, the study of globalization as a real-life phenomenon must include an investigation of the ideological projects that I have called "globalisms."

Fortunately, the tendency of the academic discourse to separate ideological and normative matters from analytical concerns has been increasingly subjected to criticism from a variety of scholars who reject a narrow scientistic approach to the study of globalization. For example, the writings of Stephen Gill and Robert W. Cox probe the extent to which neoliberal conceptions of the market have been shaping the public debate on globalization.[89] My own work also is anchored in a more interpretive approach to understanding social phenomena that does not shy away from normative and ideological matters. I seek to avoid a general discussion of globalization (the material process) without a proper recognition that the former is inextricably intertwined with the various globalisms (the ideological packages). I argue that academic efforts to capture the nature of globalization apart from the ongoing ideological claims made in the public arena reinforce, intentionally or not, the dominant market-globalist project that alternately masks and transmits a neoliberal worldview, thus making it easier for existing power interests to escape critical scrutiny. As Alan Scott notes, the separation of analytical concerns from ideological and normative matters harbors the danger that the ethos of scientific detachment might unintentionally serve politically motivated attempts to provide "people with persuasive arguments to the effect that little can be done in the face of these enormous economic, political and social developments."[90] Seeking to avoid this danger, the next chapter of this book introduces the major claims of market globalism and shows their evolution in the militaristic context of the post-9/11 world.

# CHAPTER 3

# FROM MARKET GLOBALISM
# TO IMPERIAL GLOBALISM

## MARKET GLOBALISM AND AMERICAN EMPIRE

Before we embark on our critical discourse analysis of the central claims of market globalism, let us first consider the larger political and historical context. As we briefly noted in chapter 1, the emergence of market globalism in the 1980s and 1990s was inextricably linked to the rising fortunes of neoliberal political forces in the world's sole remaining superpower. In the first decade of the new millennium, however, three related developments in the United States pushed market globalism into a more militaristic direction, thereby modifying its core ideological claims and altering its morphology. The first was the 2001 inauguration of an American president heavily influenced by a relatively small economic and military elite ably represented by his inner circle of neoconservative advisers. The second was the bellicose climate following the 9/11 al Qaeda attacks on the most recognizable symbols of American power, and the third development was evident in the ensuing "Global War on Terror" by an "American Empire," which consciously and often unilaterally exerted its unprecedented power around the globe.

The terms "empire" and "imperialism" derive from *imperium*, a Latin noun referring to "power" and "command." After the long reign of Caesar Augustus that marked the final demise of the Roman Republic by the early first century CE, *imperium* signified the emperor's legal power to enforce the law, a function he would routinely delegate to his chief military leaders and civil magistrates.[1] Operating within a Hellenic cultural framework, the Romans inherited the Stoic conception that empire was universal in the sense of partaking of universal reason and, therefore, valid for all societies. Hence, the concept of *imperium* implied a universal humanitarian mission of "spreading civilization" to the rest of the world. Romans were convinced that only the complete conquest and civilization of all "barbarians" residing beyond the borders of the empire would ultimately lead to a harmonious union of the world's peoples under Roman leadership, thus establishing peace, order, and justice on earth.[2]

Still echoing this classical ideal of establishing political domination in the name of universality, modern students of the subject define "empire" as "relationships of political control imposed by some political societies over the effective sovereignty of other political societies" and "imperialism" as political and ideological projects of "establishing and maintaining an empire."[3] To be sure, political sovereignty can be infringed on in a variety of ways—diplomatic means, economic pressure, military campaigns, and so on—but the essence of every imperial regime, ancient or modern, remains nonetheless the same: an enduring relationship of political domination and subjection.[4]

With the modern spread of liberal capitalist democracy and its professed ideals of freedom, equality, and national self-determination, "empire" acquired the rather undesirable connotation of political oppression and coercion—a charge most vehemently rejected by those powers that seem to deserve it the most. With the end of the colonial era after World War II, the world's two superpowers claimed to seek benign influence rather than domination. American and Soviet leaders eagerly attempted to substantiate their assertion that their respective nations were not involved in an "imperialist" enterprise by pointing to the lack of what had always been seen as the hallmark of empire: direct or indirect political rule over formally annexed or incorporated external territories.

During the 1950s, however, Ronald Robinson, John Gallagher, and other pioneering scholars of imperialism argued that the contemporary meaning of imperialism should not be confined to formal annexation, colonial practices, or indirect political rule. Rather, it had to include more "informal" ways of dominating others as well—largely those secured by economic means. At the same time, however, these scholars readily conceded that their theory of "informal imperialism" or "free-trade imperialism" was not meant to equate imperialism with capitalism. After all, imperialism was impossible without political pressure to "open up" previously closed markets to the allegedly "free" operation of Western competitive capitalism. For Robinson and Gallagher, politics and economics always formed a complex relationship, producing, at various historical junctures, different manifestations of imperialism. Focusing their research efforts on British imperial rule in the Victorian era, the two British political economists concluded that London usually preferred informal domination, resorting to formal political rule only when it seemed to be the only way of protecting economic interests that would otherwise be threatened.[5]

Clearly, this theory of "informal imperialism" has significance not only with regard to the nineteenth-century British Empire but also for the changing face of market globalism in a twenty-first-century world dominated by a single hyperpower. Today's raging debates over whether the United States actually constitutes an "empire"—informal or otherwise—have their origins in theoretical controversies over the precise relationship between imperialism and capitalism (and politics and economics) that reach back much further than the contemporary era of globalization.[6]

In the first decades of the twentieth century, Marxist intellectuals like Rudolf Hilferding, Rosa Luxemburg, and V. I. Lenin argued that imperialism represented the "highest stage" of capitalist development, thus implying that a rising capitalist power like the United States, by necessity, was engaged in imperialist practices. This meant that Marxists assigned politics only secondary importance because imperialism represented the logical outcome of capitalism unfolding in history. The core meaning of imperialism—political domination—was of only secondary importance. This "socialist school" was opposed by a group of liberal thinkers led by John A. Hobson, Joseph Schumpeter, and John Maynard Keynes, who regarded imperialism as an unfortunate but avoidable perversion of capitalism caused by small capitalist elites with vested interests in lucrative investment opportunities overseas that had succeeded in harnessing the state apparatus to their sinister purposes. In order to claim democratic legitimacy, these elites engaged in ideological maneuvers designed to win the masses over with patriotic flag-waving and militaristic slogans. In other words, the thinkers of this "liberal school" restored politics and ideology to the core of any systematic attempt to understand the workings of imperialism.

Even if we agreed with the liberals that the relationship between capitalism and imperialism may not necessarily be one of the former always turning into the latter, we would still have to concede that liberalism and imperialism have teamed up on many occasions in the past two centuries. With regard to the United States, prominent historians like Walter LaFeber and William Appleman Williams have drawn on the work of Robinson and Gallagher to refer to American imperialism as a continuous and largely informal process that started with the seventeenth-century settlement of the North American continent and assumed periodically politically coercive and thus more "formal" expressions. Perhaps the most obvious of these bellicose chapters in the history of American imperialism was the coercive acquisition of the Hawaiian Islands, Guam, part of Samoa, the Philippines, and Puerto Rico in a short eighteen-month period at the end of the nineteenth century.[7] A stirring speech delivered by Indiana Senator Albert J. Beveridge perfectly captures the militaristic and quite racist spirit of American Empire at the dawn of the twentieth century:

> God has not been preparing the English-speaking and Teutonic peoples for a thousand years for nothing but vain and idle self-contemplation and self-admiration. No! He has made us the master organizers of the world to establish system where chaos reigns. . . . He has made us adepts in government that we may administer government among savage and senile peoples. . . . He has marked the American people as His chosen nation to finally lead in the regeneration of the world. This is the divine mission of America . . . we will not renounce our part in the mission of the race, trustee under god, of the civilization of the world.[8]

Utilizing the useful distinction made by political scientist and former assistant secretary of defense Joseph Nye, one could say that American Empire has always oscillated between "soft power"—persuading others to want what it wants—and "hard power"—forcing others to comply with its wishes.[9] Former economic adviser to President Bill Clinton and chief economist of the World Bank Joseph Stiglitz describes these soft-power dynamics as set in motion by the informal American Empire of the "Roaring Nineties." Confessing to a colossal "mismanagement of globalization" by the neoliberal Clinton administration, Stiglitz points to the consistent application of a "double standard" behind a U.S. trade globalization agenda wearing an informal imperial design: "The United States pushed other countries to open up their markets to areas of our strength, such as financial services, but resisted, successfully so, efforts to make us reciprocate."

According to Stiglitz, President Clinton's preferred strategy was to rely on soft power: "When we needed rhetoric to justify what we wanted, we talked about free markets, but when free markets seemed to put America's firms at a disadvantage, we talked variously about 'managed trade' or 'fair trade.'"

In agriculture, for example, the administration insisted that other countries reduce trade barriers to U.S. products and eliminate the subsidies for competing products. At the same time, Stiglitz asserts, the United States kept intact "barriers for the goods produced by the developing countries" and proceeded to dole out massive subsidies to American farmers. As a second example of this "double standard," Stiglitz points to intellectual property rights such as patents and copyrights. The Clinton administration even tightened protective policies that benefited American drug companies in spite of the existence of clear evidence that such measures would actually stifle research and development of new products and thereby "harm the pace of innovation." Severely indicting extreme forms of market globalism, Stiglitz highlights the existence of a "large gap between our free trade rhetoric and our actual practice," which made the United States appear to the rest of the world as a hypocritical superpower. In his final analysis, Stiglitz points to an American informal imperialism in words that eerily echo the assessment of the liberal school a century earlier:

> America's international political economy was driven by a whole variety of special interests which saw the opportunity to use its increasing global dominance to force other countries to open their markets to its goods on its terms. America's government was seizing the opportunities afforded by the new post–Cold War world, but in a narrow way, benefiting particular financial and corporate interests.[10]

If the United States sought to conceal its imperial ambitions in the 1990s behind the largely soft-power operations of a free-trade empire anchored in the myth of the market's "invisible hand," then the gloves definitely came off after 9/11, exposing the iron fist of an irate giant. Ready to resort to hard-power tactics for the defense of "liberty, democracy, and free markets" against the "evil of terrorism," President George W. Bush abandoned the mildly isolationist position he espoused during the 2000 election campaign and adopted the bellicose views of neoconservative foreign policy hawks like Dick Cheney, Donald Rumsfeld, Paul Wolfowitz, and Richard Perle. In a way, 9/11 marked both a return to and a continuation of the neoconservative Reagan–Thatcher era, except that the enemy was no longer the "evil empire" but terrorist "evildoers" supported by the three rogue states that constituted Bush's famous "Axis of Evil." With the Soviet

Union out of the way, there was nobody left to check the global ambitions of the sole remaining superpower.

For the purposes of this book, then, it is crucial to bear in mind that neoliberalism and neoconservativism in the United States are not ideological opposites. In fact, they represent variations on the same ideological theme; their similarities often outweigh their differences. Contemporary neoconservatives in the United States are not conservative as defined by eighteenth-century thinkers like Edmund Burke, who expressed a fondness for aristocratic virtues and bemoaned radical social change, disliked republican principles, and distrusted progress and reason. Rather, American neoconservatives subscribe to a variant of muscular liberalism they connect to James Madison, Theodore Roosevelt, and Ronald Reagan. In general, neoconservatives agree with neoliberals on the importance of free markets and free trade, but they are much more inclined than the latter to combine their hands-off attitude toward big business with intrusive government action for the regulation of the ordinary citizenry in the name of public security and traditional values. In foreign affairs, neoconservatives advocate a more assertive and expansive use of both economic and military power than neoliberals, ostensibly for the purpose of promoting freedom and democracy around the world. These sentiments seem to imply a strong commitment to universalistic principles, but, as one commentator puts it,

> Unlike liberal Wilsonians, their [neoconservatives'] promotion of democracy is not for the sake of democracy and human rights in and of themselves. Rather, democracy-promotion is meant to bolster America's security and to further its world preeminence; it is thought to be pragmatically related to the U.S. national interest. The principles of these neocons [neoconservatives] are universalistic, but not so their policy, which steers clear of international organizations and is nationalist and unilateralist.[11]

On these three fundamental pillars—the global projection of American interests, unilateralism, and militarism—rests the neoconservative foreign policy vision for a post-1989 American Empire. Sketched out for the first time in a 1992 "Defense Planning Guidance" draft authored by future undersecretary of defense Paul Wolfowitz, this scheme advised deterring potential competitors—even America's traditional western European allies—from "even aspiring to a larger regional or global role."[12] The same views were reiterated in a more philosophical statement of principles issued in 1997 by the cosigners of the Project for a New American Century (PNAC), an influential neoconservative group led by Cheney, Rumsfeld, and Wolfowitz. After 9/11, this militaristic vision of a unilateral American Empire striking globally and preemptively against those it deems standing in the way of "freedom's triumph" became national policy officially enshrined in the 2001 *Quadrennial Defense Review*, the 2002 Nuclear Posture Review, and, most important, the 2002 *National Security Strategy of the United States of America* (updated 2006).

While claiming that "America has no empire to extend or utopia to establish," President Bush nonetheless welcomed the opportunity to lead the world in the "great mission" of "extending the benefits of liberty and prosperity through the spread of American values." Calling this strategy a "distinctly American internationalism that reflects the union of our values and our national interests," Bush has been fond of employing the language of religious triumphalism to put the world on notice that the United States was determined to use its "unparalleled strength and influence" to carry out its exalted mission: "Our responsibility to history is clear: to answer these attacks [of 9/11] and rid the world of evil."[13]

The ideological implications of this post-9/11 turn toward neoconservatism became evident soon after the terrorist attacks. If it were to continue as the dominant ideology in our new era of global warfare, market globalism had to be "toughened up." Just as the United States was making the transition from informal to formal empire (culminating in the establishment of a temporary territorial empire at the height of the Iraq War and subsequent occupation), market globalism was turned into imperial globalism. As militarism and the market merged in a Hummerized discursive landscape, neoconservatives joined neoliberals as the most prominent voices in the public debate about globalization. As Tom Barry and Jim Lobe suggest, "Instead of fretting over social and environmental standards in the global economy," the focus of the debate shifted to "securing U.S. national interests, particularly energy resources, and thereby ensuring continued U.S. economic supremacy."[14] David Harvey's suggestion that American Empire was "all about oil" may be putting matters too strongly, but his focus on the political and ideological maneuvers of small capitalist elites representing the interests of a narrow economic sector is right on the mark—as was the identical point made by liberal theorists of imperialism a century ago.[15] Indeed, like the late-nineteenth-century manifestation of American imperialism, the current empire requires a more militant ideology that unites the twin goals of global economic and political hegemony in the name of high-sounding ideals like strength, security, just peace, democracy, development, free markets, and free trade.[16]

## WINNING HEARTS AND MINDS

At the opening of chapter 1, we noted that the Bush administration linked the post-9/11 project of selling neoliberal globalization to a comprehensive neoconservative strategy of "winning the ideological battle" against jihadist globalism. Massive advertisement strategies to boost the global image of the United States became a major component of a widespread effort to stop the violent backlash against what many people around the world perceive as an American global arrogance and aggressive unilateralism. Rather than making serious efforts to revise its foreign policy posture, the Bush administration put forth an idealized version of "American values" as the only appropriate ideological framework for our post-9/11 world. Unwilling to engage in a genuine multicivilizational dialogue conducive to a world order anchored in human rights and the global redistribution of wealth and technology, the U.S. government opted for an imperial ideological monologue that pushes a sanitized image of American-led globality on the rest of the world. Thus, the hot Global War on Terror unfolded in tandem with a powerful market-globalist drive to sell liberty and free markets.

To that end, the Bush administration launched an unprecedented Madison Avenue–style advertising campaign aimed at branding and selling its "universal values" to audiences in the Middle East and other recalcitrant regions in the world. Originally, these efforts to sell "brand USA" were spearheaded by Charlotte Beers, a former chief executive officer (CEO) of J. Walter Thompson and Ogilvy & Mather, two of the world's top ten advertising companies. Sworn in as undersecretary of state for public diplomacy and public affairs in the immediate aftermath of 9/11, Beers's primary objective was to utilize her budget of over $500 million to overhaul the deteriorating public image of the United States abroad. While extremely important during the Cold War, public diplomacy operations were largely abandoned after 1989. Ten years later, even the once formidable U.S. Information Agency was abolished. After 9/11, however, public diplomacy has again achieved a high-priority status. In addition to creating Beers's office in the State Department, the Bush administration engaged in the ill-fated attempt to establish a Defense Department–led office to influence public global opinion by any means necessary—including deliberate misinformation in order to generate foreign support. In January 2003, President Bush established by executive order a second public diplomacy institution—the White House Office of Global Communications.

Beers's boss, Secretary of State Colin Powell, countered criticism of appointing a politically inexperienced advertising executive to such an important post by saying, "There is nothing wrong with getting somebody who knows how to sell something." "After all," he added, "we are selling a product. We need someone who can rebrand foreign policy, rebrand diplomacy. And besides, Charlotte Beers got me to buy Uncle Ben's rice."[17] Thus, treating "American values" such as liberty, diversity, and pluralism as consumer "products" that simply needed to be marketed more effectively to the rest of the world, Secretary Beers signed off on various projects designed to demonstrate "the global opportunities that result from democratization, good governance, and open markets."[18] Perhaps her most famous project was the creation of the Middle East radio network "Sawa" (Arabic for "together") in March 2002, which targets listeners of age thirty and under. Programming is music driven with five- to ten-minute newscasts twice an hour, twenty-four hours a day, that present the U.S. government's view on important political issues. In addition, she collaborated with California-based Globe TV to fund an exchange of Arab and U.S. journalists, including the prominent anchorwoman from "Good Morning Egypt." Finally, Beers's office embarked on a systematic search for thousands of foreign professionals, students, and artists who had participated in past decades in U.S. government–sponsored exchange programs, in the hope that they could be pressured into serving in their respective countries as "mini-ambassadors" for the United States.

Convinced that four decades in the advertising industry had been the perfect preparation for her new position, Beers saw herself as the salesperson in chief, hawking America's "intangible assets—things like our belief system and our values" to her "target audience" in the Muslim world. Thus, a hybrid monologue of Empire mixing martial and consumerist images and metaphors was born. As Jan Nederveen Pieterse reminds us, "Neoliberal empire is a marriage of convenience with neoliberalism, indicated by inconsistent use of neoliberal policies, and an attempt to merge America whose business is business with the America whose business is war, at a time when business is not doing great."[19] Indeed, for Beers, public diplomacy and commercial advertising were linked by the same market logic: "You'll find that in any great brand, the leverageable asset is the emotional underpinning of the brand—or what people believe, what they think, what they feel when they use it. I am much more comfortable with that dimension of the assignment, because I have dealt with it before."[20]

When Beers resigned unexpectedly in March 2003—ostensibly for health reasons—commentators were united in their negative assessment of her campaign. After all, world opinion polls actually pointed to *intensifying* anti-American sentiments. The war in Iraq and the difficult occupation of the country by coalition forces made matters only worse. Even in the United Kingdom, America's closest and most sympathetic partner, positive attitudes toward the United States dropped from 75 percent in July 2002 to 58 percent in March 2004.[21] These numbers have not improved in subsequent years. In 2007, 60 percent of Australians held a mainly negative view of the U.S. role in the world.[22] Still, Beers's successors Margaret Tutwiler and Karen Hughes continued to run American public diplomacy in the same mode of imperial globalism.

## FROM MARKET GLOBALISM TO IMPERIAL
## GLOBALISM: ANALYZING IDEAS AND CLAIMS

Having examined the shift from market globalism to imperial globalism on the macrolevel of politics and policy, let us now explore these ideologies on the microlevel of ideas and concepts. After introducing what I consider to be the core ideological claims of market globalism, I subject them to a "critical discourse analysis." This method is anchored in hermeneutics, critical theory, and poststructuralist studies and designed to explore systematically the patterns of ideological discourse. As Michael Freeden points out, "discourse" refers to the communicative practices through which ideology is exercised. The central idea behind such a critical discourse analysis is "to conceive of language as a communicative set of interactions, through which social and cultural beliefs and understandings are shaped and circulated."[23]

Thus, recognizing the importance of communication through the modern media, this method focuses on the interpretation of coherent units of spoken and written language and places them in their historical and political context. As Andrew Chadwick notes, by scrutinizing texts in the public domain, critical discourse analysis is particularly suited to help researchers comprehend the role played by language use in producing and reinforcing asymmetrical power relations that sustain certain forms of social and political identity. Rejecting a sharp distinction between the realm of "real politics" and "ideas," Chadwick suggests that any analysis of political practice is incomplete if it does not refer to the discourses that surround and construct it.[24] However, this does not mean that all meaning is the product of language alone. Rather, as Freeden puts it, "ideological meaning is a joint product of the degree of analytical rigor possessed by its formulators, of the linguistic flexibility of language, and of the historical context."[25] Consequently, our critical discourse analysis of market globalism takes seriously the ideational and linguistic dimensions of globalization while at the same time recognizing the importance of material factors such as politics and economics.

Let us then turn to our analysis of the utterances, speeches, and writings of influential advocates of market globalism before and after 9/11. As we noted in chapter 1, these global power elites function as ideological codifiers who seek to imbue the concept of globalization with values, beliefs, and meanings that support the global spread of free-market principles by a hegemonic American Empire. Although these meanings undergo ceaseless contestation and redefinition in the public arena, the dominant party of this ideological struggle enjoys the advantage of turning its assertions into the foundation of a widely shared framework of understanding. Thus, the core claims of market globalism serve as an important source of collective and individual identity.[26]

Some critics might object to my discussion below as an attempt to present my audience with a greatly exaggerated account of market globalism. Others might object to my exposition as a project of building up a straw person that can be easily dismantled. In his insightful study of economic globalization, Michael Veseth responds to the same objection by pointing out that this artificial straw person is actually the product of the globalists' own making.[27] In other words, globalists themselves construct these claims to sell their political agenda. It may be true that no single market globalist speech or piece of writing contains all the assertions discussed below. But all of them contain some of these claims.

## CLAIM NUMBER ONE: GLOBALIZATION IS ABOUT THE LIBERALIZATION AND GLOBAL INTEGRATION OF MARKETS

This first claim of market globalism is anchored in the neoliberal ideal of the self-regulating market as the normative basis for a future global order. According to this perspective, the vital functions of the free market—its rationality and efficiency as well as its alleged ability to bring about greater social integration and material progress—can only be realized in a democratic society that values and protects individual freedom. For Friedrich Hayek and his neoliberal followers, the free market represents a state of liberty because it is "a state in which each can use his knowledge for his own purpose."[28] Thus, the preservation of individual freedom depends on the state's willingness to refrain from interfering with the private sphere of the market. Liberal thinkers like Isaiah Berlin refer to this limitation on governmental interference as "negative liberty." This concept defends the protection of a private area of life within which one "is or should be left to do or be what he is able to do or be, without interference by other persons."[29] Since neoliberals allege that the free market relies on a set of rational rules applying equally to all members of society, they consider it both just and meritocratic. While the existence of the market depends on human action, its resulting benefits and burdens are not products of human design. In other words, the concrete outcomes of market interactions are neither intended nor foreseen but are the result of the workings of what Adam Smith famously called the "invisible hand."

Opposing the expansion of governmental intervention in the economy that occurred in Western industrialized nations during the first three-quarters of the twentieth century, globalists in the 1990s called for the "liberalization of markets"—that is, the deregulation of national economies. In their view, such neoliberal measures would not only lead to the emergence of an integrated global market but also result in greater political freedom for all citizens of the world. As Milton Friedman notes, "The kind of economic organization that provides economic freedom directly, namely competitive capitalism, also promotes political freedom because it separates economic power from political power and in this way enables the one to offset the other."[30] This citation highlights the crucial neoliberal assumption that politics and economics are separate realms. The latter constitutes a fundamentally nonpolitical, private sphere that must remain sheltered from the imposition of political power. Governments ought to be limited to providing an appropriate legal and institutional framework for the fulfillment of voluntary agreements reflected in contractual arrangements.

A passage in a *BusinessWeek* editorial implicitly conveys this neoliberal suspicion of political power in defining globalization in market terms: "Globalization is about the triumph of markets over governments. Both proponents and opponents of globalization agree that the driving force today is markets, which are suborning the role of government. The truth is that the size of government has been shrinking relative to the economy almost everywhere."[31] Claiming that it is the liberalization of markets that "makes globalization happen," the British *Financial Times* reporter Martin Wolf conveys a similar perspective to his mass readership. He argues that globalization "marks the worldwide spread of the economic liberalization that began nearly fifty years ago in western Europe with the Marshall Plan." Celebrating the most "precious right of democracy, the right to be left alone," the British journalist Peter Martin takes Wolf's argument a step further: "The liberal market economy is by its very nature global. It is the summit of human endeavor. We should be proud that by our work and by our votes we have—collectively and individually—contributed to building it."[32] In short, market globalist voices present globalization as a natural economic phenomenon whose essential qualities are the liberalization and integration of global markets and the reduction of governmental interference in the economy. Privatization, free trade, and unfettered capital movements are portrayed as the best and most natural way for realizing individual liberty and material progress in the world.

Globalists usually convey their assertion that globalization is about the liberalization and global integration of markets in the form of moral demands and rational imperatives. For example, President George W. Bush argues in the 2002/2006 *National Security Strategy of the United States of America* (*NSSUS*), "The concept of 'free trade' arose as a moral principle even before it became a pillar of economics."[33] Former president Clinton's U.S. Trade Representative Charlene Barshefsky admonished her audiences in both the United States and the global South to realize that globalization requires a rational commitment "to restructure public enterprises and accelerate privatization of key sectors—including energy, transportation, utilities, and communication—which will enhance market-driven competition and deregulation."[34] Asserting that the realization of "open, dynamic economies" constitutes "the very essence of globalization," International Monetary Fund (IMF) managing director Michael Camdessus argued that in order "to optimize the opportunities and reduce the risks of globalization, we must head towards a world with open and integrated capital markets."[35]

Perhaps the most eloquent exposition of the neoliberal claim that globalization is about the liberalization and global integration of markets can be found in Thomas Friedman's best sellers on the subject, including *The Lexus and the Olive Tree* and the more recent *The World Is Flat 3.0: A Brief History of the Twenty-First Century*. Indeed, many commentators see Friedman as the "official narrator of globalization" in the United States today.[36] Although the award-winning *New York Times* correspondent claims that he does not want to be considered as "a salesman of globalization," he eagerly admonishes his readers to acknowledge the factuality of existing global realities and "think like globalists."[37] For Friedman, this means that people ought to accept the following "truth" about globalization:

The driving idea behind globalization is free-market capitalism—the more you let market forces rule and the more you open your economy to free trade and competition, the more efficient your economy will be. Globalization means the spread of free-market capitalism to virtually every country in the world. Therefore, globalization also has its own set of economic rules—rules that revolve around opening, deregulating, and privatizing your economy, in order to make it more competitive and attractive to foreign investment.[38]

Asserting that, for the first time in history, "virtually every country in the world has the same basic hardware—free-market capitalism," Friedman predicts that globalization will result in the creation of a single global marketplace. He informs his readers that this feat will be achieved by means of the "Golden Straitjacket"—the "defining political–economic garment of this globalization era."[39] Stitched together by Anglo-American neoliberal politicians and business leaders, the Golden Straitjacket forces every country in the world to adopt the same economic rules:

> [M]aking the private sector the primary engine of its economic growth, maintaining a low rate of inflation and price stability, shrinking the size of its state bureaucracy, maintaining as close to a balanced budget as possible, if not a surplus, eliminating and lowering tariffs on imported goods, removing restrictions on foreign investment, getting rid of quotas and domestic monopolies, increasing exports, privatizing state-owned industries and utilities, deregulating capital markets, making its currency convertible, opening its industries, deregulating its economy to promote as much domestic competition as possible, eliminating government corruption, subsidies and kickbacks as much as possible, opening its banking and telecommunications systems to private ownership and competition and allowing its citizens to choose from an array of competing pension options and foreign-run pension and mutual funds. When you stitch all of these pieces together you have the Golden Straitjacket.[40]

Friedman concludes his pitch for the liberalization and global integration of markets by pointing out that today's global market system is the result of "large historical forces" that gave birth to a new power source in the world—the "Electronic Herd." Made up of millions of faceless stock, bond, and currency traders sitting behind computer screens all over the globe, the Electronic Herd also includes the executive officers of large TNCs who shift their production sites to the most efficient, low-cost producers. In order to succeed in the new era of globalization, countries not only have to put on the Golden Straitjacket but also have to please the Electronic Herd. Friedman explains, "The Electronic Herd loves the Golden Straitjacket, because it embodies all the liberal, free-market rules the herd wants to see in a country. Those countries that put on the Golden Straitjacket are rewarded by the herd with investment capital. Those that don't want to put it on are disciplined by the herd—either by the herd avoiding or withdrawing its money from that country."[41]

While acknowledging the shift toward imperial globalism after 9/11, both market globalists and their ideological challengers on the Left emphasize the continued viability of the project of market liberalization and global integration. For example, the Indian writer and social activist Arundhati Roy, one of the most eloquent critics of corporate globalization, argues that the neoliberal project of "breaking open different markets" has merely received more open U.S. military backing in the ongoing Global War on Terror. Claiming that "there isn't a country on God's earth that is not caught in the cross-hairs of the American cruise missile and the IMF checkbook," Roy insists that those nations with the greatest reserves of natural wealth are most at risk: "Unless they surrender their resources willingly to the corporate machine, civil unrest will be fomented or war will be waged."[42]

Approaching the subject from the opposing ideological perspective in his updated account of globalization in "the age of terrorism," Thomas Friedman nonetheless agrees with Roy's assessment that the neoliberal "globalization system" defined as the liberalization and global integration of markets is still "alive and well" in the post-9/11 era: "Not only will September 11 not be remembered for ending the process of global financial, trade, and technological integration, but it may well be remembered for bringing some sobriety to the anti-globalization movement." But perhaps the most important reason why globalization is alive and well, Friedman continues, is that the two biggest countries in the world—India and China—have long moved beyond the question of "*whether* countries should globalize [emphasis added]." Citing India's leading globalist voices, like Sanjay Baru, the editor of India's *Financial Express*, and Jairam Ramesh, the Congress Party's top economic adviser, Friedman concludes that most countries in the world are still fond of globalization, given their "great desire for participation in the economic expansion process."[43]

By forcing the West to add military muscle to its globalist project, Friedman contends, the terrorist attacks have actually strengthened the resolve of the United States and its allies to transform the world's most egregious tyrannies into "pluralistic free-market democracies." At the same time, however, Friedman insists that the Global War on Terror is not the "real war" because the eradication of terrorism amounts only to the elimination of a "tool." Reiterating the official Bush line that the "real war" is a "war of ideas," Friedman concludes that the decisive battles will be waged on the terrain of ideology: "We're fighting to defeat an ideology: religious totalitarianism. . . . The opposite of religious totalitarianism is an ideology of pluralism."[44]

Indeed, a close analysis of President Bush's public utterances before and after 9/11 provides much evidence for Friedman's assertion that the administration's turn to imperial globalism has not really affected the neoliberal drive to liberalize and globally integrate markets. During his 2000 presidential campaign, Bush consistently promised to "work tirelessly to open up markets all over the world" and "end tariffs and break down barriers everywhere, entirely, so the whole world trades in freedom."[45] A few months before the terrorist attacks, the president formalized the proposal of expanding the North American Free Trade Association to a Free Trade Area for the Americas, then projected to encompass thirty-four countries and 800 million people by the end of the decade. Even after 9/11, Bush promised to "ignite a new area of global economic growth through free markets and free trade." Strongly affirming the importance of "opening societies to commerce and investment" in his *NSSUS*, the president spells out a plethora of new neoliberal initiatives over several pages. Merging market discourse with security slogans, the document culminates in the credo of imperial globalism: "Free markets and free trade are key priorities of our national security strategy."[46] Indeed, Ben Bernanke, chair of the Federal Reserve, recently lauded the continued expansion of global trade and finance, adding that the "pace of globalization is faster and more sweeping now than at any other time in world history."[47] Bush's post-9/11 commitment to the neoliberal project of prying open markets has been dutifully echoed in similar speeches given by world leaders as different as Paul Martin, Canada's minister of finance; Thabo Mbeki, president of South Africa; and Goh Chok Tong, prime minister of Singapore. Indeed, the latter hailed the "growing trend of trade liberalization negotiations" by China, Japan, and the United States, adding that this phenomenon reflects "more creative and constructive directions for the region's strategic balance."[48]

A critical discourse analysis of the market globalist claim that globalization is about the liberalization and global integration of markets might begin by contrasting the neoliberal rhetoric of liberty with Friedman's depiction of globalization proceeding by means of the Golden Straitjacket, or, even worse, by unilateral military action. If the liberalization of trade and markets depends on coercive measures employed by the United States and its allies, then this form of liberty comes dangerously close to Jean-Jacques Rousseau's famous idea that only in obeying the "general will"—even under duress—is a person truly free. Yet, for the French philosopher, in order to count as a truly universal expression, the general will must come from all citizens and not merely from a partisan Electronic Herd or the government of a hyperpower that seeks to impose its ideology on the rest of the world.

In selling their will as the general will, market globalists condemn alternative ways of organizing the economy. Their project of "opening up economies" is advocated as an endeavor of universal applicability, for it supposedly reflects the dictates of human freedom in general. Thus, it must be applied to all countries, regardless of the political and cultural preferences expressed by local citizens. As President Bush notes, "Policies that further strenghten market incentives and market institutions are relevant for all economies—industrialized countries, emerging markets, and the developing world."[49] However, such efforts to stitch together a neoliberal economic straitjacket—one-size-fits-all countries—are hardly compatible with a process of globalization that is alleged to contribute to the spread of freedom, choice, and openness in the world.

Second, as Friedman concedes, the message of liberalizing and globally integrating markets is realizable only through the political project of engineering free markets. In order to advance their enterprise, market globalists must be prepared to utilize the powers of government to weaken and eliminate those social policies and institutions that curtail the market. Since only strong governments are up to this ambitious task of transforming existing social arrangements, the successful liberalization of markets depends on the intervention and interference of centralized state power. The assertion that governments can best contribute to the process of market liberalization by simply getting out of the way represents, therefore, a clear example of ideological distortion. Such remarks reflect a neoliberal idealization of the limited role of government, which stands in stark contrast to government's role in the actual social arena. In truth, market globalists do expect governments to play an extremely active role in implementing their political agenda. The activist character of neoliberal administrations in the United States, the United Kingdom, Australia, and New Zealand during the 1980s and 1990s attests to the importance of strong governmental action in engineering free markets.[50] Indeed, promarket governments serve as indispensable catalysts of "globalization from above." In their pursuit of market liberalization and integration, both neoliberal and neoconservative power elites violate their own principles of decentralization, limited government, and negative liberty.

Finally, the neoliberal claim that globalization is about the liberalization and global integration of markets serves to solidify as "fact" what is actually a contingent political initiative. Market globalists have been successful because they have persuaded the public that their neoliberal account of globalization represents an objective or at least neutral diagnosis rather than a direct contribution to the emergence of the very conditions it purports to analyze. To be sure, neoliberals may indeed be able to offer some "empirical evidence" for the "liberalization" of markets. But does the spread of market principles really happen because there exists an intrinsic, metaphysical connection between globalization and the expansion of markets? Or does it occur because globalists have the political and discursive power to shape the world, largely according to their ideological formula:

$$\text{liberalization} + \text{integration of markets} = \text{globalization}$$

This economistic-objectivist representation of globalization detracts from the multidimensional character of the phenomenon. Ecological, cultural, and political dimensions of globalization are discussed only as subordinate processes dependent on the movements of global markets. Even if one were to accept the central role of the economic dimension of globalization, there is no reason to believe that these processes must necessarily be connected to the deregulation of markets. An alternative view offered by justice globalists instead suggests linking globalization to the creation of a global regulatory framework that would make markets more accountable to international political institutions.

The setting of a successful political agenda always occurs simultaneously with concerted efforts to sell to the public the general desirability of a particular system of ideas. Market globalism is no exception. Like all ideologies, its values and beliefs are conveyed through a number of justificatory claims, usually starting with one that establishes what the phenomenon is all about. As international relations expert Edward Luttwak points out, there is a good reason why the spectacular advance of "turbo-capitalism" in the world is accompanied by so much talk about globalization in the public arena. The presentation of globalization as an enterprise that liberates and integrates global markets as well as emancipates individuals from governmental control is the best way of enlisting the public in the market-globalist struggle against those laws and institutions these dominant elites find most restrictive.[51] By engineering popular consent with the help of the corporate global media, they only rarely resort to open forms of coercion. The Golden Straitjacket and the U.S.-led Global War on Terror will do splendidly to keep dissent to a minimum. For those who remain skeptical, market globalists have another ideological claim up their sleeves: Why doubt a process that proceeds with historical inevitability?

## CLAIM NUMBER TWO: GLOBALIZATION IS INEVITABLE AND IRREVERSIBLE

At first glance, the belief in the historical inevitability of globalization seems to be a poor fit for a globalist ideology based on neoliberal principles. After all, throughout the twentieth century, liberals and conservatives have consistently criticized Marxism for its determinist claims that devalue human free agency and downplay the ability of noneconomic factors to shape social reality. In particular, neoliberals have attacked the Marxist notion of history as a teleological process that unfolds according to "inexorable laws" that hasten the demise of capitalism, ultimately leading to the emergence of a classless society on a global scale.

However, a close study of the utterances of influential market globalists reveals their reliance on a similar monocausal, economistic narrative of historical inevitability. While disagreeing with Marxists on the final goal of historical development, they nonetheless share with their ideological opponents a fondness for such terms as "irresistible," "inevitable," and "irreversible" to describe the projected path of globalization. As Ulrich Beck points out, "In a way, neoliberal globalism thus resembles its archenemy: Marxism. It is the rebirth of Marxism as a management ideology."[52] By focusing on the "logic" of technology and markets, market globalists minimize the role of human agency and individual choice—the centerpiece of liberal thought from John Locke and John Stuart Mill to Milton Friedman.

According to the market-globalist perspective, globalization reflects the spread of irreversible market forces driven by technological innovations that make the global integration of national economies inevitable. In fact, market globalism is almost always intertwined with the deep belief in the ability of markets to use new technologies to solve social problems far better than any alternative course.[53] When, two decades ago, British prime minister Margaret Thatcher famously pronounced that "there is no alternative," she meant that there no longer existed a theoretical and practical alternative to the expansionist logic of the market. In fact, she accused those nonconformists who still dared to pose alternatives as foolishly relying on anachronistic, socialist fantasies that betrayed their inability to cope with empirical reality. Governments, political parties, and social movements had no choice but to "adjust" to the inevitability of globalization. Their sole remaining task was to facilitate the integration of national economies in the new global market. States and interstate systems should, therefore, serve to ensure the smooth working of market logic.[54] Indeed, the multiple voices of globalism convey to the public their message of inevitability with tremendous consistency. Below are some examples.

In a speech on U.S. foreign policy, President Clinton told his audience, "Today we must embrace the inexorable logic of globalization—that everything from the strength of our economy to the safety of our cities, to the health of our people, depends on events not only within our borders, but half a world away."[55] On another occasion he emphasized that "globalization is irreversible. Protectionism will only make things worse."[56] Stuart

Eizenstat echoed the assessment of his boss: "Globalization is an inevitable element of our lives. We cannot stop it any more than we can stop the waves from crashing on the shore. The arguments in support of trade liberalization and open markets are strong ones—they have been made by many of you and we must not be afraid to engage those with whom we respectfully disagree."[57]

Frederick W. Smith, chairman and CEO of FedEx Corporation, suggests that "globalization is inevitable and inexorable and it is accelerating. . . . Globalization is happening, it's going to happen. It does not matter whether you like it or not."[58] Thomas Friedman comes to a similar conclusion: "Globalization is very difficult to reverse because it is driven both by powerful human aspiration for higher standards of living and by enormously powerful technologies which are integrating us more and more every day, whether we like it or not."[59] But Friedman simply argues by asserting that there is something inherent in technology that requires a neoliberal system. He never considers that, for example, new information technologies could just as easily be used to enhance public-service media as utilized in commercial, profit-making enterprises. The choice depends on the nature of the political will exerted in a particular social order.

Neoliberal elites in non-Western countries faithfully echo the market-globalist language of inevitability. For example, Rahul Bajaj, a leading Indian industrialist, insists that "we need much more liberalization and deregulation of the Indian economy. No sensible Indian businessman disagrees with this. . . . Globalization is inevitable. There is no better alternative." He adds that "India and Indian companies have to recognize that the forces of globalization are irreversible. I think the agenda for India is not whether globalization is on, but what to do about it, what are the implications of networking and alliances."[60] Manuel Villar Jr., Speaker of the House of Representatives in the Philippines, agrees: "Of course, we cannot simply wish away the process of globalization. It is a reality of a modern world. The process is irreversible."[61] Masaru Hayami, governor of the Bank of Japan, concurs: "The essence of globalization is the integration of markets worldwide and the deepening of various interdependent relations. . . . Thus, the move toward globalization is an inevitable reality, and not likely to be reversed."[62]

The neoliberal portrayal of globalization as some sort of natural force, like the weather or gravity, makes it easier for market globalists to convince people that they must adapt to the discipline of the market if they are to survive and prosper. Hence, the claim of inevitability serves a number of important political functions. For one, it neutralizes the challenges of alterglobalist opponents by depoliticizing the public discourse about globalization: neoliberal policies are above politics because they simply carry out what is ordained by nature. This view implies that, instead of acting according to a set of choices, people merely fulfill world-market laws that demand the elimination of government controls. There is nothing that can be done about the natural movement of economic and technological forces; political groups ought to acquiesce and make the best of an unalterable situation. Since the emergence of a world based on the primacy of market values reflects the dictates of history, resistance would be unnatural, irrational, and dangerous.

As John Malott, former U.S. ambassador to Malaysia, puts it, "Some people think that the debate about globalization is whether it is good or bad. To me, globalization just is. We cannot stop it; we have to accept it, and adjust to it. Those countries, those companies, those people who adjust to a changing world will do better. Those who resist will suffer." For Malott, "adjustment" refers to the implementation of deregulatory policies that allow for "less rather than more government control and influence over business decision-making."[63] Thus, market globalists utilize the idea of the historical inevitability of globalization in order to better advance their thoroughly political project of implementing neoliberal economic policies. For the masses, however, market globalists prescribe an attitude of political passivity in the face of inevitability. This makes it easier for market globalists to admonish the general public to "share the burdens of globalization." In short, market-globalist ideology constitutes high politics while presenting itself in nonpolitical garb.

By turning the market into a natural force, market globalists suggest that human beings are at the mercy of external imperatives they cannot control. As the neoliberal economist Alain Lipietz emphasizes, the modern market economy is an autonomous realm that is "defined by immutable economic laws, behaviors and tendencies."[64] The strategy seems to be working. Even prolabor voices, such as AFL-CIO director of public policy David Smith, have accepted the globalist claims of inevitability and irreversibility: "Globalization is a fact. . . . We're not going to turn these tides back. We shouldn't want to turn these tides back; even if we wanted to, we couldn't."[65]

In a lucid article that appeared in the *Atlantic Monthly*, theologian Harvey Cox argues that the claim of market inevitability bears a striking resemblance to religious narratives found in Genesis, St. Paul's Epistle to the Romans, and St. Augustine's *City of God*. According to Cox, Christian stories of human origins and the fall from grace, as well as doctrines of sin and redemption, find their contemporary expression in neoliberal discourses about the creation of wealth, the seductive temptations of statism, captivity to economic cycles, and, ultimately, salvation through the advent of the global free market. Both narratives are sustained by a belief in an inner meaning of human history determined by the unalterable will of a transcendental force. Endowing it with the divine attributes of omnipotence, omniscience, and omnipresence, globalists assign to "The Market" a "comprehensive wisdom that in the past only the gods have known. . . . It has risen above these demigods and chthonic spirits to become today's First Cause." Of course, the divine attributes of "The Market" are not always completely evident to mortals but must be trusted and affirmed by neoliberal faith. "Farther along," an old gospel song says, "we'll understand why."[66]

And yet the market is neither an ahistorical nor an asocial manifestation of blind natural forces that transcend human understanding. Markets are the creation of human interactions; they do not dictate policy. Global economic integration is not a natural process. Rather, it is driven by decisions of governments that have removed barriers to cross-border movements of capital and goods. People who are organized in powerful social groups facilitate the process of neoliberal globalization. They demand—in the name of "The Market"—the implementation of economic policies favorable to their interests.

Finally, the claim that globalization is inevitable and irresistible is inscribed within a larger evolutionary discourse that assigns a privileged position to those nations that are in the forefront of "liberating" markets from political control. For example, Lorenzo Zambrano, the Mexican CEO of CEMEX Corporation, the world's largest cement producer, strongly supports this idea: "I agree that globalization is inevitable and that it may be inherent to the evolution of a civilization and that it has been brought about by progress in telecommunications allowing instantaneous contact to be established."[67]

Some American globalists are more culturally explicit than Zambrano. For them, the United States and its philosophy of free-market capitalism is spearheading the inevitable historical progress toward the creation of a global "market civilization." Francis Fukuyama represents an extreme perspective on this issue. He insists that globalization is really a euphemism that stands for the irreversible Americanization of the world: "I think it has to be Americanization because, in some respects, America is the most advanced capitalist society in the world today, and so its institutions represent the logical development of market forces. Therefore, if market forces are what drives globalization, it is inevitable that Americanization will accompany globalization."[68] Friedman, too, ends his best seller *The Lexus and the Olive Tree* with a celebration of America's unique role in a globalizing world: "And that's why America, at its best, is not just a country. It's a spiritual value and role model. . . . And that's why I believe so strongly that for globalization to be sustainable America must be at its best—today, tomorrow, all the time. It not only can be, it must be, a beacon for the whole world."[69]

These statements reveal the existence of a strong link between the market-globalist claim of inevitability and the American pursuit of global cultural hegemony. As John Gray observes, neoliberal forces have successfully "appropriated America's self-image as the model for a universal civilization in the service of a global free market."[70] History looks kindly on the "shining city on the hill" because it has been listening to the voice of the market. As a reward, objective market forces have chosen the United States to point all other nations in the right direction. In what appears to be the market-globalist version of the old American theme of manifest destiny, U.S. political and business leaders proclaim to the rest of the world, Adopt our American values and neoliberal policies and you, too, can become "America."

By activating what Ricoeur calls the ideological function of integration, market globalists favor the creation of an American-style market identity that is designed to eclipse most other components of personal, group, or class identity. As Steven Kline points out, global marketing efforts particularly attempt to provide young people with the identity of the consuming global teenager. Coca-Cola, Levi-Strauss, McDonald's, and Disney "have become the source of endless campaigns to enfranchise youth in the globalizing democracy of the market."[71] Why should mere consumers be interested in strengthening civic ties and working for global justice if such endeavors are not profitable? Why show moral restraint and solidarity if "we," the consumers, are incessantly told that we can have it all? As Benjamin Barber emphasizes, by broadly endorsing happiness that comes with shopping and consuming, this market identity takes on distinct cultural features because "America" and "American culture" are best-selling commodities in the global marketplace. American films, American television, American software, American music, American fast-food chains, American cars and motorcycles, American apparel, and American sports—to name but a few of those cultural commodities—are pervading the world to such an extent that even ordinary Indonesians have become convinced that they also can become "cool" by drinking Coke instead of tea. In Budapest, people are breathlessly watching *The Bill Cosby Show* reruns, and the Russian version of *Wheel of Fortune* offers lucky winners Sony DVDs into which they can load their pirated versions of wildly popular American films.[72]

And so it appears that market-globalist forces have been resurrecting the nineteenth-century paradigm of Anglo-American vanguardism propagated by Herbert Spencer and William Graham Sumner. The main ingredients of classical market liberalism are all present in market globalism. We find inexorable laws of nature favoring Western civilization, the self-regulating economic model of perfect competition, the virtues of free enterprise, the vices of state interference, the principle of laissez-faire, and the irreversible, evolutionary process leading up to the survival of the fittest. And yet today's market globalists translate a decidedly global imaginary into concrete political agendas. Equipped with a quasi-Marxist language of historical inevitability, market globalists look forward to the final realization of their *global* free-market utopia. They are confident that human history will end on a positive note—in spite of some undeniable risks and conflicts inherent in the process of globalization.

Indeed, some of these risks became glaringly apparent during the 2001–2002 corporate scandals in the United States involving such major corporations as Enron, WorldCom, and Arthur Andersen or the 2007–2008 subprime mortgage crisis that wreaked havoc on the world's financial architecture. Suddenly, the myth of the supposed self-regulating market exploded, as did the notion that the regulatory system set up to prevent abuses was far from immune to malignant political pressures. Other risks became transparent on September 11, causing some commentators to prematurely proclaim "the end of the globalization era." To some extent, the terrorist attacks undermined the claim of globalization's inevitability and irreversibility, and even noted neoliberal economists Robert J. Samuelson wrote in his widely read *Newsweek* column that previous globalization processes had been stopped by such cataclysmic events as the 1914 assassination of the Austrian archduke Franz Ferdinand in Sarajevo.[73]

On the other hand, the Global War on Terror allowed the Bush administration to weave the determinist language of market globalism into belligerent pronouncements of the inevitable triumph of the forces of good over evil. In presidential assurances that the United States and its allies would prevail in the War on Terror and "smoke Osama bin Laden out of his hole," the old soft-power discourse of *economic* inevitability reemerged confidently in the new hard-power narrative of *military* inevitability. Constant assurances that the United States and its allies would prevail in the Global War on Terror reverberated through the global media landscape. On his state visit to the United Kingdom in November 2003, President Bush emphasized the political and cultural ties between the two nations and predicted the inevitable realization of the vision of the "forces of freedom," for they "share a mission in the world beyond the balance of power or the simple pursuit of interest."[74] Christopher Shays, Republican congressman from Connecticut and chair of the House Subcommittee on National Security, expressed his similar belief that the "fight against global terrorism" would inevitably end in a "safer world" characterized by "broad-based free expression and free markets." After all, Shays added, the "toxic zeal" of the terrorists "can only be defeated by market forces, the relentless inevitability of free peoples pursuing their own enlightened self-interest in common cause."[75]

## CLAIM NUMBER THREE: NOBODY IS IN CHARGE OF GLOBALIZATION

Market globalism's deterministic language offers another rhetorical advantage. If the natural laws of "The Market" have indeed preordained a neoliberal course of history, then globalization does not reflect the arbitrary agenda of a particular social class or group. In other words, market globalists merely carry out the unalterable imperatives of a transcendental force much larger than narrow partisan interests. People are not in charge of globalization; markets and technology are. Certain human actions might accelerate or retard globalization, but in the last instance (to paraphrase none other than Friedrich Engels), the invisible hand of the market will always assert its superior wisdom. Robert Hormats, vice chairman of Goldman Sachs International, agrees: "The great beauty of globalization is that no one is in control. The great beauty of globalization is that it is not controlled by any individual, any government, any institution."[76]

In the early part of *The Lexus and the Olive Tree*, Friedman imagines himself engaged in a spirited debate with the former prime minister of Malaysia, who had accused Western powers of manipulating markets and currencies during the 1997–1998 Asian crisis in order to destroy the vibrant economies of their overseas competitors. Friedman tells his readers how he would respond to Prime Minister Mahatir Mohamad's charge:

> Ah, excuse me, Mahatir, but what planet are you living on? You talk about participating in globalization as if it were a choice you had. Globalization isn't a choice. It's a reality. . . . And the most basic truth about globalization is this: No one is in charge. . . . We all want to believe that someone is in charge and responsible. But the global marketplace today is an Electronic

Herd of often anonymous stock, bond and currency traders and multinational investors, connected by screens and networks.[77]

Of course, Friedman is right in a formal sense. There is no conscious conspiracy orchestrated by a single evil force to disempower Asian nations. But does this mean that nobody is in charge of globalization? Is it really true that the liberalization and integration of global markets proceeds outside the realm of human choice? Does globalization, therefore, absolve businesses and corporations from social responsibility? A critical discourse analysis of Friedman's statement reveals how he utilizes a realist narrative to sell to his audience a neoliberal version of globalization. He implies that anyone who thinks that globalization involves human choice is either hopelessly naïve or outright dangerous. Such persons might as well apply for permanent residence on Prime Minister Mohamad's alien planet.

For Friedman, the real player in the global marketplace is the Electronic Herd. But he never offers his readers a clear picture of the Herd's identity. Throughout his book, he portrays the Herd as a faceless crowd of individual profit maximizers whose human identity remains hidden behind dim computer screens. Apparently, these traders and investors are solely interested in moneymaking; they don't seem to be part of any politically or culturally identifiable group. Although they wield tremendous power, they are not in charge of globalization. Ah, excuse me, Tom, but where is the "realism" in your description?

Writing about the importance of unfettering financial markets in the emerging global economic order, Steward Brand, the cofounder of California-based Global Business Network, also asserts that "nobody is in charge of globalization." According to Brand, there exists "no policy body nor even an agreed-on body of theory to constrain the activity of world markets; the game continues to evolve rapidly, with none of the players ever quite sure what the new rules are."[78] Notice how this statement denies the existence of alterglobalist challengers who propose the regulation of markets. Moreover, Brand's argument implies that the "players" of the globalization "game" do not make the rules themselves. Presumably, they merely adjust to the new rules dictated to them by the impersonal logic of evolving markets.

Neo-Marxist thinkers Michael Hardt and Antonio Negri remind their readers that it is important to be aware of the two extreme conceptions of global authority that reside on opposite ends of the ideological spectrum. One is the market-globalist notion that nobody is in charge because globalization somehow rises up spontaneously out of the natural workings of the hidden hand of the world market. The other is the idea that a single evil power dictates to the world its design of globalization according to a conscious and all-seeing conspiratorial plan.[79] Both conceptions are distortions.

Still, even some neoliberal commentators concede that the market-globalist initiative to integrate and deregulate markets around the world is sustained by asymmetrical power relations. Backed by powerful states in the North, international institutions such as the World Trade Organization, the IMF, and the World Bank enjoy the privileged position of making and enforcing the rules of the global economy. In return for supplying much-needed loans to developing countries, the IMF and the World Bank demand from their creditors the implementation of neoliberal policies that further the material interests of the global North. Unleashed on developing countries in the 1990s, these policies are often referred to as the "Washington Consensus." It consists of a ten-point program that was originally devised and codified by John Williamson, an IMF adviser in the 1970s. The program was directed mostly at countries with large remaining foreign debts from the 1970s and 1980s, with the purpose of reforming the internal economic mechanisms of these countries so that they would be in a better position to repay the debts they had incurred. In practice, the terms of the program spelled out a new form of colonialism. The ten areas of the Washington Consensus, as defined by Williamson, required Third World governments to enforce the following reforms:

1. A guarantee of fiscal discipline and a curb to budget deficits
2. A reduction of public expenditure, particularly in the military and public administration
3. Tax reform, aiming at the creation of a system with a broad base and with effective enforcement
4. Financial liberalization, with interest rates determined by the market
5. Competitive exchange rates to assist export-led growth
6. Trade liberalization, coupled with the abolition of import licensing and a reduction of tariffs
7. Promotion of foreign direct investment
8. Privatization of state enterprises, leading to efficient management and improved performance
9. Deregulation of the economy
10. Protection of property rights[80]

That this program is called the "Washington Consensus" is no coincidence. The United States is by far the most dominant economic power in the world, and the largest TNCs are based in the United States. As the British journalist Will Hutton points out, one of the principal aims of the Economic Security Council set up by President Clinton in 1993 was to open up ten countries to U.S. trade and finance. Most of these "target countries" are located in Asia and the Middle East.[81] Again, this is not to say that the United States is in complete control of global financial markets and, therefore, rules supreme over this gigantic process of globalization. But it does suggest that both the substance and the direction of economic globalization are, indeed, to a significant degree shaped by American foreign and domestic policy. As we shall see in the new imperial-globalist claim number six, this is especially true after 9/11. Substantiation of increasing U.S. hegemony comes from no less an observer than Friedman, who, in later passages of his book, surprisingly contradicts his previous account of a leaderless, anonymous Electronic Herd. Speaking in glowing terms about the global leadership of the United States, he suddenly acknowledges the existence of a captain at the helm of the global ship:

> The Golden Straitjacket was made in America and Great Britain. The Electronic Herd is led by American Wall Street Bulls. The most powerful agent pressuring other countries to open their markets for free trade and free investments is Uncle Sam, and America's global armed forces keep these markets and sea lanes open for this era of globalization, just as the British navy did for the era of globalization in the nineteenth century.[82]

Toward the end of his book, Friedman becomes even more explicit: "Indeed, McDonald's cannot flourish without McDonnell Douglas, the designer of the U.S. Air Force F-15. And the hidden fist that keeps the world safe for Silicon Valley's technologies to flourish is called the U.S. Army, Air Force, Navy, and Marine Corps. And these fighting forces and institutions are paid for by American taxpayer dollars."[83] In other words, global neoliberalism does not rely blindly on a hidden hand of the self-regulating market. When the chips are down, globalism seems to prefer the not-so-hidden fist of U.S. militarism.

Yet Friedman is not the only globalist who oscillates between the claim that "nobody is in charge" and the admission that "America is in control" (or that it should be). After telling a U.S. congressional subcommittee that globalization proceeds in a neutral arena allowing access to "many players," Joseph Gorman, chairman and CEO of TRW Inc., a large Cleveland-based manufacturing and service company of high-tech products, urges his audience to strengthen the leadership role of the United States. His ten-page statement is divided into sections that bear the following titles:

- "To win in the global economy, the United States must lead liberalization efforts."
- "International trade and investment agreements are still needed to open foreign markets for American companies and their workers."
- "If the United States is not at the table, it can't play and it can't win."
- "Success in the global economy is critical for the American economy, its companies, and its workers."
- "The global economy is real, and the United States is part of it."
- "Because the United States is the world's most competitive nation, we have the most to gain from the global economy and from trade and investment liberalization."
- "Developing countries in particular hold huge promise."[84]

The interpretive possibilities arising from a critical discourse analysis of Gorman's testimony are almost limitless. Images of the world as a gambling table that can be accessed only by the best "players" are as telling as his neo-imperialist desire to cash in on "promising" developing nations. As far as the integrative, identity-giving function of ideology is concerned, Gorman's testimony seeks to persuade its audience that one's loyalty to market principles allows one to be both a patriot defending American interests and a market globalist. Although class conflicts continue to be a very real phenomenon in the daily world of commodity production, Gorman's market rhetoric nonetheless conjures up a harmonious common identity. Businesspeople, workers, and farmers of the world unite around your consumer identity!

But if nobody is in control of globalization, why does Gorman try so hard to make a case for U.S. leadership? One obvious answer is that the claim of a leaderless globalization process does not reflect social reality. Rather, the idea that nobody is in charge serves the neoliberal political agenda of defending and expanding American global hegemony. Like the market-globalist rhetoric of historical inevitability, the portrayal of globalization as a leaderless process seeks to both depoliticize the public debate on the subject and demobilize global justice movements. The deterministic language of a technological progress driven by uncontrollable market laws turns political issues into scientific problems of administration. Once large segments of the population have accepted the globalist image of a self-directed juggernaut that simply runs its course, it becomes extremely difficult to challenge what Antonio Gramsci calls the "power of the hegemonic bloc." As ordinary people cease to believe in the possibility of choosing alternative social arrangements, market globalism gains strength in its ability to construct passive consumer identities. This tendency is further enhanced by assurances that globalization will bring prosperity to all parts of the world.

After September 11, however, it became increasingly difficult to maintain the assertion that "nobody is in charge of globalization." While a number of corporate leaders still reflexively talked about the "leaderless market," imperial globalists close to the Bush adminstration openly proclaimed that global security and a global liberal order "depend on the United States—that 'indispensable nation'—wielding its power."[85] After all, if America spearheaded the cause of universal principles, then it had a responsibility to make sure that the spread of these values was not hampered by ideological dissenters. Indeed, President Bush ends his preface to the *National Security Strategy of the United States of America* by glorifying U.S. global leadership: "Today, humanity holds in its hands the opportunity to further freedom's triumph over all these [terrorist] foes. The United States welcomes our [sic] responsibility to lead in this great mission."[86] In other words, on the issue of expanding American influence around the world, the ideology of American Empire found common ground with market discourse.

Armed U.S. world hegemony was not only good for business—particularly the American military-industrial complex—but it also made sense for a variety of political reasons. September 11 changed the terms of the discourse in that it enabled neoconservatives to put their global ambitions explicitly before a public traumatized by the terrorist attacks and thus vulnerable to what Claes Ryn, chairman of the National Humanities Institute, calls the "neo-Jacobin spirit" of the Bush administration. Many market globalists were willing to adapt to this new militancy—after all, the French Jacobins also wanted greater economic freedom.[87]

The resulting move toward imperial globalism meant that the claim "nobody is in charge of globalization" had to be abandoned and replaced by Bush's aggressive pronouncement of global leadership. However, the replacement of claim number three with a more aggressive pronouncement of global Anglo-American leadership should not be read as a sign of market globalism's ideological weakness. Rather, it reflects its ideational flexibility and growing ability to respond to a new set of political issues. Indeed, like all full-fledged political belief systems, market globalism was increasingly bearing the marks of an "ideational family" broad enough to contain the more economistic variant of the 1990s as well as its more militaristic post-9/11 manifestation.

## CLAIM NUMBER FOUR: GLOBALIZATION BENEFITS EVERYONE

This claim lies at the very core of globalism because it provides an affirmative answer to the crucial normative question of whether globalization represents a "good" or a "bad" phenomenon. Globalists frequently connect their arguments in favor of the integration of global markets to the alleged benefits resulting from the liberalization and expansion of world trade. At the 1996 G-7 Summit in Lyon, France, the heads of state and government of the seven major industrialized democracies issued a joint communiqué that contains the following passage:

> Economic growth and progress in today's interdependent world is bound up with the process of globalization. Globalization provides great opportunities for the future, not only for our countries, but for all others too. Its many positive aspects include an unprecedented expansion of investment and trade; the opening up to international trade of the world's most populous regions and opportunities for more developing countries to improve their standards of living; the increasingly rapid dissemination of information, technological innovation, and the proliferation of skilled jobs. These characteristics of globalization have led to a considerable expansion of wealth and prosperity in the world. Hence we are convinced that the process of globalization is a source of hope for the future.[88]

The dominant discourse on globalization reverberates with such generalizations. Here are some more examples. In 1999, then U.S. Secretary of the Treasury Robert Rubin asserted that free trade and open markets provide "the best prospect for creating jobs, spurring economic growth, and raising living standards in the United States and around the world."[89] Denise Froning, trade-policy analyst at both the Center for International Trade and Economics and the Heritage Foundation, suggests that "societies that promote economic freedom create their own dynamism and foster a wellspring of prosperity that benefits every citizen."[90] Alan Greenspan, former chairman of the U.S. Federal Reserve Board, insisted that "there can be little doubt that the extraordinary changes in global finance on balance have been beneficial in facilitating significant improvements in economic structures and living standards throughout the world."[91] President Bush, in a recent visit to India's high-tech industry centers around Hyderabad, emphasized that "globalization provides great opportunities."[92]

However, not one of the speakers cited previously addresses the ideological assumptions behind their key concepts. Who exactly is "every citizen"? What does "great opportunities" mean? As discussed in more detail in chapter 4, dissenting voices argue that income disparities between nations are actually widening at a quicker pace than ever before in recent history.[93] Two of the most thorough scientific assessments of changes in global income distribution have arrived at sharply conflicting results. Columbia University economist Xavier Sala i-Martin argues that his evidence shows that inequality across the world's individuals is declining, but according to World Bank economist Branko Milanovic, global inequality has risen slightly.[94] Jay Mazur, the president of the U.S. Union of Needletrades, Industrial, and Textile Employees, argues that "the benefits of the global economy are reaped disproportionately by the handful of countries and companies that set rules and shape markets. . . . Of the 100 largest economies in the world, 51 are corporations. Private financial flows have long since surpassed public-development aid and remain remarkably concentrated."[95]

There are many indications that the global hunt for profits actually makes it more difficult for poor people to enjoy the benefits of technology and scientific innovations. Consider the following story. A group of scientists in the United States has warned the public that economic globalization may now be the greatest threat to preventing the spread of parasitic diseases in sub-Saharan Africa. They pointed out that U.S.-based pharmaceutical companies are stopping production of many antiparasitic drugs because developing countries cannot afford to buy them. For example, the U.S. manufacturer for a drug to treat bilharzia, a parasitic disease that causes severe liver damage, has stopped production because of declining profits—even though the disease is thought to affect over 200 million people worldwide. Another drug used to combat damage caused by liver flukes has not been produced since 1979 because the "customer base" in the Third World does not wield enough "buying power."[96]

While market globalists typically acknowledge the existence of unequal global distribution patterns, they nonetheless insist that the market itself will eventually correct these "irregularities." As John Meehan, chairman of the U.S. Public Securities Association, puts it, while such "episodic dislocations" are "necessary" in the short run, they will eventually give way to "quantum leaps in productivity."[97] Although he admits that problems of global and domestic inequality created by such dislocations constitute a "legitimate concern," the former Speaker of the House of Representatives Newt Gingrich is quick to add that the "reality" of globalization is made visible in "a rising general standard of living for everybody." Ignoring the glaring contradiction arising from his recognition of global inequality while at the same time including "everybody" in the pool of globalization's beneficiaries, Gingrich launches into a masterpiece of market-globalist distortion:

> That is why people overall are generally better off than they have ever been—but in the short run, in a period of great transition those who are more successful pull away, and get even wealthier faster. But the historical pattern is that everybody else begins to catch up over time, and I think if you know what you are doing you don't become a "have not," and if you don't know what you are doing transferring welfare to you does not solve the problem. We've got to find a way to have more people understand the information age and participate in it.[98]

In the end, Gingrich justifies the real human costs of globalization as the short-term price of economic liberalization. Such ideological statements are disseminated to large audiences by what Benjamin Barber calls the profit-oriented "infotainment telesector." Television, radio, and the Internet frequently place existing economic, political, and social realities within a neoliberal framework, sustaining the claim that globalization benefits everyone through omnipresent affirmative images and sound bites. As a popular television commercial suggests, "the whole world is Ford country." Market globalist ideology appears as "videology," the product of popular culture driven by commercial interests that incessantly instills in its audience the values, needs, and desires required for the expansion of markets.[99] The alleged benefits of globalization are also touted on television, on the Internet, and in film. Shopping malls and theme parks glorify the new global market as enhancing consumer choice and facilitating individual self-realization. The past few years have seen an enormous expansion of the celebrity "gossip market," which presents viewers and readers with the riveting private lives and heartrending troubles of global celebrities such as Paris Hilton, Lindsay Lohan, Britney Spears, Martha Stewart, and Kobe Bryant. These stories have become more real and newsworthy than the persistence of poverty, inequality, displacement, and environmental degradation.

Actual economic and social conditions matter little; TNCs that control global information and communications can conjure up an ideal world of the global village inhabited by beautiful people who live long and fulfilling lives as mindless consumers. In fact, market globalists such as Friedman even pretend to know beyond the shadow of a doubt that the poor in developing countries are itching to assume the identity of Western consumers: "[L]et me share a little secret I've learned from talking to all these folks [in the Third World]: With all due respect to revolutionary theorists, the 'wretched of the earth' want to go to Disney World—not the barricades. They want the Magic Kingdom, not Les Misérables."[100]

The market-globalist claim that globalization benefits everyone remained remarkably stable throughout the 2000s. As the prominent economist Jagdish Bhagwati notes in his best-selling book *In Defense of Globalization*, "economic globalization is on balance socially benign."[101] September 11 and the Global War on Terror did not have much impact on market-globalist claim number four; in fact, it seems that the terrorist attacks actually added to the fervor with which market globalists speak of the supposed benefits accruing from the rapid liberalization and global integration of markets. Indeed, throughout their respective terms in office, both Bill Clinton and George W. Bush have consistently argued that "[f]ree trade and free markets have proven their ability to lift whole societies out of poverty—so the United States will work with individual nations, entire regions, and the entire global trading community to build a world that trades in freedom and therefore grows in prosperity."[102]

## CLAIM NUMBER FIVE: GLOBALIZATION FURTHERS THE SPREAD OF DEMOCRACY IN THE WORLD

This market-globalist claim is anchored in the neoliberal assertion that freedom, free markets, free trade, and democracy are synonymous terms. Persistently affirmed as common sense, the compatibility of these concepts often goes unchallenged in the public discourse. The most obvious strategy by which neoliberals and neoconservatives generate popular support for the equation of democracy and the market is by discrediting traditionalism and socialism. The contest with both precapitalist and the anticapitalist forms of traditionalism, such as feudalism, has been won rather easily because the political principles of popular sovereignty and individual rights have been enshrined as the crucial catalyst for the technological and scientific achievements of modern market economies. The battle with socialism turned out to be a much tougher case. As late as the 1970s, socialism provided a powerful critique of the elitist, class-based character of liberal democracy, which, in its view, revealed that a substantive form of democracy had not been achieved in capitalist societies. Since the collapse of communism in Eastern Europe, however, the ideological edge has shifted decisively to the defenders of a neoliberal perspective who emphasize the relationship between economic liberalization and the emergence of democratic political regimes.

Francis Fukuyama, for example, asserts that there exists a clear correlation between a country's level of economic development and successful democracy. While globalization and capital development do not automatically produce democracies, "the level of economic development resulting from globalization is conducive to the creation of complex civil societies with a powerful middle class. It is this class and societal structure that facilitates democracy."[103] But Fukuyama's argument hinges on a limited definition of democracy that emphasizes formal procedures such as voting at the expense of the direct participation of broad majorities in political and economic decision making. This "thin" definition of democracy is part of what William I. Robinson has identified as the Anglo-American neoliberal project of "promoting polyarchy" in the developing world. For the critical political economist, the concept of polyarchy differs from the concept of "popular democracy" in that the latter posits democracy as both a process and a means to an end—a tool for devolving political and economic power from the hands of elite minorities to the masses. Polyarchy, on the other hand, represents an elitist and regimented model of "low-intensity" or "formal" market democracy. Polyarchies not only limit democratic participation to voting in elections but also require that those elected be insulated from popular pressures so that they may "effectively govern."[104]

This focus on the act of voting—in which equality prevails only in the formal sense—helps to obscure the conditions of inequality reflected in existing asymmetrical power relations in society. Formal elections provide the important function of legitimating the rule of dominant elites, thus making it more difficult for popular movements to challenge the rule of elites. The claim that globalization furthers the spread of democracy in the world is based largely on a narrow, formal-procedural understanding of "democracy." Neoliberal economic globalization and the strategic promotion of polyarchic regimes in the Third World are, therefore, two sides of the same ideological coin. They represent the systemic prerequisites for the legitimation of a full-blown world market. The promotion of polyarchy provides market globalists with the ideological opportunity to advance their neoliberal projects of economic restructuring in a language that ostensibly supports the "democratization" of the world.

Friedman's discussion of the democratic potential of globalization represents another clear example of such ideological maneuvering. Assuring his readers that globalization tends to impose democratic standards (like voting) on undemocratic countries, he argues that the integration of countries such as Indonesia and China into the global capitalist system has shown that the global market forces on authoritarian regimes the rules-based business practices and legal standards they cannot generate internally. Friedman coins the term "globalution" to refer to today's "revolutionary process" by which the powerful Electronic Herd contributes to building the "foundation stones of democracy":

> The Electronic Herd will intensify pressures for democratization generally, for three very critical reasons—flexibility, legitimacy, and sustainability. Here's how: The faster and bigger the herd gets, the more greased and open the global economy becomes, the more flexible you need to be to get the most out of the herd and protect yourself from it. While one can always find exceptions, I still believe that as a general rule the more democratic, accountable, and open your governance, the less likely it is that your financial system will be exposed to surprises.[105]

It is not difficult to notice the instrumentalist tone of Friedman's argument. Devoid of any moral and civic substance, democracy represents for Friedman merely the best shell for the imperatives of the market. His use of the term "accountability" hardly resonates with the idea of participatory democracy. Rather, he equates accountability with the creation of social and economic structures conducive to the business interests of the Electronic Herd. Moreover, he uses "flexibility" as a code word for deregulatory measures and privatization efforts that benefit capitalist elites but threaten the economic security of ordinary citizens. Granted, the "flexibility" of labor markets may well be an important factor in attracting foreign investment, but it is hardly synonymous with the successful creation of popular-democratic institutions in developing nations.

After September 11, the claim that the liberalization and integration of markets furthers the spread of democracy in the world became firmly linked to the Bush administration's controversial security agenda culminating in the famous "Bush doctrine" that legitimated the use of "preemptive strikes" against potential enemies. To be sure, the president did not mince words in "Securing Freedom's Triumph," his *New York Times* op-ed piece a year after the attacks: "As we preserve the peace, America also has an opportunity to extend the benefits of freedom and progress to nations that lack them. We seek a peace where repression, resentment and poverty are replaced with the hope of democracy, development, free markets and free trade."[106] Several months later, Bush reaffirmed this "forward strategy for freedom" by referring to his country's unwavering "commitment to the global expansion of democracy" as the "third pillar" of America's "peace and security vision for the world." The same claim takes center stage in Bush's 2005 Inaugural Address: "The best hope for peace in our world is the expansion of freedom in all the world. . . . So it is the policy of the

United States to seek and support the growth of democratic movements and institutions in every nation and culture, with the ultimate goal of ending tyranny in our world."[107] Indeed, Bush's definition of globalization as "the triumph of human liberty stretching across national borders" remained the same before and after 9/11, yet the emphasis shifted from freedom's "promise of delivering billions of the world's citizens from disease and want" to a militarized security narrative.[108] Indeed, the idea of securing "freedom" through an American-led drive for political and economic "democratization" around the globe—thus connecting the military objectives of the War on Terror to the neoliberal agenda—emerged as the conceptual hallmark of imperial globalism. As Richard Falk notes, such a design

> combines ideas of American dominance associated with economic globalization, that were prevalent before September 11, with more militarist ideas associated with the anti-terrorist climate of the early 21st century. . . . While not abandoning the ideological precepts of neoliberal globalization, the Bush administration places its intense free market advocacy beneath the security blanket that includes suspect advice to other governments to devote their resources to non-military activities.[109]

Cultural theorist William Thornton concurs: "Empire keeps all the major features of globalization, plus one: it stands ready to enforce market privileges the old-fashioned way. . . . Emphatically, however, power economics did not surrender the field to resurgent power politics. Rather the two joined forces in the common cause of Empire."[110]

And so it appears that the market globalist claim of spreading freedom and democracy has become a convenient narrative for the Bush administration and its supporters in Congress to secure and expand its influence and power globally by combining military interventions and market liberalization. Indeed, "expansion" is the logic that holds these two dimensions together. These operations amount to what Claes Ryn calls American "armed world hegemony" exercised by imperialist ideologues in Washington who have convinced themselves and who seek to convince others that their country's turbo-capitalism and military might are the greatest forces for freedom in human history.[111] In combating the evil forces of terrorism, the United States and its allies spearhead the cause of universal principles—of course, democracy and free markets being first and foremost among them.

## CLAIM NUMBER SIX: GLOBALIZATION
## REQUIRES A WAR ON TERROR

At this point, it is not difficult to grasp why, in the post-9/11 context, it became necessary for globalist forces to add this claim to their existing discursive arsenal. If globalization, understood as the liberalization and global integration of markets, was to remain a viable project (as demanded by neoliberals), then the full coercive powers of the state had to be employed against those who threatened it—both justice dissenters and jihadist globalists. To be sure, massive state intervention on behalf of corporate interests would constitute a glaring contradiction of a central tenet of classical liberalism, but many market globalists were willing to strike a compromise on this point as long as such political interventions not only maintained their access to established markets but also opened up new markets in populous and resource-rich regions of the world.

As noted previously, the "necessary elimination" of "terrorists" and other "radical forces" hostile to the spread of democracy and the free market have made untenable the claim that nobody is in charge of globalization. Putting the public on notice that the War on Terror would be a long-term commitment for the United States, the Bush administration left no doubt that it had taken it on itself to protect the free market against the new barbarian forces bent on destroying Western civilization. The necessary military infrastructure to engage in an open-ended, global conflict was already in place. As political scientist Chalmers Johnson points out in his sobering analysis of the American Empire, the United States currently operates at least 725 military bases worldwide and maintains some form of military presence in 153 of 189 member countries of the United Nations.[112]

Power elites around the world put forward the contention that globalization requires a global war on terror on countless occasions and in numerous contexts. Let us consider three versions of presenting American-led perpetual warfare as the necessary bodyguard of corporate-led globalization. The first comes from neoconservative veteran Robert McFarlane, President Reagan's former national security adviser. Shortly after the U.S. military's opening "shock and awe" Iraq campaign in March 2003, McFarlane, now the chairman of a Washington-based energy corporation, teamed up with Michael Bleyzer, CEO of an international equity fund management company, to write a revealing op-ed piece for the *Wall Street Journal*. Bearing the suggestive title "Taking Iraq Private," the article praises the military operations in Iraq as an "indispensable tool" for establishing security and stability in the region. According to the imperial-globalist duo, the Global War on Terror prepared the ground for the profitable enterprise of "building the basic institutions that make democracy possible."[113]

In the second version, pondering how a "Global American Empire" should "manage an unruly world" after 9/11, Robert Kaplan, an award-winning journalist and influential Pentagon insider, quickly settles on the claim that globalization requires a global war on terror. Arguing that free markets cannot spread without military power, the best-selling author advises the Bush administration to adopt the pagan warrior ethos of second-century Rome, which he distills into "ten rules" for the expansion of American Empire. These include fast-track naturalization for foreign-born soldiers fighting for the empire; training special forces to be "lethal killers one moment and humanitarians the next"; using the military to promote democracy; preventing military missions from being compromised by diplomacy; establishing the resolve to "fight on every front," including the willingness to strike potential enemies preemptively on limited evidence; dealing with the media "more strictly"; and cracking down on internal dissent, targeting justice globalists and antiwar demonstrators in particular.[114]

Hence, the most pressing problem of our time is not *whether* but *how* the world's hyperpower ought to deal with so-called crisis regions—that is, on the tactical level of military operations. Kaplan reminds his readers that military questions can no longer be treated in isolation from economic questions and vice versa:

> The purpose of [U.S.] power is not power itself; it is the fundamentally liberal purpose of sustaining the key characteristics of an orderly world. Those characteristics include basic political stability; the idea of liberty, pragmatically conceived; respect for property; economic freedom; and representative government, culturally understood. At this moment in time it is American power, and American power only, that can serve as an organizing principle for the worldwide expansion of a liberal civil society.[115]

Kaplan's suggested "ten rules" seem to culminate in the idea that the best way for the United States to maintain and expand its empire is to adopt the pagan warrior ethos of second-century Rome. What he seems to forget in the heat of his argument, however, is that neither Emperor Trajan nor Emperor Hadrian was known for his liberal inclinations. In other words, Kaplan's "pragmatic" conception of liberty ultimately renders the very concept vacuous. This, of course, is the ultimate danger of the neoliberal compromise with neoconservatism: once the empire gets hold of globalism, it may turn it into a very different ideological creature.

With regard to establishing "representative government, culturally understood," Kaplan makes unmistakably clear that what he has in mind is the American model imposed on the rest of the world. While he prefers—á la Beers—the neoliberal approach of "marketing" U.S. values and foreign policy, Kaplan leaves no doubt that this task cannot be completed without extensive military backup. As he sees it, the world's nearly 200 countries and thousands of nongovernmental organizations represent a chaos of interests. Without the organizing force of a great and self-interested liberal power, they would be unable to advance the interests of humanity as a whole.

It is important to note how Kaplan assumes to know what the "interests of humanity" really are as well as his arrogant assumption that American culture and its political institutions are universally applicable. Once again, we witness the resurrection of the old Roman-Stoic narrative of a universal empire representing order and rationality and, therefore, valid for all societies. Self-interested action aimed at political domination is interpreted as the universal humanitarian mission of "spreading civilization" to the rest of the world. The military plays a key role in this process because the success of the mission depends on the complete annihilation of all opposing forces, particularly of terrorists (today's "barbarians") residing in "nonglobalized areas." No wonder, then, that Kaplan closes his article with a panegyric to Winston Churchill and his flattery of the United States as "a worthy successor to the British Empire, one that would carry on Britain's liberalizing mission."[116]

Similarly, Norman Podhoretz, foreign policy adviser to 2008 Republican presidential candidate Rudy Giuliani, calls for the escalation of the U.S.-led Global War on Terror into a full-blown "World War IV" (apparently, "World War III" ended in the defeat of the Soviet Union). Podhoretz surveys a post-9/11 landscape teeming with "enemies" of all kinds, the two principal ones being "Islamofascism" and misguided Western leftist intellectuals critical of U.S. operations in Iraq. For the patriarch of American neoconservatism, only a "tough" and "unforgiving" approach of the kind adopted by the Bush administration might eventually succeed in "draining the swamps" of terrorism and political treachery, thus assuring the full globalization of liberal democracy and free markets.[117]

The third and perhaps most original version of the new imperial-globalist claim that globalization requires a global war on terror flows from the pen of Thomas P. M. Barnett, managing director of a global security firm and former professor of military strategy at the U.S. Naval War College. A former assistant for strategic futures in the Pentagon's Office of Force Transformations, the Harvard-educated strategist provided regular briefings to Secretary of Defense Donald Rumsfeld and the inner circle of the U.S. intelligence community. He also interacted regularly with thousands of high-ranking officers from all branches of the U.S. armed forces. *The Pentagon's New Map*, Barnett's best-selling reexamination of American national security, links the author's military expertise to his long-standing interests in economic globalization.[118] The book presents a straightforward thesis:

in the global age, America's national security is inextricably bound up with the continued global integration of markets and increasing flows of trade, capital, ideas, and people across national borders. Since 9/11, it has become abundantly clear that the one-sided identification of globalization with an "economic rule set" must be complemented by an understanding of globalization as a "security rule set" mandating the destruction of transnational terrorist networks and all states harboring them.

For Barnett, both of these "rule sets" are normatively anchored in the universal values of individual freedom, democracy, multiculturalism, and free markets. At the same time, however, these norms are also uniquely "American," for they found their political expression for the first time in human history in the eighteenth-century American experiment of an expanding democratic union of *united states*.[119] In a daring conflation of national interest with global interest that runs counter to the nation-centered mind-set of the U.S. defense establishment, Barnett presents America as "globalization's ideological wellspring" destined to bring to the world nothing less than what its citizens already enjoy today: "the individual pursuit of happiness within free markets protected from destabilizing strife by the rule of law." For the strategist, American interests are by definition global interests precisely because the country is built on universal ideals of freedom and democracy and not restricted to narrow ethnic or national identities. As the world's first truly multinational union, the United States is globalization incarnate. Moreover, the universal values at the heart of its Constitution allow the American government to judge the rest of the world in universal terms of right and wrong, good and evil: "What gives America the right [to render these judgments] is the fact that we are globalization's godfather, its source code, its original model." And so it appears that by human design and historical destiny, the United States serves as the evolutionary engine of a multicultural "world system" that ascends toward ever-higher levels of connectivity, rule-bound behavior, wealth, security, and happiness. Although Barnett considers this course likely, he disavows historical determinism by conceding that there are no guarantees. Cleary, al Qaeda and other "antiglobalization forces" committed to "a sort of permanent civilizational apartheid" are capable of derailing the globalization of individualism, democracy, and free markets. Thus, 9/11 marks a critical juncture in human history where America, "globalization's source code," is called on to guide the rest of the world toward the noble goals of "universal inclusiveness" and "global peace." Its Herculean task is to "make globalization truly global"—by any means necessary.[120]

This is, of course, where the new claim of globalization requiring a global war on terror comes in. In order to defeat the enemies of global interdependence, the Pentagon must devise a new strategy that, once and for all, abandons antiquated "international thinking." National security in the twenty-first century must be reimagined in global terms as the ruthless destruction of all forces of disconnectedness and the nurturing of the "networks of political and security connectivity commensurate with the mutually assured dependence that now exists among all states that are deeply integrated with the growing global economy." In short, the Pentagon's new global strategy requires a new map—both in a cognitive and in a geographical sense—that divides the globe into three distinct regions. Unlike the three-world order of the Cold War, however, the entire world is now fair game for U.S. military operations.

Barnett calls the first region on the Pentagon's new map the "Functioning Core," defined as "globalization thick with network connectivity, financial transactions, liberal media flows, and collective security." Featuring stable democratic governments, transparency, rising standards of living, and more deaths by suicide than by murder, the Core is made up of North America, most of Europe, Australia, New Zealand, a small part of Latin America, and, with significant reservations, possible "new core" countries like India and China. Conversely, he refers to areas where "globalization is thinning or just plain absent" as the "Non-Integrating Gap." This region is plagued by repressive political regimes, handcuffed markets, mass murder, and widespread poverty and disease. For Barnett, the Gap provides a dangerous breeding ground for "global terrorists" and other "forces of disconnectedness" opposed to the "economic and security rule sets we call globalization." This region includes the Caribbean Rim, virtually all of Africa, the Balkans, the Caucasus, parts of Central Asia, the Middle East, and parts of Southeast Asia. Along the Gap's "bloody boundaries," the military strategist locates "Seam States" such as Mexico, Brazil, South Africa, Morocco, Algeria, Greece, Turkey, Pakistan, Thailand, Malaysia, the Philippines, and Indonesia. Lacking the Core's high levels of connectivity and security, these countries are the logical entry point for terrorists plotting their attacks.[121]

Despite its horrific toll, Barnett considers 9/11 a necessary "wake-up call" that forced the United States to make a long-term military commitment to "export security" to the Gap. The Core has no choice but to treat the entire Gap region as a "strategic threat environment." Inaction or a premature retreat from Iraq and Afghanistan would jeopardize the fledgling world order based on America's universal values. For Barnett, the imperative for the Global War on Terror is rooted in the "underlying reality" of a "military-market nexus"—the dependence of "the merchant culture of the business world" on the military's "warrior culture":

> I express this interrelationship [of the military and the market] in the form of a "ten commandments of globalization": (1) Look for resources and ye shall find, but . . . (2) No stability, no markets; (3) No growth, no stability; (4) No resources, no growth; (5) No infrastructure, no resources; (6) No money, no infrastructure; (7) No rules, no money; (8) No security, no rules; (9) No Leviathan [American military force], no security; and (10) No (American) will, no Leviathan. Understanding the military-market link is not just good business, it is good national security strategy.[122]

Ultimately, Barnett proposes a "global transaction strategy" built on three basic principles. First, the United States must increase the Core's "immune system capabilities" by responding quickly and efficiently to 9/11-like "system perturbations." Second, it must pressure the Seam States to "firewall the Core from the Gap's worst exports," namely, terror, drugs, and pandemics. Finally, America must remain firmly committed to a global war on terror and its overriding objective of "shrinking the Gap." There can be no compromise or vacillation. Globalization's enemies must be eliminated, and the Gap region must be integrated into the Core. As Barnett emphasizes, "I believe it is absolutely essential that this country lead the global war on terrorism, because I fear what will happen to our world if the forces of disconnectedness are allowed to prevail—to perturb the system at will."[123]

A critical discourse analysis reveals a number of problematic assumptions and omissions in Barnett's rendition of imperial globalism. For example, consider the phrase "exporting security" to the Gap. "Security" obviously stands for massive military intervention by Core countries. The gerund "exporting" has been chosen to indicate a connection between security and commercial activity similar to exporting cars, sweaters, computers, and so on. In other words, U.S.-led military intervention has become an indispensable commodity in the Core's struggle to "shrink the Gap" and keep the Seam from "falling off this bandwagon called globalization." In other words, recipients of this export—whether they like this commodity or not—ought to consider themselves "lucky" that American troops will come in and "restore order."

What Barnett is not telling his readers, however, is that "exporting security" is unlike other commercial transactions in that it brings instant death, injury, homelessness, and other forms of suffering to scores of flesh-and-blood human beings and their possessions, many of whom are neither terrorists nor sympathizers but who just happen to find themselves caught in the crossfire of America's top export. Likewise, the technical phrase "shrinking the Gap" reveals a cold instrumentalism that conceals the fact that the "Gap" is a region populated by human beings with hopes and dreams for the future, like their counterparts everywhere. Indeed, the mixing of neoliberal market language and military jargon constitutes the brutal discursive core of imperial globalism.

Finally, Barnett's portrayal of globalization as market connectivity inextricably intermingled with collective security in military terms explains why globalization requires a war on terror. After September 11, Barnett insists, the project of expanding the Core can no longer be achieved by soft U.S. hegemony anchored in a benign Clintonian multilateralism that utilizes international economic institutions to enforce its market paradigm but that keeps the iron fist of military power firmly in the velvet glove of globalism. What is required in our new age of terrorism, Barnett argues, is a conscious switch to "hard-power" tactics rooted in unilateralism and preemptive warfare, regardless of what the rest of the world thinks. If other countries bestow on the United States the pejorative label "empire," so be it; Americans should accept it as a badge of honor.

## CONCLUSION

The six claims discussed in this chapter show that market globalism is sufficiently systematic to add up to a comprehensive political ideology. In the harsh political climate following the attacks of September 11, however, many market globalists struggled to maintain the viability of their project. One obvious solution was to toughen up their ideological claims to fit the neoconservative vision of a benign U.S. empire relying on overwhelming military power. As a result, market globalism morphed into imperial globalism. Claims one (globalization is about the liberalization and global integration of markets) and four (globalization benefits everyone)—the backbone of market globalism—are still largely intact but had to undergo hard-power facelifts. The determinist language of claim two found its new expression in the proclaimed "inevitability" of America's military triumph over its terrorist nemesis. Claim three (nobody is in charge of globalization), however, was dropped in favor of Bush's ostentatious pronouncement of U.S. global leadership. Claim five (globalization furthers the spread of democracy in the world) ascended to new heights with the hard-power mission of "building democracy" in the Gap regions. The neoconservative commitment to "American values" of freedom, security, and free markets made it necessary to add claim six (globalization requires a war on terror) to globalism's discursive arsenal. As Robert Kaplan puts it, "You also have to have military and economic power behind it, or else your ideas cannot spread."[124]

Still, this modified ideological formation retained most of its original makeup. Imperial globalism's promises of material well-being and collective security through a perpetual global war on terror are designed to sustain consensual arrangements of political rule. To argue that post-9/11 market globalism has shifted from a soft-power narrative to a hard-power discourse of empire does not mean that it enjoys undisputed ideological dominance. There exists a multiplicity of alternative stories about globalization that also aim to provide authoritative accounts of what the phenomenon is all about. As a result, market (and imperial) globalism's ideological claims have been contested both by justice globalists on the political Left and by jihadist globalists on the political Right. It is the task of the next two chapters to examine the counterarguments advanced by the challengers of the dominant ideology of our global age.

# CHAPTER 4

## CHALLENGES FROM THE POLITICAL LEFT: JUSTICE GLOBALISM

In the first chapter of this book, I suggested that ideologies represent systems of ideas, values, and beliefs that make simplified claims about politics. Putting before the public a specific agenda of things to discuss, various groups in society seek to advance their particular interests. I also emphasized that ideology should not be reduced to a nebulous construct floating in thin air above more material political or economic processes. Ideals, power interests, and physical entities all converge in concrete social practices that are both ideational and material. In our global age, market globalism—and its modified imperial version—has emerged as the dominant ideology, chiseling into the minds of many people around the world a particular understanding of globalization, which, in turn, is sustained and reconfirmed by promarket governments.

Still, no single social formation ever enjoys absolute dominance. Even the strongest ideological edifice contains small fissures that threaten to turn into dangerous cracks when a recalcitrant social environment resists the disciplinary modes contained in dominant claims and pronouncements. Growing gaps between these assertions and the lived experience of ordinary people may usher in a long-term crisis for the hegemonic paradigm. At the same time, however, such a crisis also represents a golden opportunity for dissenting social groups that propagate new ideas, beliefs, practices, and institutions.

As we have seen in the previous chapter, arguments critical of market globalism began to receive more play in the public discourse on globalization in the late 1990s. This development was aided by a heightened awareness of how extreme corporate-profit strategies were leading to widening global disparities in wealth and well-being. The growing forces of a new political Left closely aligned with an emerging "global justice movement" began to challenge market globalism in open street demonstrations in major cities around the world. From Seattle and Prague, from Chiang Mai to Melbourne, and from Honolulu to Genoa, these protesters accumulated valuable practical experience that helped them refine their ideological program emphasizing the values of social justice, equality, solidarity with the world's poor, and ecological sustainability. But before we examine the political context and the ideational structure of justice globalism in more detail, let us briefly reflect on the enduring relevance of the traditional distinction between the political Left and Right.

## THE LEFT–RIGHT DISTINCTION

The distinction between the political Left and Right originated in the French National Assembly at the outset of the revolutionary period in the late eighteenth century. Those representatives favoring radical change in the direction of more equal social arrangements congregated on the left side, or "wing," of the chamber, whereas those arguing for the traditional status quo gathered on the right wing. Deputies supporting only moderate change sat in the center. The world's political landscape has changed dramatically since 1789, and reliance on the old Left–Right metaphor as an indicator for contemporary ideological differences has undergone growing criticism, especially after the collapse of the Soviet Union in 1991.

Consciously linking his reappraisal of the Left–Right divide to this momentous event, Anthony Giddens suggested in the early 1990s that "Right" and "Left" had come to mean different things in different social and geographical contexts. In particular, the British sociologist maintained that it was very problematic to label market globalism as a right-wing ideology.

After all, neoliberal programs tend to undermine the sanctity of tradition and custom by supporting radical processes of change stimulated by the incessant expansion of markets. On the other hand, neoliberalism does depend on the persistence of some traditional values for its legitimacy. Its attachment to conservative norms is particularly obvious in the areas of religion, gender, and the family. Likewise, Giddens continued, the fuzzy boundary between the political Left and Right was also reflected in the eclectic value structures of new social movements such as environmentalism and feminism. Hence, he concluded that the Left–Right metaphor retained only limited validity in the contemporary political discourse:

> No doubt, the differentiation of left and right—which from the beginning has been a contested distinction in any case—will continue to exist in the practical contexts of party politics. Here its prime meaning, in many societies at least, differs from what it used to be, given that the neoliberal right has come to advocate the rule of markets, while the left favors more public provision and public welfare: straddling the ground of left and right, as we know, is a diversity of other parties, sometimes linked to social movements. But does the distinction between left and right retain any core meaning when taken out of the mundane environment of orthodox politics? It does, but only on a very general plane. On the whole, the right is more happy to tolerate the existence of inequalities than the left, and more prone to support the powerful than the powerless. This contrast is real and remains important. But it would be difficult to push it too far, or make it one of overriding principle.[1]

Around the same time Giddens made his comments, however, Norberto Bobbio published a celebrated defense of the continued significance of this political distinction in *Left and Right*, an enormously successful book that sold hundreds of thousands of copies in Europe. The seasoned Italian political thinker argued that it was the attitude of political groups toward the ideal of equality that constituted the most important criterion in distinguishing between the Left and the Right. According to Bobbio, members of the political Left had historically shown support for the idea that political and social institutions are socially constructed. Hence, they emphasized the power of human reason to devise workable schemes for the reduction of social inequalities such as power, wealth, educational opportunity, and so on. But, according to Bobbio, this does not mean that all members of the Left favor the complete elimination of all forms of inequality; only extreme leftists embrace such a radical position.

Representatives of the political Right, on the other hand, are more reluctant to support policies that reduce existing social inequalities. Bobbio argued that they consider many of these inequalities legitimate because they see them as anchored in a largely unalterable "natural order." Skeptical of the power of reason to change social arrangements without seriously undermining social stability, they affirm existing social arrangements based on custom, tradition, and the force of the past. Only extremist members of the Right are opposed to all social change; others support change, provided that it occurs in slow, incremental fashion over a long period of time. Thus, Bobbio suggested that the distinction between Left and Right is based on values, whereas the contrast between extremism and moderation pertains to the method of social change.[2]

Although the Italian thinker conceded that the line dividing the Left and the Right always shifted with changing historical circumstances, he nonetheless emphasized that this distinction—anchored in two fundamentally different perspectives on equality—retains its significance even in our postcommunist era of globalization:

> The communist left was not the only left; there was—and still is—another left within the capitalist horizon. The distinction has a long history which goes back long before the contrast between capitalism and communism. The distinction still exists, and not, as someone jested, simply on road signs. It pervades newspapers, radio, television, public debates, and specialized magazines on economics, politics, and sociology in a manner which is almost grotesque. If you look through the papers to see how many times the words "left" and "right" appear, even just in headlines, you will come up with a good crop.[3]

In 2008, Alain Noel and Jean-Philippe Therien published a sophisticated defense of the Left–Right distinction that extended Bobbio's thesis to global politics. Drawing on the 1999–2001 World Values Survey—a worldwide database covering cultural and political trends in seventy-eight countries—the Canadian political scientists found that the Left–Right scheme was not only consistently evoked in the global public sphere but also corresponded to clearly distinct perspectives on equality, justice, and social protection. Thus, they concluded that the Left–Right divide had survived the transformation of class structures of the past two centuries as well as the more recent rise of new postmaterialist values in advanced democracies. In short, this divide continues to help people around the world integrate into coherent patterns their attitudes and ideas about politics.[4]

In the next two chapters, I classify market globalism's challengers according to the Left–Right distinction. Indeed, my typology owes much to the insights of Bobbio, Noel, and Therien. I particularly agree with their central contention that today's conflicting political worldviews—especially on the issue of global equality—justify the drawing of this distinction. In our global age, the existing differences between these two camps are significant enough to distinguish between two principal alterglobalist groups: justice globalists on the political Left and jihadist globalists on the political Right. As I will explain in chapter 5, national populists also constitute a significant group of globalization critics on the Right. However, unlike jihadist globalists, they do not translate the rising global imaginary into a concrete ideological agenda. Clinging to the declining national imaginary, national populists are the only significant group of detractors with genuinely "anti"-globalization (rather than "alter"-globalization) views.

## FROM CHIAPAS TO SEATTLE

In the early 1990s, left-wing social activists around the world reacted to the collapse of communism with a mixture of despair, embarrassment, and relief. Although most of them were glad to see the authoritarian Soviet regime exit the world stage for good, they had hoped that Mikhail Gorbachev's *perestroika* (economic restructuring) and *glasnost* (openness) reforms would result in the transformation of Russian totalitarianism into a Scandinavian-style social democracy. When it became clear that the successor states of the Soviet Empire would be subjected to a humiliating capitalist shock therapy administered by neoliberal elites in the United States and Europe, the democratic Left found itself in an ideological quandary that seemed to bear out Margaret Thatcher's famous contention that "there is no alternative" to market globalism. Searching for new ideas, the Left began to engage in what social movement expert Sidney Tarrow calls "global framing," that is, a flexible form of "global thinking" that connected local or national grievances to the larger context of "global justice," "global inequalities," or "world peace." Tarrow argues that most of these left-wing activists could be characterized as "rooted cosmopolitans" because they remained embedded in their domestic environments while at the same time developing a global consciousness as a result of vastly enhanced contacts to like-minded individuals and organizations across national borders.[5] The organizational result of both global framing and multi-issue framing was a broader and more eclectic "global justice movement" (GJM) that began to cohere ideologically through its opposition to market globalism.

Most of the movement's leaders would later point to a number of events that had a galvanizing impact on the ideological formation of justice globalism. On January 1, 1994, the day the North American Free Trade Agreement (NAFTA) took effect, a relatively small group of guerrillas calling themselves the Zapatista Army of National Liberation launched an uprising in their native province of Chiapas in southern Mexico. Drawing on the beliefs and values of Che Guevara, Emiliano Zapata, indigenous Mayan culture, and Catholic liberation theology, the Zapatistas stitched together an interpretive framework that presented their rebellion as an act of popular resistance against their government's free-trade policies. Engaging in effective global framing, their leader, Subcomandante Marcos, announced to the world that the local struggle in Chiapas was of global significance: "[W]e will make a collective network of all our particular struggles and resistances. An intercontinental network of resistance against neoliberalism, an intercontinental network of resistance for humanity."[6] Keeping their promise, the Zapatistas managed to get their message out to other progressive forces around the world. Their efforts culminated in the 1996 First Intercontinental Meeting for Humanity and Against Neoliberalism held in the jungles of Chiapas and attended by more than 4,000 participants from nearly thirty countries. The conference set into motion further initiatives that sensitized millions of people to the suffering of poor peasants in the global South caused by market-globalist policies. Indeed, the creation of the global "Zapatista solidarity network" served as a model for dozens of other alliances that vowed to challenge "neoliberal" globalization "from below."

Another significant catalyst in the formation of the GJM and its corresponding ideology was the devastating Asian economic crisis of 1997, which we referred to briefly in previous chapters. In the early 1990s, the governments of Thailand, Indonesia, Malaysia, South Korea, and the Philippines had gradually abandoned their control over the domestic movement of capital in order to attract foreign direct investment. Intent on creating a stable monetary environment, they raised domestic interest rates and linked their national currency to the value of the U.S. dollar. The ensuing influx of foreign investments translated into soaring stock and real estate markets all over Southeast Asia. However, by 1997, many investors realized that prices had become inflated far beyond their actual value. They panicked and withdrew a total of $105 billion from these countries within days, forcing governments in the region to abandon the dollar peg. Unable to halt the ensuing free fall of their currencies, those governments used up nearly all their foreign exchange reserves. As a result, economic output fell, unemployment increased, and wages plummeted. Foreign banks and creditors reacted by declining new credit applications and refusing to extend existing loans. By the end of 1997, the entire region found itself in the throes of a financial crisis that threatened to wreak havoc on the global economy. Disaster was narrowly averted by a combination of international bailout packages and the immediate sale of Southeast Asian commercial assets to foreign corporate investors at rock-bottom prices. In addition to wrecking the regional economy for years to come, the crisis also caused serious ideological damage: power elites and ordinary citizens alike had been treated to an ominous preview of what a world run on unfettered market-globalist principles might look like.

Finally, the formation of the ideational cluster associated with the GJM owed much to a spectacular series of strikes that hit France in 1995 and 1998. Protesting government policies that had driven up unemployment while reducing social services, the striking workers and public employees received tremendous support from these new Left networks. Lasting alliances between unions and environmentalists were forged, and many new multi-issue coalitions were born. One of these novel organizational networks was the *Association pour une taxation des transactions financiers pour l'aide aux citoyens* (Association for the Taxation of Financial Transactions for the Aid of Citizens [ATTAC]). Founded by academics and intellectuals associated with *Le Monde Diplomatique*—a multilingual leftist monthly with a global circulation of over 1 million copies—ATTAC began to draft comprehensive proposals for the elimination of offshore corporate tax havens, the blanket forgiveness of developing countries' debts, and the radical restructuring of the major international economic institutions, including the Internal Monetary Fund (IMF) and the World Trade Organization (WTO). But its core demand was the leveling of a "Tobin Tax," named after its inventor, the Nobel Prize–winning economist James Tobin, on international short-term financial transactions, with proceeds going to the global South. If introduced globally, a tax from 0.1 to 0.25 percent on these transactions might have raised up to U.S.$250 billion. Within a few years, ATTAC grew into an impressive global network with tens of thousands of members and autonomous branches in more than fifty countries.

From its very inception in 1998, ATTAC was an important voice in the fight against "neoliberal globalization." It played an instrumental role in defeating the Multilateral Agreement on Investment (MAI), an international investment legislation proposal negotiated in secret among G-7 members that favored transnational corporations (TNCs) and global investors. Together with Brazilian and Asian global justice networks, ATTAC also served as a vital catalyst in the 2001 creation of the World Social Forum (WSF) in Porto Alegre, Brazil. As we discuss in more detail later, the WSF has become a central organizing space for tens of thousands of justice globalists who delighted in their annual "countersummit" to the

January meeting of the market-globalist World Economic Forum (WEF) in the exclusive Swiss ski resort of Davos.

Refusing to accept orthodox Marxist categories as the common ideological denominator of all left politics, global justice organizations like ATTAC formed responsive nodes in a decentralized, nonhierarchical, and transnational "network of networks." The ideological coherence and political dominance of market globalism allowed the various groups belonging to the GJM to pull together even more closely, in the process sharing organizational know-how, strategy, and ideas. Embedded in their national framework without being confined to it, this pluralistic "movement of movements" learned to take advantage of the ICT-mediated flow of goods, services, and ideas that their opponents associated with the "inevitable" globalization of markets. Gradually, prominent movement activists like Susan George, Naomi Klein, and Walden Bello articulated a set of principles guiding the GJM's interactions with international institutions, states, and other private and public organizations. Academic observers like Mary Kaldor announced the birth of a "global civil society"—"groups, networks and movements which comprise the mechanisms through which individuals negotiate and renegotiate social contracts or political bargains on a global level."[7] Cultivating ever closer contacts with members of distant cultures, these transnational activists traversed geographical space as well as cyberspace in search for new ways to put their ideals of global justice, equality, diversity, and pluralism into practice. Although the GJM of the 1990s incorporated most of the issues dear to feminists, environmentalists, and other "new social movement" activists of the 1960s and 1970s, it rearranged and rearticulated their concerns around the core concept of "globalization."

The potent combination of global activism and spectacular market failures created larger discursive and political openings for the fledgling GJM, which had become confident enough to call on its mass membership to participate in contentious "parallel summits" or "countersummits" held at official international meetings of high-profile market-globalist institutions like the IMF, the World Bank, the G-7 (after 1998, the G-8), the WEF, or the WTO. A clear indication of an impending, large-scale confrontation between the forces of market globalism and its challengers on the left came in June 1999, when various labor, human rights, and environmental groups organized global protests, known as "J18," to coincide with the G-8 Economic Summit in Cologne, Germany. Financial districts of cities in North America and Europe were subjected to well-orchestrated direct actions that included large street demonstrations as well as to more than

10,000 "cyberattacks" perpetrated by sophisticated hackers against the computer systems of large corporations. In London, a march of 2,000 protesters turned violent, causing dozens of injuries and significant property damage. But the spectacular "coming-out party" of the GJM took place six months later in Seattle, Washington.

## THE "BATTLE OF SEATTLE" AND ITS AFTERMATH

About 50,000 people took part in the anti-WTO protests in Seattle in late November and early December 1999. In spite of the predominance of North American participants, there was also a significant international presence. In fact, the transnational character of the Seattle demonstrations was a central feature that distinguished it from other mass protests in the recent past. Activists such as José Bové, a charismatic French sheep farmer who became an international celebrity for trashing a McDonald's outlet, marched shoulder-to-shoulder with Indian farmers and leaders of the Philippines' peasant movement. Clearly articulating justice-globalist concerns, this eclectic alliance included consumer activists, labor activists (including students demonstrating against sweatshops), environmentalists, animal-rights activists, advocates of Third World debt relief, feminists, and human-rights proponents. Especially criticizing the WTO's neoliberal position on agriculture, multilateral investments, and intellectual property rights, this impressive crowd represented more than seven hundred organizations, including groups such as Direct Action Network, The Ruckus Society, IFG, GEX, and the Rainforest Action Network. The main message of these groups was that the WTO had gone too far in setting global rules that supported corporate interests at the expense of developing countries, the poor, the environment, workers, and consumers.[8] The ensuing "Battle of Seattle" received extensive news coverage, ultimately making headlines in both the United States and abroad. For the purposes of this book, it suffices to provide a brief summary of the unfolding events.

Most commentators agree that both the WTO and Washington State officials severely underestimated both the quantitative strength and organizational skill of the protesters. On the opening day of the WTO meeting, large groups of demonstrators interrupted traffic in the city center and managed to block off the major entrances to the convention center by forming human chains. Many demonstrators had been trained in nonviolent methods of resistance and acted in accordance with a nonviolent strategy that called for blocking key intersections and entrances in order to shut the WTO meeting down before it even started. As delegates were scrambling to make their way to the conference center, Seattle police stepped up their efforts to clear the streets. Equipped with gas masks, commando boots, leg guards, combat harnesses, disposable plastic cuffs, slash-resistant gloves, riot batons, rubber-bullet stingers, tear-gas grenades, ballistic helmets, and body armor, the city's police force was indeed a frightening sight to behold. Soon it launched tear-gas cans into the crowds—even into throngs of people who were peacefully sitting on streets and pavements. Next, the force fired rubber bullets at some protesters. Having failed to accomplish its goal by early afternoon, the Seattle police force began to use batons and pepper-spray stingers against the remaining demonstrators.

To be sure, there were perhaps two hundred individuals who, having declined to pledge themselves to nonviolent direct action, delighted in smashing storefronts and turning over garbage cans. Most of these youthful protesters belonged to the anarchist Black Bloc, an Oregon-based political organization ideologically opposed to free-market capitalism and the centralized state power of modern nation-states. Wearing dark hoods and black jackboots, the spokespersons of the Black Bloc would later defend their actions by emphasizing that they were not senseless vandals but political resisters acting according to a strategic plan worked out in advance. They insisted that anarchist youths had been instructed to move only against corporations that had been identified as engaging in extremely callous business practices. For example, they spared a Charles Schwab outlet but smashed the windows of Fidelity Investments for maintaining high stakes in Occidental Petroleum, the oil company most responsible for violence against indigenous people in Colombia. They moved against Starbucks because of the company's nonsupport of fair-trade coffee (at the time) but not against Tully's. They stayed away from REI stores but inflicted damage on Gap outlets because of the company's heavy reliance on sweatshops in Asia.[9]

By late afternoon, Seattle Mayor Paul Shell declared a civic emergency in the city. Only one step away from martial law, this measure allowed Seattle's police chief to impose a rigid 7:00 PM to 7:00 AM curfew and create generous "no-protest zones" that included a twenty-five-square-block area in downtown. The closure appeared to be in stark violation of the 1996 U.S. Court of Appeals (Ninth Circuit) decision in the case of *Collins v. Jordan*, which compels municipal governments to permit protests close enough so that they can be heard and seen by the intended audience. In addition, there were some indications that the U.S. Army's Delta Force was present in Seattle. If this observation were true, it would mean that the Clinton administration violated the Posse Comitatus Act of 1887, forbidding the U.S. military any role in domestic law enforcement.[10]

When it became clear that many demonstrators refused to obey these emergency orders, police actions became even more extreme. Some police officers resorted to using their thumbs to grind pepper spray into the eyes of their victims and to kicking nonviolent protesters in the groin. Moreover, there were more than three hundred reports of beatings and other acts of brutality against protesters inside Seattle's jails.[11] In the early morning hours of December 1, the last remaining demonstrators were finally forced to vacate the city center. However, by the next morning, several thousand had regrouped in the Capitol Hill area, ready to march to the conference center. But National Guard units and police armed with AR-15 assault rifles made clear that they were no longer limiting themselves to rubber bullets. A police officer told a demonstrator that, this time, they should expect the "real thing."[12] Not only did the police prevent protesters from entering the restricted areas, they also arrested people outside these spaces for such "incendiary" actions as handing out anti-WTO leaflets. Altogether, the police arrested over six hundred protesters. Significantly, the charges against over five hundred of them were eventually dismissed. Only fourteen cases actually went to trial, ultimately yielding ten plea bargains, two acquittals, and only two guilty verdicts.[13]

Negotiations inside the conference center did not proceed smoothly either. Struggling to overcome the handicap of a late start, the WTO delegates soon deadlocked over such important issues as international labor and environmental standards. Many delegates of developing countries refused to support an agenda that had been drafted behind closed doors by the major economic powers. Caught between two rebellions, one inside and one outside the conference center, the Clinton administration sought to put a positive spin on the events. Downplaying the street demonstrations as "a rather interesting hoopla," the president agreed to meet with opposition leaders from moderate labor unions and environmental organizations.[14] While emphasizing the "obvious benefits of free trade and globalization," President Bill Clinton nonetheless admitted that the WTO needed to implement "some internal reforms." In the end, the Seattle meeting ended without the traditional joint communiqué. In her improvised closing remarks, U.S. Trade Representative Charlene Barshefsky conceded that "we found that the WTO has outgrown the processes appropriate to an earlier time. . . . We needed a process which had a greater degree of internal transparency and inclusion to accommodate a larger and more diverse membership."[15]

Ironically, the Battle of Seattle showed that many of the new technologies hailed by market globalists as the true hallmark of globalization could also be employed in the service of justice-globalist forces and their political agenda. For example, the Internet enabled the organizers of the Seattle protest to arrange for new forms of protests, such as a series of demonstrations held in concert in various cities around the globe. Justice-globalist groups and networks all over the world learned to utilize the Internet to readily and rapidly recruit new members, establish dates, share experiences, arrange logistics, and identify and publicize targets—activities that only a decade earlier would have demanded much more time and money. Other new technologies such as sophistcated cell phones allowed demonstrators not only to maintain close contact throughout an event but also to react quickly and effectively to shifting police tactics. This enhanced ability to arrange and coordinate protests without the need of a central command, a clearly defined leadership, a large bureaucracy, and significant financial resources added an entirely new dimension to the nature of justice-globalist street demonstrations. Moreover, cheap and easy access to global information raised the protesters' level of knowledge and sophistication. Justice-globalist teach-ins and street-theater performances, organized by various groups via the Internet, were particularly successful in recruiting college students for international antisweatshop campaigns. Organizations such as the California-based Ruckus Society used the video capacities of the World Wide Web to train potential Seattle protesters in the complex techniques of nonviolent direct action.

Finally, the Battle of Seattle also vindicated the old vision of forging nonhierarchical alliances among progressive groups—even among those who share a rather antagonistic history. Perhaps the best example of this new spirit of coalition building on the Left is the willingness of labor unions and environmental groups to advance a common justice-globalist agenda. There were many signs of this new cooperation in Seattle. For example, when a longshoreman from Tacoma hoisted up a banner that read "Teamsters and Turtles Together at Last," marching environmentalists enthusiastically responded with their own chant, "Turtles Love Teamsters." Likewise, the Alliance for Sustainable Jobs and the Environment—a coalition of environmental activists and steelworkers—made its presence felt in the streets of Seattle.[16] Although there remains a strong presence of protectionist voices in organized labor, it also appears that a number of American and European union leaders have learned the crucial lesson of Seattle: the best way of challenging the established framework of globalism is to build a broad international support network that includes workers, environmentalists, consumer advocates, and human-rights activists. As the representatives of this new alliance insist, any trade system of the future must be anchored in fair international rules supportive of extensive labor rights, environmental protections, and human rights.[17]

In the months following the events in Seattle, several large-scale justice-globalist demonstrations took place in rapid succession all over the world. In February 2000, the annual meeting of the WEF in Davos was targeted by thousands of protesters denouncing the globalist vision and neoliberal policies advocated by most delegates. After transforming itself from a body concerned with bland management issues into a dynamic political forum in the late 1980s, the WEF managed to attract to its annual meeting hundreds of the world's most powerful business executives and senior policymakers. The WEF also generates dozens of publications, including a yearly index that measures the economic competitiveness of all the world's countries. The annual conference in Davos provides unparalleled opportunities for global corporate elites and politicians (including dozens of heads of state and government) to streamline social and economic policies. Employing strategies similar to those of the participants in the Battle of Seattle, anti-WEF protesters clashed with police forces in the streets of the small Swiss alpine village. Surprised by the size and organizational strength of the demonstrations, Swiss security forces struggled for several days to disperse the crowds. The disturbing images of these fierce street battles featured prominently in national and international news reports, attesting to the considerable extent of the existing backlash against market globalism.

In mid-April 2000, about 25,000 justice-globalist activists from around the world attempted to shut down the semiannual meetings of the IMF and the World Bank in Washington, D.C. Planning to march into the heart of the city and protest the neoliberal policies imposed by these institutions on developing countries, the demonstrators found the entire downtown area blocked off. Forced into the northwest part of town, they attempted several times to break through the menacing phalanx of thousands of police and National Guard troops. The demonstrators' efforts to get closer to the conference center were greeted by clouds of tear gas and pepper spray. Several protesters were injured by club-wielding police officers. No doubt, District of Columbia authorities had paid close attention to the events in Seattle. As Police Chief Charles Ramsey put it, his force was "fully prepared" and "ready to defend the city." In fact, his strategic decision to shut down the city in order to guard the meetings more effectively was backed up by significant monetary commitments. In anticipation of the demonstrations, Ramsey had requested and received millions of dollars for overtime pay and new riot equipment.[18]

Police officers politely ushered conference delegates to waiting buses and escorted them to their meetings. At the same time, they shut down the protesters' headquarters, declaring that it was a "fire hazard." Overall, the police arrested about 1,200 protesters on a variety of charges, including "parading without a permit" and "obstructing traffic." After two days of clashes, the police finally claimed victory. "We didn't lose the city," Chief Ramsey announced proudly to throngs of journalists. Mayor Anthony A. Williams insisted that the police had acted with "appropriate force" and that the mass arrests of peaceful protesters the night before were justified as a "matter of prudence."[19] Dutifully, most of the next day's morning papers reported that city officials had "done their job" and that demonstrators had "failed" in their goals. Unfazed, the remaining protesters staged a victory party in the streets, celebrating the meteoric rise of the global justice movement. After all, the impressive images and sounds of their "failure" in the District of Columbia had been broadcast worldwide, leaving millions of viewers and listeners with the distinct impression that the Battle of Seattle had not been an isolated event.

After similar protests against both the Asian Development Bank in Chiang Mai, Thailand, and the Asia–Pacific Summit of the WEF in Melbourne, the struggle against globalism shifted in the autumn of 2000 to Prague. The capital of the Czech Republic had been chosen as the site for the annual meeting of the IMF and the World Bank. Many GJM networks encouraged their sympathizers to travel to Prague in order to participate in a series of demonstrations against the neoliberal policies devised by these Bretton Woods institutions. Although Czech border authorities denied entry to many would-be protesters with arrest records from previous justice-globalist rallies, over 10,000 demonstrators, most of them Europeans, managed to make their way to the Czech capital. "This is our Seattle," a young German union activist told a television reporter. "Seattle was the most amazing thing I have ever seen—people uniting to shut down a global institution."[20]

Having prepared for this occasion for weeks, an astonishing number of Czech police officers—11,000—along with advisers from the FBI and Britain's Special Branch were armed with pistols, attack dogs, and water cannons. Indeed, the police force outnumbered the demonstrators. In addition to guarding the thirty-one hotels occupied by delegates, the task of the Czech police was to keep protesters from reaching the Congress Center, where most of the weeklong sessions were held. Large areas of the city were closed to traffic, and most urban shopkeepers closed early. Authorities advised citizens to stock up on food and then bolt their doors and stay inside. Indeed, the U.S. State Department even warned Americans to avoid "unnecessary" travel to the Czech capital for the week of the meetings.[21] Although almost all of the two hundred planned protests were organized as avowedly peaceful events, the chief security coordinator for the Czech police emphasized the presence of potentially violent groups, such as the neofascist skinheads and the radical anarchists. In order to justify the size of the security operation, he claimed that as many as 20 percent of the demonstrators could be aggressive. "The foreigners are the worst," he added. "We're afraid they're teaching the Czechs their violent methods."[22]

On September 26, 2000, some street demonstrations turned violent after several protesters had been injured in confrontations with the police. Some groups pelted police with a hail of bottles and stones, while others deluged them with Molotov cocktails. In response, police in armored personnel carriers raced into position to close off the streets, showering the demonstrators with more tear gas, water cannons, and stun grenades. Soon, the narrow cobblestone streets of Prague's Old Town were flooded and the air was filled with dense clouds of smoke. Most marchers, however, refused to abandon their commitment to nonviolence, instead hurling at attacking police officers antiglobalist slogans such as "Stop the economic terror now" and the ATTAC trademark, "Our world is not for sale." As a result of the fierce street battles, the convention was ended a day before its scheduled conclusion. Over one hundred people, half of them police officers, had been injured, and 420 protesters had been arrested.[23]

Although Prague protest organizers distanced themselves from extremist groups, they conceded that acts of violence and destruction were detracting from the political message of the justice-globalist Left. While blaming the media for focusing excessively on fringe-group activities, many protesters were beginning to realize that their demonstrations were providing cover for small groups that championed entirely different causes. This usurpation of the justice-globalist agenda by extremist groups was particularly apparent during the European Union Summit in December 2000. Hundreds of Basque separatists, French anti-immigration groups, and Italian communists mingled with antiglobalist demonstrators to battle police in the streets of Nice, France. Attacking banks, looting shops, and wrecking cars, these groups rampaged through the famous Riviera resort without showing much concern for a constructive solution to the problem of global inequality.[24]

At the same time, however, the Battle of Seattle and the subsequent series of antiglobalist demonstrations had also served as a convenient excuse to radicalize police forces all over the world. Worried about their continued viability, market globalists—contrary to their laissez-faire philosophy—increasingly supported the state's coercive power against dissenters. The growing brutality and arbitrariness of police actions became especially evident at the January 2001 WEF meeting in Davos. Determined to prevent a repetition of the "embarrassing events" of the year before, Swiss authorities pledged to keep protesters out of the alpine village. In what has been described as the country's largest security operation since World War II, Swiss border units refused entry to thousands of people—often merely on the suspicion that these individuals might be participating in anti-WEF demonstrations. Police and military units set up dozens of roadblocks on all roads leading to Davos. They halted all train services to the town and placed thousands of police and military troops on alert.[25]

Notwithstanding these drastic measures, demonstrators and police did finally confront each other in Davos and Zurich. These street battles led to dozens of injuries and hundreds of arrests. At times, Swiss police even arrested demonstrators merely for handing out anti-WEF leaflets, singing protest songs, or dressing up in "fat cat" costumes with conference-style identification cards around their necks reading "Frank Suisse," "Dave Dollar," and "Mark Deutsch."[26] As in Seattle, a significant part of the Swiss protests was performative, featuring puppets, colorful costumes, and even some giant kites and paper sculptures.

The harsh treatment of peaceful protesters received intense criticism from within Switzerland and abroad. The Swiss Social Democratic Party publicly accused authorities of violating the demonstrators' right to free speech as well as encroaching on other "basic principles of democracy." Swiss newspapers denounced the police for using "methods just like a dictatorship."[27] Yet, in the aftermath of Seattle, such disproportionate official responses to justice-globalist demonstrations had become the rule by the summer of 2001. At demonstrations in Ecuador and Papua New Guinea, military and police units killed several justice-globalist protesters.

At the G-8 Summit in Genoa, the Italian government employed a contingent of over 16,000 police and military troops to "guarantee the safety" of the delegates. As world leaders were feasting on sea bass and champagne aboard a luxury liner safely anchored in the city's harbor, dozens of demonstrators and police were injured in street clashes. Twenty-three-year-old Carlo Giuliani, one of thousands of protesters taking to the streets of the Mediterranean port city, was shot to death by a twenty-year-old carabiniere. The official reaction from attending politicians was mixed, with French President Jacques Chirac wondering what was prompting so many people to turn up in the streets. However, the general tenor of the comments was predictable. Expressing his sorrow at this "tragic loss of life,"

Italian president Azeglio Ciampi urged the demonstrators to "immediately cease this blind violence." Prime Minister Silvio Berlusconi and President George W. Bush quickly followed suit, arguing that both violent and non-violent protesters embraced "policies that lock poor people into poverty."[28]

The transnational corporate media legitimized these elite views by broadcasting images from Genoa that focused almost entirely on the un-ruly behavior of relatively few hard-core anarchists. It mattered little to neoliberal outlets like CNN or Fox that their stories did not tally with ac-tual events. Systematic acts of police brutality and torture employed against nonviolent demonstrators received little media coverage until the Roman newspaper *La Repubblica* started its own investigation. None of the major television networks in the United States paid close attention to re-ports like the one filed by Walden Bello describing how, in the middle of the night, police had barged into the press center of the Genoa Social Forum—the Italian group that lined up six hundred groups behind a pledge of nonviolence—forced everyone to the floor, and then proceeded to humiliate and mistreat those activists.[29] For Enrica Bartasaghi, mother of a young nonviolent protester, the summit was still a "bleeding wound" two years later. "My twenty-one-year-old daughter . . . was beaten by the police," she lamented, "arrested, brought to the hospital and then taken to the Bolzaneto barracks, where she disappeared for two days. There she was threatened and tortured by the police."[30]

Moreover, it seemed to be of no concern to the powerful media voices of neoliberalism that the overwhelming majority of those people who par-ticipated in the series of justice-globalist demonstrations from Seattle to Genoa were firmly committed to nonviolent means of protest. Nor was it big news when Italian Green Party Senator Francisco Martone told the BBC that he had credible evidence for the Italian government's use of infiltrators and provocateurs both to cement the public image of violent, cobblestone-throwing "Black Bloc" anarchists and to justify extreme police reactions. Finally, there were credible reports of police collusion with radical right-wing organizations, including neofascist groups, not to speak of subse-quent political persecution of several protest organizers. And yet, two months later, the Italian parliament approved a report absolving the police of wrongdoing during the G-8 Summit.[31]

## RESISTING IMPERIAL GLOBALISM AFTER 9/11: DOHA AND BEYOND

In the first few months following the 9/11 attacks, even dyed-in-the-wool justice globalists like Naomi Klein worried that the cataclysmic events of that day might have a negative effect on the size and strength of the GJM. Suddenly, she noted, obituaries of the movement appeared in newspapers around the world, proclaiming that "anti-globalization is so yesterday."[32] Indeed, most demonstrations planned for September and October 2001 were canceled in deference to the mood of mourning and out of fear of stepped-up police violence. Moreover, the November 2001 WTO meeting had been arranged in remote Doha, the capital of the tiny Persian Gulf state of Qatar. Only a handful of carefully picked representatives of nongovernmental organizations were allowed into the country.

The Doha meeting was hailed as a great success because the 143 members of the WTO arrived at the unanimous decision to launch a new round of world trade talks. Called the "Doha development agenda," this round of negotiations was designed to seek further trade liberalization and a review of trade rules by January 2005. However, it is important to keep in mind that a trade round is not a new set of rules, principles, or procedures for global trade but rather a catchall term for the painstaking discussions that aim to result in such rules. The last successful attempt, the Uruguay Round of the General Agreement on Tariffs and Trade, ran from 1986 to 1993 before the WTO itself was formed in 1995. Attempts to set up a Seattle Round in 1999 floundered under the weight of international protests and internal disagreements. Partly because of the impact of the GJM, trade talks were no longer simply about the economic technicalities of demolishing tariff barriers and agreeing on subsidies. As reflected in the Doha agreement, issues including environmental concerns and poverty-reduction policies were as high on the WTO's agenda as basic freedom of trade. Moreover, the striking imbalance of political and economic power between the global North and South increasingly facilitated more intense cooperation among developing countries. Indeed, one of the most remarkable features of the Doha meeting was the strength, sophistication, and unity among a large number of the global South representatives, particularly the countries of the so-called Africa Group.[33]

As the initial shock of 9/11 slowly wore off in 2002, justice-globalist protesters returned to various meetings of international economic organizations, although their numbers were generally smaller than before the attacks. Perhaps the largest of these demonstrations took place during the 2002 WEF conference. The Swiss forum leaders had moved the meeting from the Swiss Alps to New York City, ostensibly to show solidarity with the city in the wake of the al Qaeda strikes. More than 10,000 protesters faced thousands of police and concrete barriers that made the venue—the luxurious Waldorf-Astoria Hotel—an impenetrable fortress. Still, protesters sought to stop traffic in the vicinity and thus drew the ire of hundreds of police officers who indiscriminately descended on protesters at various locations and arrested more than 150 people.[34] However, perhaps the most notable thing about the 2002 WEF meeting in New York was how many of the delegates inside the Waldorf picked up on the complaints voiced by the demonstrators on the streets. None of these powerful corporate and political leaders suggested dropping neoliberal globalization, but most of them conceded that reforms were in order. Some admitted that global poverty and hopelessness had contributed to the 9/11 attacks. Indeed, a few of them even went so far as to warn the Bush administration that it was courting disaster by restricting its Global War on Terror to military campaigns without dealing with social and economic issues or solving underlying dynamics like the Israeli–Palestinian conflict.[35] On cue, two months after the WEF meeting, thousands of justice-globalist protesters blended with tens of thousands of Arab American marchers in a huge demonstration against what they perceived as a disproportionate military action in Afghanistan and the administration's one-sided support of Israel.[36]

As the year drew to a close, the merger of the antiwar movement and the GJM was but the mirror image of the convergence of the neoconservative security agenda and the market-globalist economic project in what I have previously referred to as "imperial globalism." In response, the rapid growth of a united Left front against market globalism and militarism was particularly apparent at the October 2002 IMF and World Bank meeting in Washington, D.C. Over 15,000 protesters carried signs and chanted slogans like "No more wars, no more corporate exploitation" or "Drop the debt, not bombs." This blending of peace issues and the antiglobalist agenda culminated in early 2003 when it became clear that the Bush administration was set on a collision course with Iraq. On February 15, 2003, an estimated 15 million to 20 million people in over sixty countries—a remarkable conglomerate of peace activists and justice globalists—took to the streets to register their firm opposition to a U.S.-led war against Iraq. Cities like London and Barcelona registered the largest crowds of protesters in their entire history.

Justice-globalist resistance against the WTO came to a surprising climax six months later at the World Trade Summit in Cancún, Mexico. In addition to thousands of Mexican farmers who had marched on the city to demand that rich nations end hypocritical farm subsidies that hurt millions of farmers in the global South, at least 10,000 justice-globalist activists from all over the world came to Cancún. The roads leading to the city were dotted with security checkpoints, and thousands of police sealed off the conference center. Reacting to these massive attempts to keep dissenters away from the meeting, protesters creatively responded by setting up a parallel conference site where they camped out and held a running series of seminars on the problems of free trade and possible alternatives. Eventually, however, clashes broke out during a march at a security fence six miles from the convention center, culminating in the arrest of dozens of people by scores of Mexican police willing to use considerable force to disperse the crowd. In a dramatic act of desperation, fifty-five-year-old South Korean farmer Lee Kyung Hae scaled the security fence and committed suicide by stabbing himself in the chest.[37]

Inside the conference, the trade talks did not proceed smoothly. The G-22—a group of twenty-two developing countries led by Brazil, India, Nigeria, and China—mounted a quiet revolt, demanding that their proposal to cut rich nations' farm subsidies be openly debated and not shunted aside through the invocation of procedural rules. They raised other issues as well—most notably the unfair WTO rules on foreign investment that favored the interest of TNCs over those of Third World countries and the issue of intellectual property rights that prevented poor countries from gaining access to generic medicines to combat AIDS and other diseases—but the core problem was the question of agricultural subsidies.

After all, according to the market-globalist gospel of free trade, developing countries should have an advantage in agriculture, given that they have lower land and labor costs that allow them to produce more cheaply. And yet farming has remained the most protected sector of the economies of the rich global North. Not only do countries like the United States, France, and Japan maintain high agricultural tariffs that block imports, but they also spend billions on subsidies to their own farmers. During the 2000s, for example, U.S. cotton farmers received an average of $3 billion a year in subsidies, allowing them to vastly undersell African countries on the world market.[38] It is estimated that the total agricultural subsidies of the world's wealthiest nations in this decade have amounted to $300 billion every year, thus devastating agriculture-based economies in the global South. In 2002, President Bush signed into law a new farm policy that increased permanent subsidies to U.S. farmers by $40 billion a year. Bush's protectionism may not be surprising considering that the political contributions from agribusiness in the United States to the two main parties jumped from $37 million in 1992 to $53 million in 2002, with the Republican Party's share rising from 56 percent to 72 percent.[39]

In the end, Cancún proved to be a watershed, showing that developing countries were no longer willing to knuckle under to hypocritical WTO rules largely created and maintained by the global North. After days of unsuccessful attempts to pressure the global North into making concessions on the issue of agricultural subsidies, G-22 representatives walked out of the meeting, thus causing the world trade talks to collapse and casting a dark cloud on the future of the Doha Round that was slated to end in major agreements in January 2005. Instead of admitting to his country's double standard on free trade, then U.S. Trade Representative Robert Zoellick blamed the G-22, arguing that they had deliberately "stalled the talks" with "tactics of inflexibility and inflammatory rhetoric."[40] While hoping that these countries would eventually "come around," Zoellick also put the world on notice that the breakdown of the Cancún trade talks would cause the U.S. administration to shift its focus from the multilateral framework of the WTO to an individualistic posture of hammering out bilateral and multinational deals without the blessing of global economic institutions.[41] Once again, Zoellick's threats revealed the unilateral underpinnings of imperial globalism. Only a few committed market globalists like Jagdish Bhagwati were not willing to go along with such policies. Claiming that "the process of trade liberalization is becoming a sham," the Columbia University economist accused TNCs of essentially hijacking free-trade principles and turning them into their own agenda for unrestricted exploitation.[42]

Unsurprisingly, on January 1, 2005, the original deadline for a successful completion of the Doha Round, it was clear to all participants that the talks needed to be extended if they were to yield positive results. But subsequent meetings failed to produce the desired outcomes, and at its meeting on July 27–28, 2006, Director-General Pascal Lamy suspended further negotiations. When a hastily convened summit in Potsdam in June 2007 involving representatives from the European Union, the United States, India, and Brazil foundered on the old thorny issue of European and American agricultural subsidies, experts pronounced Doha dead. Much to the surprise of these pundits, however, President Bush announced in early 2008 that the United States was willing to make agricultural concessions to reach a new world trade deal if other countries opened their markets to more American exports. European Union leaders followed suit. Even Roberto Azevedo, Brazil's chief negotiator, showed some optimism, stating that while there was no certainty of success, negotiators were closer than ever to reaching agreement. It remains to be seen, however, if President Bush's bold prediction that the Doha Round will be succesfully concluded by the end of 2008 will actually materialize.[43] After all, the $290 billion U.S. farm bill proposed for 2009 offers the usual subsidies to farmers, thus clearly contradicting trade liberalization principles.

## WHAT DOES THE GLOBAL JUSTICE MOVEMENT WANT? THE CORE CLAIMS OF JUSTICE GLOBALISM

Let us now turn from the political context in which the GJM has operated for a decade to an examination of the ideological structure of justice globalism. We proceed with our critical discourse analysis by focusing primarily on textual passages involving two influential codifiers of justice globalism: American consumer activist and repeat presidential candidate Ralph Nader and the WSF's Charter of Principles.

For the past few decades, Ralph Nader, named by *Life* magazine as one of the hundred most influential people of the twentieth century, has been a prominent spokesperson for the democratic Left in the United States. Born in Connecticut to Lebanese immigrants, Nader showed extraordinary intellectual promise as a student. He received his BA degree (magna cum laude) from Princeton University and his law degree from Harvard University. In 1963, he abandoned a conventional law practice for a consulting job with the Department of Labor's assistant secretary, Daniel Patrick Moynihan. The young lawyer also freelanced as a journalist, writing regular articles for Left-liberal journals such as *The Nation* and progressive newspapers such as the *Christian Science Monitor*. In 1965, he published his best-selling book *Unsafe at Any Speed: The Designed-In Dangers of the American Automobile*, in which he targeted the American auto industry for covering up serious safety hazards in order to protect its profits. After prevailing in an ensuing lawsuit involving General Motors, Nader used the settlement money he received to launch the modern consumer movement in America.

His reputation as a relentless critic of corporate America grew over the next decades as Public Citizen, his major nonprofit organization, successfully lobbied Congress for the passage of new consumer-protection laws. By the 1990s, more than 150,000 people were actively involved in Public Citizen's six major divisions. One of these branches, Global Trade Watch, is dedicated to educating the American public about the negative impact of neoliberal economic globalization on job security, the environment, public health and safety, and democratic accountability. Founded in 1993 as a direct response to the passage of NAFTA in Congress, Global Trade Watch has emerged as a leading watchdog organization monitoring the activities of the IMF, the World Bank, and the WTO. Nader has established himself as one of the principal Left critics of these organizations, arguing that their main purpose lies in promoting a neoliberal, corporatist agenda at the expense of the interests of ordinary citizens all over the world.

After his botched presidential campaign of 1996, Nader ran again as the

Green Party presidential candidate four years later. This time, he and his party managed to put together a vigorous national campaign. On Election Day 2000, the justice-globalist consumer advocate received 3 percent of the national vote, which amounted to about 3 million votes nationwide. Many political pundits argued that in such hotly contested states as Florida and New Hampshire, Nader's candidacy ultimately lost the election for the Democratic presidential candidate, Vice President Al Gore. In 2004 and 2008, Nader ran again for president. This time, however, the Green Party did not nominate him as its offical candidate.

In his official statement announcing his 2000 candidacy for president, Nader presented himself as a defender of democratic principles against the "neoliberal forces of globalism."[44] Unlike national populists on the Right who sought to stoke the fires of popular resentment against ethnic minorities, recent immigrants, or welfare recipients, Nader's leftist populism invoked the inclusive spirit of the Green Party platform, which "opposes those who seek to divide us for political gain by raising ethnic and racial hatreds, blaming immigrants for social and economic problems."[45] The justice-globalist dimension of Nader's populism is also evident in his conscious attempt to avoid the Right's exaggerated patriotism. In spite of his occasional tendency to play to the chauvinistic passions of his campaign audiences by defending the "self-determination of nations" against the "domination of global corporations," Nader regularly returns to the idea that market globalism must be opposed by a *global* alliance of egalitarian forces. For example, in his acceptance speech at the 2000 Green Party convention, he noted that the values of "deep democracy" and social justice, the elimination of poverty, and the protection of the environment constitute moral imperatives that ought to transcend the narrow conceptual framework of nationalism or regionalism.[46]

With regard to the role of corporate elites, however, Nader's leftist populism finds itself precariously close to Patrick Buchanan's brand of national populism, which we discuss in the next chapter. In a joint online interview given to *Time* magazine on the evening of the 1999 Seattle anti-WTO protests, both men affirmed that underlying their antagonistic ideological positions was a common understanding of the market-globalist agenda as undermining the power of the people.[47] The main difference, however, is that Nader's understanding of "people" goes far beyond Buchanan's narrow focus on "Americans." Time and again, Nader directs the brunt of his message against the market-globalist claims that nobody is in charge of globalization and that globalization furthers the spread of democracy in the world. For the consumer advocate, globalization is driven by powerful global corporate elites who subordinate human rights, labor rights, consumer rights, environmental rights, and democratic rights to the imperatives of global trade and investment. As he points out, of the top one hundred economic entities in the world, fifty-two are corporations and only forty-eight are countries. Moreover, the gross annual sales of such huge TNCs as General Motors exceed the gross domestic product of countries such as Norway, South Africa, and Saudi Arabia. Shaping the globalization of commerce and finance in an authoritarian fashion, these transnational companies contribute to a widening "democracy gap" between ordinary people and their political institutions:

> The global corporatists preach a model of economic growth that rests on the flows of trade and finance between nations dominated by giant multinationals—drugs, tobacco, oil, banking, and other services. The global corporate model is premised on the concentration of power over markets, governments, mass media, patent monopolies over critical drugs and seeds, the workplace, and corporate culture. All these and other power concentrates homogenize the globe and undermine democratic processes and their benefits.[48]

In Nader's view, the worldwide implementation of the "corporate model of globalization" goes hand in hand with the creation of autocratic institutions of political governance that push a neoliberal agenda of economic development. For example, the establishment of the WTO reflects the formalization and strengthening of corporate power. For Nader, such institutions were designed by market-globalist forces in order to eliminate "the oppositional factors we call democracy—to have an international system of autocratic governance that undermines open judicial courts and replaces them with [the] secret tribunals [of the WTO]." In this way, he notes, corporate globalization establishes supranational limitations and impinges deeply on the ability of ordinary people around the world to control commercial activity with democratically enacted laws. The tactic of market globalists is to eliminate democratic decision making and accountability over matters as intimate as the safety of food, pharmaceuticals, and motor vehicles, or the way a country may use or conserve its land, water and minerals, and other resources. What we have now, Nader concludes, is a slow-motion coup d'état, a low-intensity war waged to redefine free society as subordinate to the dictates of international trade—that is, "big business über alles."[49]

Noting the rise of political-action committees in the United States from four hundred in 1974 to about 9,000 in 2000, Nader claims that this "huge, beefed up corporate-lobby presence in Washington" successfully pressured

Congress and the president to steer on a neoliberal course. A "massive avalanche of [corporate] money" has buried the democratic system of the United States:

> Government has been hijacked to a degree beyond anything we have seen in the last 70 years. It's been hijacked by corporate power, the multinationals mostly. They have their own people in government. They run their own people, they appoint their own people, they get corporate lawyers to agree to become judges. And when that happens you no longer have a countervailing force called government arrayed against excesses of what Jefferson called "the moneyed interest." Instead, you have this convergence, almost a phalanx, of business controlling government and turning it against its own people.[50]

If even the world's sole remaining superpower has been captured by transnational corporate interests, Nader continues, one should not be surprised to see the growth of unaccountable corporate power all over the world. Rather than living up to their market-globalist claim of stimulating the spread of democratic values, Western corporatist governments have propped up authoritarian, oligarchic regimes in the developing world that ensure social conditions conducive to foreign direct investment. Pitting states against each other, powerful TNCs have created a "race to the bottom" in which governments attempt to attract foreign investment by lowering wage levels, imposing the lowest pollution standards, and cutting business taxes to an absolute minimum. Thus, American standards of living and the standards of justice have been pulled down "to the level of other countries that happen to be authoritarian and dictatorial. That is why, for example, globalization does not ban trade produced by child labor. That's why it does not ban trade produced by brutalizing working conditions."[51]

Responding to neoliberal figures that suggest a worldwide rise in living standards, Nader employs his own data effectively against the market-globalist claim that globalization benefits everyone. Referring to rising levels of inequality in America alone, Nader notes that the United States ranks thirty-seventh among nations in the world regarding the quality of health care. Forty-seven million workers, over one-third of the U.S. workforce, make less than $10 per hour and work 160 hours longer per year than did workers in 1973. The low U.S. unemployment rate in the 1990s, often cited by globalists as evidence for the economic benefits of globalization, is masked by low wages and millions of part-time laborers who are registered as employed if they work twenty-one hours a week and cannot get a full-time job. At the same time, the average salary of a chief executive officer employed in a large corporation has exploded. In 2000, it was 416 times higher than that of an average worker. The financial wealth of the top 1 percent of American households exceeds the combined wealth of the bottom 95 percent, reflecting a significant increase in the last twenty years.[52]

But Nader habitually goes beyond the national imaginary by addressing the increase of global inequalities brought on by corporate globalization. Some of the numbers he uses are readily available from annual editions of the UN *Human Development Report*. For example, he notes that the world income distribution among households in the past ten years has shown a sharp rise in inequality. The economic gap between rich and poor is widening in most countries. At the same time, economic growth has stagnated in many developing countries, leading to an increase in income disparities between rich and poor countries by orders of magnitude out of proportion to anything previously experienced. Just before the onset of globalization in 1973, the income ratio between the richest and poorest countries was at about forty-four to one. Twenty-five years later it had climbed to seventy-four to one. In the period since the end of the Cold War, the number of persons subsisting below the international poverty line rose from 1.2 billion in 1987 to 1.5 billion today and, if current trends persist, will reach 1.9 billion by 2015. This means that, at the dawn of the twenty-first century, the bottom 25 percent of humankind lives on less than $140 a year. Meanwhile, the world's two hundred richest people have doubled their net worth to more than $1 trillion between 1994 and 1998. The assets of the world's top three billionaires are worth more than the combined gross national product of all least developed countries and their 600 million people.[53]

Despite the seemingly hopeless social dynamic expressed in these statistics, Nader refuses to accept the market-globalist claim that globalization equals the liberalization and integration of markets and that this dynamic is inevitable and irresistible. But a successful challenge to the concentration of global corporate power over governments requires a "revitalized citizen democracy in the United States and movement building across national borders."[54] Rather than emphasizing the central role of strong political leaders, Nader invokes the efforts of countless, locally based GJM groups where ordinary people struggle together to overcome steep concentrations of undemocratic power. He also points to recent, worldwide mass mobilizations against market globalism and its institutions as evidence for ordinary people's ability to halt, reverse, or redirect the allegedly inexorable march of the corporate juggernaut.

Time and again, Nader challenges his audience to participate in open forms of resistance against the dominant order. He attempts to delegitimize the ideological claims of market globalism by drawing on the central elements of justice globalism, which are rooted in leftist traditions of the previous two centuries: citizen participation, grassroots democracy, racial and gender equality, ecological balance, community-based economics, and distributive justice. Nader is nonetheless not above fighting the ideological distortions of market globalism with equally contorted, Manichaean images of a "selfish corporate oligarchy" responsible for all the ills in society, including economic decline, the debasement of politics, and the betrayal of the democratic heritage.[55] Again, the populist streak in his vision of justice globalism contains the danger of hyperbole and demonization of political opponents.

On the other hand, Nader's ideological enterprise also contains a constructive, integrative function that seeks to transform people's one-dimensional consumer identities. At the heart of his struggle for the creation of a new identity lies his moral commitment to "putting human values first." Emphasizing the importance of ethical, cosmopolitan ideals guiding political action, Nader directs his justice-globalist message especially at young people:

> I say, beware of being trivialized by the commercial culture that tempts you daily. I hear you saying often that you're not turned on to politics. The lessons of history are clear and portentous. If you do not turn on to politics, politics will turn on you. The fact that we have so many inequalities demonstrates this point. Democracy responds to hands-on participation. And to energized imagination. That's its essence. We need the young people of America to move into leadership positions to shape their future as part of this campaign for a just society.[56]

When Nader announced his candidacy for president in early 2004, many of those sympathetic voices in the Green Party who had embraced his campaign four years earlier turned against him. For one, arguing that a united front against President Bush was needed, they grudgingly supported Democratic candidate John Kerry. Fearing that a Nader candidacy would help Bush retain his office, many progressive voices pleaded with the maverick not to run. Yet Nader decided to mount another campaign. Failing to secure the Green Party's nomination, he turned to Buchanan's Reform Party, which promptly endorsed him, thus putting Nader automatically on the ballot in seven states. Many justice globalists were outraged, arguing that Dennis Kucinich's run for president as a Democratic candidate in both

2004 and 2008 made Nader's initiative superfluous. Indeed, Kucinich's progressive credentials were impeccable.

Having been elected mayor of Cleveland in 1977 at age thirty-one—the youngest person ever elected to lead a major American city—Kucinich made national headlines in 1978 when he resisted selling Cleveland's seventy-year-old municipally owned electric system to its private competitor. Partly as a result of this bold posture, Kucinich lost his reelection bid a year later. However, in 1998, the Cleveland City Council honored him for "having had the courage and foresight to refuse to sell the city's municipal electric system," noting that it provided low-cost power to almost half the residents of Cleveland. In the early 1990s, Kucinich made a political comeback by winning election to the Ohio State Senate, followed by his election to the U.S. House of Representatives as a Democrat for several terms. For his continuous work toward world peace and the reduction of poverty worldwide, the congressman was awarded the 2003 Gandhi Peace Award, a distinction Kucinich shares with such engaged individuals as Eleanor Roosevelt, A. J. Muste, Dorothy Day, Cesar Chavez, and Dr. Benjamin Spock.

Kucinich's presidential platforms in 2004 and 2008 spelled out core justice-globalist objectives, including calls for "confronting the global trade regime" in order to facilitate fair trade and end sweatshop conditions worldwide. He favored a repeal of NAFTA but opposed protective measures that benefit Americans at the expense of foreign workers. Emphasizing that "government must reclaim its rightful role as regulator in the public interest," he vowed to take on corporate power and make it accountable to ordinary citizens. Like Nader, Kucinich supported not only the massive increase of U.S. contributions to the UN World Food Program but also the immediate cancellation of all bilateral debts of countries facing hunger as well as cancellation of debts to the IMF and World Bank.[57] As we shall see next, these demands echo those included in the WSF's Charter of Principles. On U.S. foreign policy issues, too, Kucinich was more justice-globalist minded than Nader. Kucinich insisted that the United States ought to promote international cooperation as well as affirm and ratify global treaties, including the controversial Kyoto Treaty on Global Climate Change, the Landmine Ban Treaty, the Anti-Ballistic Missile Treaty, and the Biological/Chemical Weapons Conventions. Opposing the Bush administration's extensive military operations, Kucinich proposed trimming the Pentagon budget by 15 percent, or $60 billion. He argued that the most effective security strategy consists of a coordinated, multilateralist effort in the Global War on Terror involving as many nations as possible. For Kucinich, genuine "homeland security" ought to refer also to the expansion of domestic social programs (including free health care and education for all Americans). He called for the establishment of a U.S. Department of Peace, dedicated to furthering the goal of "global human development" and the control of violence by "supporting disarmament, treaties, peaceful co-existence and peaceful consensus building." Moreover, Kucinich believed that the Department of Peace should also address the unique concerns of the world's women and children.[58] Thus outlined, Kucinich's program encapsulates the major ideological claims associated with the WSF. Before considering these in greater detail, let us briefly recall its general organizational structure and purpose.

Founded as the counterpart to the WEF in 2001, the WSF established itself as both the key ideological site and the transnational social space from which to develop such justice-globalist policy proposals as the cancellation of Third World debt and the taxation of international capital flows. Candido Grzybowski, the executive director of the Brazilian Institute for Social and Economic Analysis and cofounder of the WSF, noted that the transnationalization of civil society in the 1990s was a crucial precondition for the creation of the WSF. Grzybowski argued that the world's civil societies were beginning to view themselves within the framework of globalization, increasingly enabling ordinary people to articulate the rising global imaginary in political terms. As he pointed out, one of the primary goals of justice globalism was to produce a counterhegemonic discourse that would challenge the dominant deterministic claims of market globalism and contribute to the emergence of a more egalitarian global consciousness. Grzybowski believed that people at the grass roots can affect the course of globalization but only by means of forging transnational alliances that reach across geographic, ethnic, and class boundaries:

> Forging another kind of globalization within civil society is possible. To do that we must reaffirm the primacy of the ethical principles constituting democracy: Equality, freedom, participation, and human diversity and solidarity. They are capable of touching the hearts and minds of civil society's different groups and sectors. These principles should regulate power and market and be upheld and practiced throughout the world. The priority task is to counterpose a deepening process of global democracy and of planetary-scale cultural change to worldwide neo-liberal disorder.[59]

The first WSF was held in Porto Alegre in January 2001, attracting about 5,000 participants from 117 countries and thousands of Brazilian activists. Indeed, the efforts of eight Brazilian civil society organizations close to the Workers' Party proved to be instrumental in setting up the

WSF as an "open space" for citizens worldwide to explore the negative impacts of global neoliberal restructuring on their local and national experiences while expanding transnational dialogues and social movement networking to address key global problems from global climate change to political violence and terrorism to poverty and surging food prices.[60] The figures from the second forum showed momentous growth, rising to over 12,000 official delegates from 123 countries and tens of thousands of participants, mostly from Brazil. The third forum in January 2003 attracted over 20,000 official delegates and approximately 100,000 participants in total. The global media impact of the second and third forums was significantly stronger than in the first year.

At the 2004 WSF in Mumbai, India, the global peace movement and justice globalists joined forces after making the event a transnational coordination space for the worldwide protest against the Iraq War. At that meeting, a variety of new initiatives were discussed, including the idea of launching a World Parliamentary Forum. Most importantly, the conference participants stressed the importance of poking holes in the dominant market-globalist discourse and disseminating to people around the world a coherent "alter-globalist" vision. As Bernard Cassen, a co-organizer of the WSF meetings and president of ATTAC, put it, "We are here to show the world that a different world is possible."[61] In 2005, the WSF returned, successfully, to Porto Alegre. The year 2006 saw a series of large-scale continental social forums rather than a global forum, but the 2007 WSF was once again a unified event held in Nairobi, Kenya. In 2008, a "Global Action Day" replaced the global forum, but another WSF meeting will be held in 2009 in Belém, Brazil.

By 2008, there were 150 civil society organizations from around the world associated with the WSF. These organizations represent different interests, possess distinctive structures, pursue various projects, and are based in different geographical regions. They include labor unions (such as the Australian ACTU and the American AFL-CIO), environmental groups (such as Greenpeace), agricultural co-ops (such as the All Arab Peasants and Agricultural Cooperatives Union), think-tanks and educational organizations (such as Focus on the Global South and the Transnational Institute), indigenous peoples' assemblies (such as Congreso Nacional Indigena de Mexico), financial watchdog groups (such as ATTAC and Bankwatch Network), feminist and women's networks (such as World March of Women), human-rights organizations (such as Public Citizen and Oxfam International), religiously affiliated groups (such as Caritas International), migration associations (such as the Forum des Organisations de Solidarité Internationale Issues des Migrations), peace networks (such as Peace Boat), alternative public policy organizations (such as Global Policy Network), global democracy advocacy groups (such as the Network Institute for Global Democratization), North-South networks (such as North-South Centre and Solidar), and poor people's movements (such as Poor People's Economic Human Rights Campaign). Diverse as they are in many respects, these organizations nonetheless inhabit overlapping discursive spaces—framed around globalization and its social and environmental impacts—from which they address various transnational publics.

There is virtual unanimous agreement in the authoritative literature on the significance of the WSF as the intellectual and organizational epicenter of the GJM, constituting its largest and most diverse organizational umbrella.[62] While there exist other large global justice networks such as the International Confederation of Free Trade Unions, the Amsterdam-based Transnational Institute, or Friends of the Earth International, these organizations are focused on particular sectoral concerns. The WSF brings together a vast diversity of social sectors, spanning North and South, crossing a range of linguistic divides. It is also politically diverse: unlike other global justice formations, it draws together a broad range of political orientations and tendencies. Although much of its membership is in Latin America, Europe, and North America, there is also significant involvement from African and Asian groups. Indeed, no other global justice coalition comes close to the geographical, ethnic, and linguistic reach and diversity existing at the WSF.

Unlike other large global justice coalitions, the WSF was consciously established as an *ideological* antithesis to the market-globalist WEF. Indeed, the fourteen clauses of its Charter of Principles constitute a particularly rich source of justice-globalist claims. Let us now analyze some of these claims. The Charter invokes in its first clause a global "we" defined as "social forces from around the world" and "organizations and movements of civil society from all the countries in the world" that are committed to "building a planetary society directed toward fruitful relationships among humankind and between it and the Earth." These general declarations of global subjectivity are then further specified in a special 2001 WSF "Call to Mobilization" to "women and men, farmers, workers, unemployed, professionals, students, blacks, and indigenous peoples, coming from the South and from the North."[63]

Thus, the movement's affirmation of a "global we" becomes tied to its irreducible plurality and diversity. In her careful analysis of five similar documents authored by transnational networks that belong to different sectors of the GJM, Donatella della Porta also underlines the construction of a global collective self respectful of differences of views and cultural and political traditions: "[M]ultifacetedness becomes an intrinsic element of the movement's collective identity, so intrinsic that it becomes implicit."[64] Clause 8 of the Charter drives home this point by declaring, "The World Social Forum is a plural, diversified, non-confessional, nongovernmental, and nonparty context that, in a decentralized fashion, interrelates organizations and movements engaged in concrete action at levels from the local to the international to build another world." Insisting that the means must be consistent with the end, the Charter claims to translate its commitment to diversity and decentralization through "nonviolent social resistance" to corporate globalization. The goals of justice globalism are clearly spelled out: "solve the problems of exclusion and social inequality that the process of capitalist globalization with its racist, sexist, and environmentally destructive dimensions is creating internationally and within countries." Committed to the ideal of "planetary citizenship," the WSF encourages its participant organizations and movements to introduce into the global agenda "change-inducing practices" for the "building of a new world in solidarity." In short, the Charter envisions an engagement in the world as a whole that is fundamentally different from the "inevitable" economic integration along market-globalist lines.[65]

Hence, at the center of the justice-globalist critique of the dominant paradigm lies the unshakable conviction that the liberalization and global integration of markets leads to greater social inequalities, environmental destruction, the escalation of global conflicts and violence, the weakening of participatory forms of democracy, the proliferation of self-interest and consumerism, and the further marginalization of the powerless around the world. The Charter makes clear that the crucial ideological task of the GJM is to undermine the premises and ideological framework of the reigning neoliberal worldview by disseminating an alternative translation of the global imaginary based on the core principles of the WSF: equality, social justice, diversity, democracy, nonviolence, solidarity, ecological sustainability, and planetary citizenship.

Although the Charter identifies "neoliberalism," "imperialism," and the "domination of the world by capital" as the main obstacles on the path toward global democracy, it specifically rejects old Marxist or Leninist formulas derived from "reductionist views of economy" or a "totalitarian" disregard for human rights. Susan George, an American-French author and one of the driving citizen-activists behind WSF and ATTAC, rarely misses an opportunity to point to the difference between Marxism's radical anti-market rhetoric and a justice-globalist position critical of markets: "The issue as I see it is not to abolish markets. . . . Trying to ban markets would rather be like banning rain. One can, however, enforce strict limitations on what is and is not governed by market rules and make sure that everyone can participate in exchange." George also shows no hesitation to dispense with Marx's agent of social change—the international working class—as "more wishful thinking than reality." Scientific socialism's revolutionary expectation of the inevitable collapse of capitalism strikes her as a "global accident" unlikely to occur. Neither is such a doomsday scenario to be cheerfully contemplated, for it would entail "massive unemployment, wiped-out savings, pensions and insurance; societal breakdown, looting, crime, misery, scapegoating and repression, most certainly followed by fascism, or at the very least, military takeovers." George ends her extended criticism of old-Left thinking with a ferocious broadside against the "totalitarian systems" of "state-socialism." In her view, the gulags and killing fields of the Soviet Union, Mao's China, and other purportedly "revolutionary" Third World regimes belie their supposed humanist ideals. But the 1960s activists do not fare well either in George's hard-nosed approach to changing the world. For example, she counters the New Age slogan of "personal transformation" as the perquisite for "enlightened" political action with Kant's famous statement of unavoidable human fallibility—the "crooked timber of humanity, from which no straight thing was ever made." While acknowledging the far-reaching cultural and social effects of the 1960s, she reminds her global audience that the political and ideational framework of nation-based movements was not strong enough to withstand the worldwide offensive of market globalism.[66]

Indeed, the justice-globalist vision is neither about reviving a moribund Marxism nor about a return to the good old days of 1968. Although it contains ideational elements of Third World liberationism and traditional European social democracy, it goes beyond these ideologies in several respects—most importantly in its ability to bring together a large number of Left concerns around a more pronounced orientation toward the globe as a single, interconnected arena for political action. As the WSF slogan suggests, "Another *World* is possible." One example of its strong global focus is the GJM's publicity campaign to highlight the negative consequences of deregulated global capitalism on the planet's environmental health. But the programmatic core of the ideological claims of justice globalism is a "global Marshall Plan" that would create more political space for people around the world to determine what kind of social arrangements they want. Millions of justice globalists believe that "another world" has to begin with a new, worldwide Keynesian-type program of taxation and redistribution, exactly as it was introduced at the national level in Western countries a century ago. As we noted previously, the necessary funds for this global regulatory framework would come from the profits of TNCs and financial markets—hence the justice-globalist campaign for the introduction of the global Tobin Tax. Other proposals include the cancellation of poor countries' debts; the closing of offshore financial centers offering tax havens for wealthy individuals and corporations; the ratification and implementation of stringent global environmental agreements; the implementation of a more equitable global development agenda; the establishment of a new world development institution financed largely by the global North and administered largely by the global South; the establishment of international labor protection standards, perhaps as clauses of a profoundly reformed WTO; greater transparency and accountability provided to citizens by national governments and global economic institutions; making all governance of globalization explicitly gender sensitive; and the transformation of "free trade" into fair trade. Thus, justice globalism as articulated at the WSF offers an alternative translation of the rising global imaginary, one that not only is critical of market-globalist claims but also rejects the national-populist and jihadist-globalist visions of the political Right.

# CHAPTER 5

## CHALLENGES FROM THE POLITICAL RIGHT: NATIONAL POPULISM AND JIHADIST GLOBALISM

### WHAT IS NATIONAL POPULISM?

Although justice globalists made up the vast majority of those millions who protested worldwide against market globalism, they were not the only political camp opposed to it. At the Battle of Seattle, for example, there also marched a number of people who championed the nationalist perspective of the radical right. Even hard-edged soldiers of neofascism such as Illinois-based World Church of the Creator founder Matt Hale, who was convicted in Illinois in 2004 for instigating the killing of a judge, encouraged their followers to come to Seattle and "throw a monkey wrench into the gears of the enemy's machine." The dangerous neo-Nazi group National Alliance was represented as well. White supremacist leader Louis Beam praised the demonstrators, emphasizing that the "police state goons" in Seattle were paid by international capital to protect "the slimy corporate interests of 'free trade' at the expense of free people." In the sea of signs

131

bearing leftist slogans, there were occasional posters bitterly denouncing the "Jewish Media Plus Big Capital" and the "New World Order."[1] Indeed, at the dawning of the twenty-first century, market globalism became the principal target not only for these marginal right-wing radicals but also for a growing number of more moderate "national populists" like the prominent American journalist and former Republican Party and Reform Party presidential candidate Pat Buchanan, who called on his supporters to join his economic protectionist cause against the World Trade Organization (WTO).

National populists like Buchanan belong to one of the two major ideological camps within the political Right that are critical of market globalism. They tend to blame "globalization" for most of the social, economic, and political ills afflicting their home countries.[2] Threatened by the slow erosion of old social patterns and traditional ways of life, they denounce free trade, the increasing power of global investors, and the neoliberal "internationalism" of transnational corporations as unpatriotic practices that have contributed to falling living standards and moral decline. Fearing the loss of national self-determination and the destruction of a circumscribed national culture, they pledge to protect the integrity of their nation from those "foreign elements" that they identify as responsible for unleashing the forces of globalization.

National populists focus on the challenges and dislocations brought about by globalization dynamics to appeal to those segments of the population most in danger of losing their status in the conventional social hierarchies of the nation-state. As we shall discuss in this chapter, they respond to people's growing sense of fragmentation and alienation by presenting themselves as strong leaders capable of halting the erosion of conventional social bonds and familiar cultural environments. Lending an authoritarian voice to their audiences' longing for the receding world of cultural uniformity, moral certainty, and national parochialism, they refuse to rethink community in light of the rising global imaginary. Indeed, national populists put the well-being of their own citizens above the construction of a more equitable international order based on global solidarity.

In the United States, Patrick Buchanan and the popular CNN host Lou Dobbs are perhaps the most prominent of the national populists representing this position. Elsewhere, nationalist-populist parties such as Jörg Haider's Austrian Freedom Party (since 2005 he has been heading up the new Alliance for the Future of Austria Party), Jean-Marie Le Pen's French National Front, Gerhard Frey's German People's Union, Christoph Blocher's Swiss People's Party, Gianfranco Fini's Italian National Alliance, Pauline

Hanson's Australian One Nation Party, and Winston Peters's New Zealand First Party have expressed their opposition to "American-style globalization" and its alleged tendency to produce a multicultural "New World Order." Their resistance to globalization has only increased with the rise of imperial globalism after 9/11. In the global South, one finds similar voices on the Right that blame neoliberal globalization and the expansion of American economic and military power for triggering economic crisis and cultural decay and undermining regional autonomy. Venezuelan president Hugo Chávez's "Bolivarian" brand of national populism represents one such highly visible example.[3]

Deriving from the Latin *populus*—"the people"—populism has been associated with a variety of phenomena including "an ideology," "a social movement," "a strategy of political mobilization," "a political outlook," "a mentality," "a political syndrome," and "an emotional appeal."[4] But none of these associations has achieved universal acceptance. Margaret Canovan, perhaps the world's foremost authority on the subject, has pointed out that the meaning of populism varies from context to context, thus demanding different kinds of analysis.[5] Others have argued that populism and democracy refer to virtually synonymous "modes of articulation" that divide the social into two camps: "power and the underdog."[6] However, even a cursory perusal of modern political history reveals that populists have been reluctant to endorse the rules of representative democracy. In fact, their hostility to representative politics could be seen as one of populism's most prominent features.[7] And yet the fundamental democratic notion of political power residing in the people can be made to fit the temperaments of both radical egalitarians in favor of people's direct, unmediated rule and staunch authoritarians claiming to speak and act on behalf of the entire *populus*. Latin American strongmen like Juan Peron or Hugo Chávez, for example, portrayed their repeated violations of basic constitutional liberties as necessary measures to carry out "the will of the people" against the power interests of corrupt social elites. Seizing on emotionally charged issues that are modified or even disavowed according to changing political conditions, populists have been branded "political chameleons" who routinely change their colors in searching for prey. To be sure, populism is not the only political discourse that thrives on passions, but, perhaps more than others, it relies on an "extra emotional ingredient" to attract normally apolitical people to its vision of society's deplorable decline and its necessary "great renewal."[8]

Although populism cuts across the ideological spectrum, its latest and most powerful manifestations have been skewed toward the Right. Indeed, the alleged concern of contemporary national populists with the "corrupt party system" or the "liberal media" mixes all too easily with the fondness of right-wing authoritarians for paternalist policies, their aversion to participatory and critical debate, pluralism, compromise between conflicting interests, and their hostility toward the political agenda of liberals, feminists, gays and lesbians, and multiculturalists.[9] In spite of its rhetorical power, however, national populism lacks the developed ideational structure of comprehensive political belief systems. As Paul Taggart points out, national populism's "empty heart" is responsible for both its conceptual thinness and its potential ubiquity.[10] Incapable of standing on its own ideological feet, it attaches itself to various host vessels in the form of a "persistent yet mutable style of political rhetoric."[11]

As we shall see in this chapter, national populists routinely perform at least three mutually reinforcing rhetorical maneuvers. The first involves the construction of unbridgeable political differences. Fond of airtight Manichaean divisions between Good and Evil, they divide the population into the vast majority of ordinary people ("us") and a small but powerful elite ("them"). "The people" are idealized as decent, good-natured folk susceptible to the corrupt machinations of the privileged few. Thus, they require protection and guidance from a personalized leader or a dedicated vanguard of moral warriors fighting "intellectuals," "speculators," "politicians," "city dwellers," "Jews," "cosmopolitans," "globalists," and other "enemies of the people." Domestic political elites are frequently taken to task for allowing "our community" to be infiltrated by immigrants, guest workers, ethnic minorities, or foreign radicals—allegedly for material gain and other self-serving, unpatriotic reasons. Hence, "the Establishment" stands for corruption, abuse of power, parasitism, arbitrariness, and treachery, whereas "the people" radiate honesty, purity, piety, resourcefulness, resilience, quiet wisdom, willingness to play by the rules, fondness for religion and tradition, and hard work.

Second, national populists attack their enemies from a moralistic high ground rather than facing them on a political level playing field. Reluctant to associate with traditional political parties, they spark short-lived movements or parties against moral corruption and the alleged abuse of power. Couched in absolutist terms, the battle is never just about political and cultural differences but over fundamental moral disagreements. Casting themselves as the defenders of the people's collective traditions, national populists blame "them" for the alleged moral decay of the community. Keen to awaken "the common man" from his perilous slumber, they construct emotional charges armored in deep-seated stereotypes and prejudices. As Chip Berlet observes, such techniques include demonizing, scapegoating, and the spinning of conspiracy tales. And yet, in the end, it is always the victim who stands accused of hatching some insidious plot against the people while the scapegoater is valorized as a paragon of virtue for sounding the alarm.[12]

The third rhetorical maneuver routinely performed by national populists involves the evocation of an extreme crisis that requires an immediate and forceful response. Usually directed to segments of the population most threatened by the forces of modernization, such appeals thrive on the alleged discrepancy between the idealized values of the "heartland" and existing political practices.[13] Finally, national populists imagine "the people" as a homogeneous national unit welded together by a common will, a single interest, an ancestral heartland, shared cultural and religious traditions, and a national language. However, the common "we" applies only to those persons deemed to belong to the nation. The presumed identity of "our" people-nation—often conveyed in racial terminology—allows populists to fuel and exploit existing hostilities against those whose very existence threatens their essentialist myth of homogeneity and unity.[14] Let us now examine the workings of the national-populist rhetoric in the writings and speeches of two prominent self-proclaimed American "antiglobalists."

## THE NATIONAL POPULISM OF PAT BUCHANAN
## AND LOU DOBBS

Associated with the nationalist wing of the Republican Party since the early 1960s, Patrick J. Buchanan served as an aide and speechwriter for President Richard Nixon from 1966 to 1974. After Nixon's resignation, he became a successful newspaper columnist and popular TV talk-show host. In the mid-1980s, he briefly interrupted his media career to serve as President Ronald Reagan's director of communications. Buchanan has been credited with scripting Reagan's controversial remarks that German SS soldiers buried in Bitburg Veterans' Cemetery in Germany were victims, "just as surely as the victims in the concentration camps." In 1992, Buchanan mounted an impressive challenge to President George H. W. Bush for the presidential nomination of the Republican Party. Four years later, he defeated Senator Robert Dole in the important New Hampshire Republican presidential primary. Although Buchanan ultimately lost the primary contest, he received almost a quarter of the national Republican primary vote. By the late 1990s, Buchanan had emerged as the most prominent leader of right-wing populism in the United States.

After serious disagreements with leading Republicans on issues of free trade and immigration, Buchanan left the Republican Party to pursue the presidential nomination of the Reform Party, the brainchild of Texas billionaire H. Ross Perot, who had captured an astonishing 19 percent of the national vote as an independent presidential candidate in 1992. Perot had built the Reform Party on an ideological platform that combined familiar populist themes with strong nationalist-protectionist appeals to protect the economic national interest and reduce the exploding trade deficit. Most famously, he opposed the expansion of the regional free-trade agreement between the United States and Canada. Convinced that the North American Free Trade Agreement (NAFTA) carried the "virus of globalism," he argued that the inclusion of Mexico would lead to a massive flight of manufacturing capital to the South in search of cheap labor. Emerging as one of the principal spokespersons of the anti-NAFTA campaign, Perot forged tactical alliances with organized labor, environmentalists, and import-competing agricultural and industrial interests. His public utterances on the subject often conveyed thinly veiled anti-immigration sentiments.

Although Buchanan eventually won the Reform Party nomination in the summer of 2000, his positions on a variety of social and economic issues proved to be highly controversial with many party delegates. Consequently, a sizable splinter group held a rival conference and nominated a different candidate for president. It took a formal ruling by the Federal Election Commission to confirm Buchanan as the official nominee, allowing him to gain access to the disputed $12.6 million federal subsidy that went with the Reform Party's presidential nomination. Having inherited the remains of the Reform Party, he emerged as one of the chief spokespersons of the national-populist Right in the United States. This remained true even after Buchanan ended his political career as a result of his disappointing showing in the 2000 presidential elections, where he took only 1 percent of the vote. Throughout the 2000s, his best-selling books and popular blogs conveyed his fierce opposition to a "Darwinian world of the borderless economy, where sentiment is folly and the fittest alone survive. In the eyes of this rootless transnational elite, men and women are not family, friends, neighbors, fellow citizens, but 'consumers' and 'factors of production.'" Turning the ideological table on free-trade Republicans who were dismissing his arguments as "antiquated protectionism," Buchanan reminded his former comrades of the Republican Party's traditional perspective on trade policy. "For not only was the party of Lincoln, McKinley, Theodore Roosevelt, Taft, and Coolidge born and bred in protectionism, it was defiantly and proudly protectionist." For Buchanan, "Protectionism is the structuring of trade policy to protect the national sovereignty, ensure economic self-reliance and 'prosper America first."[15]

Buchanan refers to his position as "economic nationalism"—the view that the economy should be designed in ways that serve, first and foremost, the nation. Indeed, he defines economic nationalism as tax and trade policies that put America before the global economy and the well-being of our own people before what is best for humankind. "Our trade and tax policies should be designed to strengthen U.S. sovereignty and independence and should manifest a bias toward domestic, rather than foreign, commerce."[16] Indeed, Buchanan claims that his economic nationalism reflected the "noble ideas" that "Washington, Hamilton, and Madison had taken to Philadelphia and written into the American Constitution, and that Henry Clay had refined to create 'The American System' that was the marvel of mankind."[17] When the Democrats regained their congressional majority after their memorable trouncing of the Republicans during the 2006 midterm elections, Buchanan, a fierce critic of George W. Bush's "globalism," celebrated the demise of the "free-trade Republican-controlled Congress" as the beginning of a "new era of economic nationalism." A year later, he approvingly noted that both Hillary Clinton and Barack Obama were promising to revise NAFTA along more protectionist lines: "The trade issue is back, big-time. For to blue-collar workers in industrial states like Ohio, NAFTA is a code word for betrayal—a sellout of them and their families to CEOs [chief executive officers] panting to move production out of the United States to cheap-labor countries like Mexico and China."[18]

Buchanan's writings and speeches of the past decade convey his Manichaean conviction that there exists at the core of contemporary American society an "irrepressible conflict between the claims of a New American nationalism and the commands of the Global Economy." Assuring his audience that he considers himself a strong proponent of a free-market system operating within a national context, he insists that global markets must be harnessed in order to work for the good of the American people. This means that the leaders of the United States have to be prepared to make economic decisions for the benefit of the nation, not in the interests of "shameless cosmopolitan transnational elites" who are sacrificing "the interests of their own country on the altar of that golden calf, the Global Economy."[19]

For Buchanan, American economic nationalism is anchored in the resolute rejection of the European ideology of free trade—an "alien import, an invention of European academics and scribblers, not one of them ever built a great nation, and all of whom were repudiated by America's greatest statesmen, including all four presidents on Mt. Rushmore."[20] Surprisingly, the American national populist does not seem to be bothered by the fact that the central intellectual features of economic nationalism were also designed by Europeans—most importantly, by the early-nineteenth-century German thinkers J. G. Fichte and Friedrich List. He argues that the greatness of modern nations such as the United States has always been built on a staunchly nationalist economic philosophy that favors low taxes and prescribes high tariffs on imports in order to protect domestic manufacturers. After all, he asserts, the United States experienced its greatest economic successes when anti–free trade sentiments prevailed in the Protectionist Era of 1865 to 1913 and during the 1920s. Chiding his former party, he wonders "How long before the GOP wakes up to the reality that globalism is not conservatism, never was, but is the pillar of Wilsonian liberalism, in whose vineyards our faux conservatives now daily labor."[21]

Mirroring the strategy of his market-globalist opponents, Buchanan relies on an endless stream of "hard data" to make his protectionist case to the public. Giving the first chapter of his recent best-selling book the suggestive title "How Nations Perish," the author hurls an endless stream of data at his readers as evidence against the globalist claim that globalization benefits everyone.[22] Arguing that globalization benefits only the wealthy transnational elites, he notes that since its onset in the late 1970s, real wages of working Americans have fallen by as much as 20 percent. By the mid-1990s, top CEO salaries skyrocketed to 212 times over an average worker's pay, and corporate profits more than doubled between 1992 and 1997. In 2007, the U.S. trade deficit with Mexico and China soared to a record $73 billion and $256 billion, respectively. Under the "globalist presidency" of George W. Bush, he continues, 3 million American manufacturing jobs were lost, inflation shot up, foreclosures mounted, credit card debt exploded, oil surged to nearly $150 a barrel, and the dollar fell by 50 percent against the euro. As Buchanan puts it, "The chickens of globalism are coming home to roost." Bemoaning the loss of economic independence and national sovereignty as a result of free-trade policies, he ends his litany with a predictable nationalist-populist punch:

> America rose to power behind a republican tariff wall. What has free trade wrought? Lost sovereignty. A hollowing out of U.S. manufacturing. Stagnant wages. Wives forced into the labor market to maintain the family income. Mass indebtedness to foreign nations, and a deepening dependency on foreign goods and borrowings to pay for them. We have sacrificed our country on the altar of this Moloch, the mythical Global Economy.[23]

Buchanan's populist focus on the "treacherous" activities of the neoliberal "Washington Establishment" serves as the foundation for his rejection of the market-globalist claim that nobody is in charge of globalization. He points his finger at "greedy global mandarins who have severed the sacred ties of national allegiance" to be found among the members of the U.S. Council on Foreign Relations and the Business Roundtable. Their elitist conspiracy, he insists, has eroded the power of the nation-state and replaced it with a neoliberal new world order. As a result, most mainstream American politicians are beholden to transnational corporate interests that are undermining the sovereignty of the nation by supporting the WTO and other international institutions. He accuses the Washington Establishment of channeling billions of dollars to the International Monetary Fund (IMF) and the World Bank for the purpose of bailing out undeserving developing countries in Africa, Latin America, and Asia. Evoking the wrath of "the little man"—in this case the "American taxpayer" who is saddled with the costs of these bailouts—Buchanan demands severe punishment for the market globalists at the helm of the American government and international economic institutions like the IMF, WTO, and World Bank. Remarkably, the American national populist even considers the global warming crisis an invention of scheming elites: "This, it seems to me, is what the global-warming scare and scam are all about—frightening Americans into transferring sovereignty, power and wealth to a global political elite that claims it alone understands the crisis and it alone can save us from impending disaster."[24]

Finally, in the familiar nationalist-populist move of scapegoating outsiders, Buchanan accuses the nation's "liberal advocates of multiculturalism" of tolerating and even encouraging the influx of "12 to 20 million illegal immigrants roosting here." His fundamentally inegalitarian and nativist message is especially obvious in his derogatory language toward irregular migrants from the global South. Making them responsible for the economic and moral decline of the United States, he evokes the specter of the cultural dissolution of the United States: "With the 45 million Hispanics here to rise to 102 million by 2050, the Southwest is likely to look and sound more like Mexico than America. Indeed, culturally, linguistically and ethnically, it will be part of Mexico."[25] In fact, during the acrimonious public debate over the 2006–2007 immigration reforms in the United States, Buchanan accused Latinos of Mexican extraction of promoting the cultural and political *reconquista* of the U.S. Southwest. He insisted that most of "them" lacked a passionate attachment to the core of America—its land, people, its past, its heroes, literature, language, traditions, culture, and customs.[26] Hence, it is not surprising that the American national populist declares himself in favor of drastic anti-immigration policies designed to "strengthen the Border Control, lengthen the 'Buchanan Fence' on the southern frontier, repatriate illegals, and repair the great American melting pot. The twenty-seven million who have come into our nation since the 1970s shall be assimilated and Americanized, introduced fully into our history, culture, the English language, and American traditions."[27]

As we noted previously, such a retroactive construction of a homogeneous "heartland" based on an idealized picture of the past represents a common theme in nationalist-populist narratives. Moreover, their implied moralism lends itself to the easy incorporation of religious and mystical themes that resonate particularly well with conservative or anti-intellectual audiences. Still, as Buchanan's writings show, the evocation of faith and tradition does not necessarily result in an endorsement of the religious establishment. As we shall see in our ensuing ideological analysis of jihadist globalism, religiously inspired populist rhetoric often favors militant sectarianism. Apocalyptic narratives and millennial visions, generally downplayed in mainstream religions, loom large in such discourses. In Buchanan's antiglobalization rhetoric, such visions are often expressed in terms of the demographic "catastrophe" resulting from "the baby boom among these black and brown peoples" that is changing the face of the West forever: "More arresting is that the white population is shrinking not only in relative but also in real terms. Two hundred million white people, one in every six on earth—a number equal to the entire population of France, Britain, and Germany—will vanish by 2060. The Caucasian race is going the way of the Mohicans." Thus Buchanan's succinct conclusion: "If demography is destiny, the West is finished."[28]

Another of these apocalyptic narratives in the United States can be linked to assocations such as the John Birch Society, the Christian Coalition, the Liberty Lobby, and so-called patriot and militia movements; all these groups are convinced that globalization lies at the root of an incipient anti-American new world order. Regarding neoliberal internationalism as an alien and godless ideology engulfing the United States, they fear that globalism is relentlessly eroding individual liberties and the "traditional American way of life." For example, Pat Robertson, the undisputed leader of the million-member Christian Coalition, published in the early 1990s a best-selling book that described globalization as part of a diabolical conspiracy among transnational corporate elites to create "a new order for the human race under the domination of Lucifer and his followers."[29]

In recent years, Buchanan has been joined on the American national-populist stage by Lou Dobbs, the charismatic host of CNN's prestigious news show *Lou Dobbs Tonight*, watched by millions every weeknight. He also served as the anchor of *Moneyline*, a wildly successful business-news program that aired worldwide on CNN in the early 2000s. In addition, Dobbs anchors a nationally syndicated financial news radio report, *The Lou Dobbs Financial Report*, and is a columnist for *Money* magazine, the *New York Daily News*, and *U.S. News and World Report*. In the past decade, he has won nearly every major award for television journalism, including the Luminary Award of the *Business Journalism Review*. Over the past few years, Dobbs has emerged as a pivotal national-populist figure in the increasingly fractious debate over the future immigration policy in the United States. Politicians from both American major political parties have openly acknowledged the power of his national-populist views: "He definitely influenced politicians who were watching him and listening to him," New York Republican Congressman Peter King conceded, "and I think he had an impact."[30]

Dobbs has devoted large portions of *Lou Dobbs Tonight* to investigative series with such suggestive titles as "Exporting America," "Broken Borders," and "A Crowded Nation." As a result of these reports, the audience for his show has grown by 73 percent between 2003 and 2007, and his two most recent books have become best sellers. Impressed by his growing stature, CBS television hired him as a commentator on its popular *Early Morning Show*.[31] The persistent message of these reports is that ordinary Americans are being hurt by two related phenomena: the market-globalist strategy of outsourcing jobs and the massive influx of foreign high-tech workers and undocumented laborers. On his official website, Dobbs maintains a blacklist of more than two hundred companies that are "exporting America." He charges these firms with "either sending American jobs overseas, or choosing to employ cheap labor overseas, instead of American workers." However, Dobbs fails to tell his viewers that, in his *Lou Dobbs Money Letter*, he has urged subscribers to invest in some of the same companies that appear on his list of unpatriotic market globalist corporations.[32]

Framing the debate in apocalyptic terms as a "battle for the American soul," Dobbs directs his economic nationalism to ordinary Americans in easily digestible slogans, such as "As politicians talk, jobs walk."[33] In his view, corporate, political, and intellectual elites eager to spread the gospel of market globalism have been waging a relentless "war on the American middle class." His uncanny ability to adjust his national-populist message to the hyperpatriotic post-9/11 landscape was on dramatic display during a controversial 2002 episode of *Moneyline* when he demanded on air that the Bush administration change the phrase "War against Terror" to "War against Islamists and all who support them."[34]

An even more egregious incident occurred in 2005 when Dobbs's show ran a report alleging that 7,000 new cases of leprosy had been reported in the past three years and that most of these cases could be linked to illegal immigrants. An investigative report undertaken by a *New York Times* journalist revealed that Dobbs seems to have deliberately shortened the number of years from thirty to three. In fact, the director of the National Hansen's Disease Program pointed out that the reported cases have been dropping steadily in the last decade, averaging scarcely 100 per year. But even when Dobbs was confronted with the outcome of this investigation on CBS's *60 Minutes*, he not only failed to apologize but insisted that his original report had been factually correct. Hence, it is not surprising that the prominent civil rights group Southern Poverty Law Center has long been critical of Dobbs, accusing him of giving airtime to white supremacy sympathizers and misrepresenting the facts in order to stigmatize "them"—be it immigrants or "the Establishment." For example, Dobbs recently alleged that one-third of the inmates in the U.S. federal prison system are illegal immigrants. But, according to the U.S. Justice Department, only 6 percent of prisoners are noncitizens, and the crime rate is actually lower among immigrants than among natives.[35]

No doubt, this explosive mixture of nativism and economic nationalism in the United States continues to resonate in a country where 78 percent of the population have not traveled to another country in the past five years, where only 26 percent follow foreign news closely, and where 45 percent believe that international events do not affect them—even after September 11.[36] Dobbs and Buchanan target especially parochial, conservative elements in both the business community and organized labor—the "old" constituencies of the Republican and Democratic parties. As far as business is concerned, they call for the replacement of the market-globalist outlook with the old corporate mind-set that was decidedly nationalist protectionist. In other words, U.S.-based corporations ought to be pressured to show their patriotic loyalty by "putting America first." However, Buchanan and Dobbs always make sure to couple their idealistic appeals to patriotic loyalty with the more tangible assurance that old-style protectionism will produce profits for business and workers alike.

With regard to labor issues, both Dobbs and Buchanan embrace major parts of the antiglobalization agenda espoused by such union leaders as John Sweeney, president of the AFL-CIO, and James Hoffa, head of the

Teamsters. Echoing the same concerns of the old industrial working class, Buchanan's and Dobbs's slogans are tailored to fit the backward-looking mood of small-town America. Their arguments for greater social equality in their country rest on their implicit willingness to tolerate high levels of international inequality. These inegalitarian tendencies are reflected in speeches that contain racist code words and anti-Semitic allusions. For example, Buchanan told a crowd of American steelworkers that "Asian invaders" were dumping devalued steel on American markets in a concerted effort to destroy the U.S. steel industry. In permitting these "illegal practices" to continue, the Washington Establishment had turned a blind eye to the "wholesale sacrifice of the United Steelworkers of America" in order "to make the world safe for Goldman Sachs." During the April 2000 anti-IMF protests in Washington, D.C., Buchanan told cheering members of the Teamsters union that, as president, he would tell the Chinese to either shape up or "you guys have sold your last pair of chopsticks in any mall in the United States." He also assured the appreciative crowd that he would appoint their boss, James Hoffa, as America's top trade negotiator. In spite of his prolabor rhetoric, however, Buchanan has a long record of refusing to endorse such basic workers' demands as raising the minimum wage. Much in the same vein, Dobbs suggested that the 2006–2007 immigration reforms in the United States were part of a supposed "Mexican plot" to reclaim the American Southwest. One of the correspondents on *Lou Dobbs Tonight* even referred to an official visit of the Mexican president to Utah as a "Mexican military incursion." By mixing opinions and facts into such a potent national-populist concoction, Dobbs and Buchanan carry on a nativist tradition in the United States that has long used stereotyping and scapegoating as a weapon against undesirable "outsiders."[37]

A number of writers have suggested that the global surge of national populism can be explained as an extreme reaction against both the structural and the institutional development of contemporary capitalism. With the onset of globalization in the 1970s, mid-twentieth-century American industrial-welfare capitalism was rapidly transformed into the postindustrial individualized capitalism of the early twenty-first century. A similar transformation also occurred on the cultural level with the spread of multiculturalism and the rise of a postmodern culture whose central features include the collapse of high culture to mass culture, increased advertising and commercialization, and the individualization of choice and lifestyle.[38] According to this interpretation, then, the antiglobalization voices of the national-populist camp represent an antiquated authoritarian response to the economic hardships and dislocations brought about by globalization.

Experiencing considerable anxiety over the dissolution of secure bound-aries and familiar borders, groups such as industrial workers and small farmers are losing their former privileged status in traditional social hierar-chies. As people's old identities are subjected to a growing sense of frag-mentation and alienation, one possible response to the new challenges of our shrinking world lies in assigning blame to internal and external Others for the desecration of the familiar.

In their appeal to "globalization losers," Buchanan, Dobbs, and other successful national populists are calling for a halt to the mighty dynamic of globalization. Capitalizing on these people's sense of powerlessness in the face of massive structural change, they give voice to the authoritarian longing for a bygone world of cultural uniformity, moral certainty, and na-tional superiority. Mark Worrell notes that although national-populist leaders wear an egalitarian label and valorize the power of grassroots democracy, they actually contribute to the decline of participatory democ-racy: "Buchananism does not promise collective and democratic participa-tion, but redemption by the hero."[39]

Championing the simplistic idea of social change through the deeds of great men, Buchanan and Dobbs attack market globalism as the doctrine of hedonistic economic determinists who lack not only the motive but also the will and the courage to resist the forces of globalization. Promising to lead America's struggle against neoliberal internationalism, Buchanan told the Daughters of the American Revolution, "It is time Americans took their country back. Before we lose her forever, let us take America back from the global parasites of the World Bank and the IMF who siphon off America's wealth for Third World socialists and incompetents. And, let us take her back from the agents of influence who occupy this city [Washington, D.C.] and do the bidding of foreign powers."[40]

Indeed, the national-populist critique of market globalism is both "re-actionary" and "conservative" in that it seeks to retain the familiar national framework at any cost. Stuck in the old paradigm, its proponents fail to provide their audiences with an alternative globalist vision. Still, their pro-jection of community as the traditional nation should not lead us to con-clude that all styles of populism have to remain inevitably nationalist. While all forms of populism remain inescapably tied to some conceptual-ization of "the people," there is no compelling reason why the concept should *always* and *necessarily* refer to a *national* community. As we noted in the previous chapter, the more encompassing imagining of "the people" offered by justice globalists clearly transcends the national framework. The same is true for jihadist globalists like Osama bin Laden who incorporate into their militant version of political Islam a populist style of rhetoric that decontests "the people" as the umma of *tawhid*—the *global* Islamic community of believers in the oneness of the one and only God. Unlike national populism, however, this religiously inspired style of populist rhetoric has been merged with political Islam to create a comprehensive ideology capable of translating the rising global imaginary into concrete political terms and programs. Today, jihadist globalism represents market globalism's most formidable ideological challenger from the political Right.

## AL QAEDA'S JIHADIST GLOBALISM

After the al Qaeda attacks of 9/11, scores of commentators around the world pointed to radical Islamism as one of the most potent ideological challengers to market globalism. Nevertheless, except for al Qaeda's worldwide network, most of these voices saw nothing "global" in bin Laden's worldview. Rather, they castigated his brand of Islamism as "backward" and "parochial," typical of a religious fanatic who represented one of the reactionary forces undermining globalization. As we will argue here, however, al Qaeda's potent political belief system powered by religious symbols and metaphors not only represents the second and more powerful camp of market globalism's challengers from the political Right but also reflects the complex dynamics of globalization. For this reason, this ideology can best be described as "jihadist globalism." The famous post-9/11 "bin Laden videotapes" broadcast worldwide between 2001 and 2008 testifies to al Qaeda's immediate access to sophisticated information and telecommunication networks that kept the leadership informed, in real time, of relevant international developments. Bin Laden and his top lieutenants may have denounced the forces of modernity with great conviction, but the smooth operation of his entire organization was entirely dependent on advanced forms of technology developed in the last two decades of the twentieth century.

To further illustrate the global dynamics reflected in al Qaeda's jihadism, consider bin Laden's personal appearance. The October 7, 2001, videotape shows him wearing contemporary military fatigues over traditional Arab garments. In other words, his dress reflects contemporary processes of fragmentation and cross-fertilization that globalization scholars call "hybridization"—the mixing of different cultural forms and styles facilitated by global economic and cultural exchanges. In fact, the pale colors of bin Laden's mottled combat dress betrayed its Russian origins, suggesting that he wore the jacket as a symbolic reminder of the fierce guerrilla war waged by him and other Islamic militants against the Soviet occupation forces in Afghanistan during the 1980s.

His ever-present AK-47 Kalashnikov, too, was probably made in Russia, although dozens of gun factories around the world have been building this popular assault rifle for over forty years. By the mid-1990s, more than 70 million Kalashnikovs had been manufactured in Russia and abroad. At least fifty national armies include such rifles in their arsenals, making Kalashnikovs truly weapons of global choice. Thus, bin Laden's AK-47 could have come from anywhere in the world. However, given the astonishing globalization of organized crime during the past two decades, it is quite conceivable that bin Laden's rifle was part of an illegal arms deal hatched and executed by such powerful international criminal organizations as al Qaeda and the Russian Mafia. It is also possible that the rifle arrived in Afghanistan by means of an underground arms trade similar to the one that surfaced in May 1996, when police in San Francisco seized 2,000 illegally imported AK-47s manufactured in China.

A close look at bin Laden's right wrist reveals yet another clue to the powerful dynamics of globalization. As he directs his words of contempt for the United States and its allies at his handheld microphone, his retreating sleeve exposes a stylish sports watch. Journalists who noticed this expensive accessory have speculated about the origins of the timepiece in question. The emerging consensus points to a Timex product. However, given that Timex watches are as American as apple pie, it seems rather ironic that the al Qaeda leader should have chosen this particular brand. After all, Timex Corporation, originally the Waterbury Clock Company, was founded in the 1850s in Connecticut's Naugatuck Valley, known throughout the nineteenth century as the "Switzerland of America." Today, the company has gone multinational, maintaining close relations to affiliated businesses and sales offices in sixty-five countries. The corporation employs 7,500 employees located on four continents. Thousands of workers—mostly from low-wage countries in the global South—constitute the driving force behind Timex's global production process.[41]

Our brief deconstruction of some of the central images on the videotape makes it easier to detect the global within the apparently anachronistic expressions of a supposedly "antiglobalist" terrorist. In his subsequent taped appearances, bin Laden presented himself more as a learned Muslim cleric than a holy warrior. In a September 2007 tape, he even went so far as to show off his neatly trimmed and dyed beard. But even this softened image of one of the world's most famous mujahideen ("holy warriors") does not change the overarching reality of intensifying global interdependence. Just as bin Laden's romantic ideology of a "pure Islam" is itself an articulation of the global imaginary, so has our global age, with its insatiable appetite for technology, mass-market commodities, and celebrities, indelibly shaped the ideological structure of jihadist globalism. But let us start our investigation with an exploration of the political context.

The origins of al Qaeda can be traced back to the *Maktab al-Khidamat* (MAK; "Office of Services"), a Pakistan-based support organization for Arab mujahideen fighting invading Soviet troops in Afghanistan. Set up in 1980 by bin Laden and his Palestinian teacher and mentor Abdullah Azzam, MAK received sizable contributions from the government of Saudi Arabia as well as private donors from other Islamic countries. It also enjoyed the protection of Pakistan's Inter-Service Intelligence Agency intent on replacing, with support from the Central Intelligence Agency, the communist puppet regime in Kabul with an Islamist government friendly to Pakistan. Thus, al Qaeda and other radical Islamist groups operating at the time in this region should be seen as creatures of the Cold War which eventually outlived the purpose assigned to them by their benefactors. Left without much support after the withdrawal of the Soviet troops in 1989, the multinational coalition of Arab-Afghani fighters found itself put out of business by its own success. Stranded in a country devastated by decades of continual warfare, the victorious mujahideen lacked a clear sense of purpose or mission.

As can be gleaned from the burgeoning literature on the subject, the term "Islamism" has been used in many different ways by both Muslim and non-Muslim scholars to refer to various "movements" and "ideologies" dedicated to the revival of Islam and its full political realization. Related terms currently in circulation include "political Islam," "Islamic fundamentalism," "Islamist purism," and "Islamo-fascism."[42] Our focus on al Qaeda's jihadist globalism is meant neither to downplay the diversity of ideational currents within Islamism nor to present a single brand as its most representative or authentic manifestation. Rather, our interest in bin Laden's doctrine attests to the tremendous political and ideological influence of jihadist globalism around the world. Second, it highlights the rise of new political ideologies resulting from the ongoing deterritorialization of Islam. Third, it recognizes the religious Right's most successful ideological attempt yet to articulate the rising global imaginary around the core religious concepts of umma (Muslim community), jihad (armed or unarmed "struggle" against unbelief purely for the sake of God and his umma), and *tawhid* (the absolute unity of God). Indeed, the label "jihadist globalism" applies also to those Christian fundamentalist ideologies that seek to establish a global Christian community by means of a violent "struggle" against the forces of secularism and "false belief."

Osama bin Laden was born in 1957 the seventeenth son of Muhammed bin Laden, a migrant laborer from Yemen who created a multibillion-dollar construction empire in his adopted Saudi Arabia. Bin Laden's early experiments with libertarian Western lifestyles ended abruptly when he encountered political Islam in classes taught by Abdallah Azzam and Muhammad Qutb at King Abd al-Aziz University in Jiddah. After earning a graduate degree in business administration, the ambitious young man proved his managerial talent during a short stint in his father's corporation. But his professional successes were soon trumped by his fervent religious vocation, expressed in his support of the Arab mujahideen in their struggle against the Soviet-backed Afghan regime. Acquiring extensive skill in setting up guerrilla training camps and planning military operations, bin Laden saw battle on several occasions and quickly acquired a stellar reputation for his martial valor. Euphoric at the Soviet withdrawal from Afghanistan but bitterly disappointed by the waning support of the United States and Arab countries, bin Laden returned to Riyadh in 1990 as a popular hero, his close ties to the Saudi regime still intact.

At the time, Saddam Hussein's occupation of Kuwait was threatening the balance of power in the Middle East. To counter the threat, the House of Saud invited half a million "infidels"—American and other foreign troops—into their country, ostensibly for a short period of time and solely for protective purposes. To ensure religious legitimacy for its decision, the government then pressured the Saudi *ulema* (learned interpreters of the sacred texts) to approve of the open-ended presence of foreign troops in the Land of the Holy Two Sanctuaries (Mecca and Medina). The scholars complied, ultimately even granting permission for Muslims to join the U.S.-led "Operation Desert Storm" against Iraq in 1991.

Stung by the royal family's rejection of his proposal to organize thousands of Arab-Afghan veterans and outraged by their enlistment of foreign infidels in defense of the kingdom against a possible Iraqi attack, bin Laden severed all ties with the Saudi regime. Like tens of thousands of angry religious dissenters, bin Laden, too, denounced these acts of "religious heresy" and "moral corruption" and openly accused the rulers of selling out to the West. The Saudi government immediately responded to these accusations with political repression, arresting several opposition leaders and shutting down their organizations. Bin Laden and his closest associates fled to Sudan, where the sympathetic Islamist government of Hassan al-Turabi offered them political exile and the opportunity to create dozens of new training camps for militants. Stripped of his Saudi citizenship in 1994, bin Laden forged a lasting alliance with Ayman al-Zawahiri, the charismatic leader of the radical Egyptian group Islamic Jihad. This partnership would eventually lead to the formation of the World Islamic Front, with main branches in Pakistan and Bangladesh and an unknown number of affiliated cells around the world.

Forced to leave Sudan in 1996 as a result of mounting U.S. pressure on the Turabi regime, bin Laden and his entourage returned to Afghanistan, where they entered into an uneasy relationship with the Taliban, whose forces, led by Mullah Omar, managed to capture Kabul in the same year. Imposing a strict version of shari'a (God-given, Islamic law) on the Afghan population, the Taliban based its rule on the "true tenets of Islam" alleged to have been realized in the world only once before by the seventh-century *salaf* (pious predecessors) who led the umma for three generations following the death of the Prophet. By the end of the 1990s, bin Laden had openly pledged his allegiance to the Taliban, most likely in exchange for the regime's willingness to shelter his organization from U.S. retaliation following the devastating 1998 al Qaeda bombings of the American embassies in Kenya and Tanzania. To show his gratitude to his hosts, bin Laden referred to the Taliban leader Mullah Omar as the "Commander of the Faithful"—one of the honorific titles of the caliph, the Islamic ruler of both the religious and the civil spheres. Since this designation was deprived of its last bearer in 1924 when the modernist Turkish leader Kemal Ataturk replaced the Ottoman caliphate with a secular nation-state, bin Laden's fondness for it signifies nothing less than his rejection of eight decades of Islamic modernism—in both its nationalist and its socialist garbs—as well as his affirmation of Taliban-ruled Afghanistan as the nucleus of a global caliphate destined to halt the long decline of the Islamic world and the corresponding ascendancy of the West. His anti-Western convictions notwithstanding, bin Laden never hesitated to use modern technology to communicate his message.

As Bruce Lawrence notes, the bulk of bin Laden's writings and public addresses emerged in the context of a "virtual world" moving from print to the Internet and from wired to wireless communication. Largely scriptural in mode, the sheikh's "messages to the world" are deliberately designed for the new global media. As we have seen, they appear on video and audio tapes, websites, and handwritten letters scanned onto computer disks and delivered to Arabic-language news outlets of global reach. Bin Laden conveys his ideological claims in carefully crafted language that draws on the five traditional types of Muslim public discourse: the declaration, the juridical degree, the lecture, the written reminder, and the epistle. Disdainful of ghostwritten tracts of the kind supplied by professional speechwriters to many politicians, he produces eloquent pieces of Arabic prose that speak in the "authentic, compelling voice of a visionary, with what can only be called a powerful lyricism."[43] Bin Laden's writings over the past fifteen years amount to a coherent doctrine appealing to millions of Muslims. His post-9/11 messages, in particular, contain specific instructions to the faithful on how to resist the advances of the American Empire, the "New Rome."

The ideological edifice of jihadist globalism rests on the populist evocation of an exceptional crisis: the umma has been subjected to an unprecedented wave of attacks on its territories, values, and economic resources. Although he blames the global "Judeo-Crusader alliance," bin Laden considers its assault on Islam to be the expression of an evil much larger than that represented by particular nation-states or imperialist alliances.[44] At the same time, however, he and his lieutenants insist that the forces of "global unbelief" are led by specific individuals like President George W. Bush or by concrete "hegemonic organizations of universal infidelity" such as the United States and the United Nations.[45] In their view, the collapse of the Soviet Empire—attributed directly to the efforts of the Arab-Afghan mujahideen—has made America even more haughty and imperialistic:

> [I]t has started to see itself as the Master of this world and established what it calls the new world order. . . . The U.S. today, as a result of this arrogance, has set a double standard, calling whoever goes against its injustice a terrorist. It wants to occupy our countries, steal our resources, install collaborators to rule us with man-made laws, and wants us to agree on all these issues. If we refuse to do so, it will say we are terrorists.[46]

Bin Laden cites as evidence for such "Satanic acts of aggression" the open-ended presence of American troops on the Arabian peninsula, the ongoing Israeli oppression of the Palestinian people, the 1993 American operations against Muslim warlords in Somalia, the Western indifference to the slaughter of thousands of Bosnian Muslims during the 1991–1995 Yugoslav civil war, and the economic sanctions imposed by the West on Iraq after the first Gulf War that contributed to the death of countless innocent civilians. Indebted to the discursive legacy of Third World liberationism, the sheikh considers these immoral and imperialist acts inflicted by Western powers on the umma but the latest crimes in a series of humiliations that can be traced back to the Great Powers' division of the Ottoman Empire after World War I and the post–World War II establishment of the Jewish state in Palestine. But what makes today's "attacking enemies and corrupters of religion and the world" even more dangerous than the medieval Christian crusaders or the thirteenth-century Mongol conquerors of the mighty Abbasid Empire is their all-out "campaign against the Muslim world in its entirety, aiming to get rid of Islam itself."[47] Rather than supporting the umma at this critical point in history when the Judeo-Crusader alliance has "violated her honor, shed her blood, and occupied her sanctuaries," Saudi Arabia and other Islamic countries have colluded with the infidel enemy. Abandoning the umma in her hour of need, these "apostate rulers" have desecrated the true religion of God's messenger and thereby lost their political legitimacy. Likewise, Islamic scholars and clerics who lent their learned voices to the defense of these "defeatist Arab tyrannies" deserve to be treated as "cowardly heretics" and "traitors to the faith."

In true populist fashion, bin Laden directs his first public letter intended for a wider audience against the appointed head of Saudi Arabia's collaborationist ulema. In addition to accusing the mufti of spiritual corruption, he also objects to his alleged willingness to turn a blind eye to the moral decay of modern Islamic societies, most visibly reflected in their toleration of practices of usury expressly prohibited in the Qur'an. The letter also laments the ulema's unwillingness to resort to more drastic measures to prevent the further intrusion of Western values at the expense of Muslim principles. In several poignant passages, bin Laden identifies as the worst feature of the present age of *jahiliyya* (ignorance; pagan idolatry) "the degree of degradation and corruption to which our Islamic *umma* has sunk."[48]

But what, precisely, does bin Laden mean by "umma"? After all, this core concept, together with *jihad* and *tawhid*, serves as the ideational anchor of his political belief system. In the sheikh's major writings, one finds ample textual evidence for his populist understanding of umma.[49] As Mohammed Bamyeh notes, the concept of the "Islamic community" has functioned historically as an equivalent of the Western idea of "the people," empowered to set limits to the tyrannical tendencies of governing elites.[50] Drawing on this traditional understanding of the umma, bin Laden emphasizes that political authority can never rest on "popular sovereignty," for political rule is not the exclusive property of the people. Rather, the righteous umma exercises political power in the name of God only, thus building its political institutions on the foundation of Islamic sovereignty.[51] Since God's authority transcends all political borders and any humanly designed lines of demarcation, the umma supersedes not only ancient tribal solidarities and traditional kinship structures but, most importantly, modern Western conceptions of community rooted in the national imaginary.

To be sure, contemporary Muslims carry national passports, but their primary solidarity must lie with the umma, a community that encompasses the entire globe: "You know, we are linked to all of the Islamic world, whether that be Yemen, Pakistan, or wherever. We are part of one unified *umma*."[52]

This central idea of "the people of the Qur'an" having been commanded by God to safeguard His sovereignty and to resist the sinful influences of despots, heretics, and infidels usurping God's ultimate sovereignty received its most radical modern interpretation in the writings of the Egyptian political Islamist Sayyid Qutb, the older brother of bin Laden's influential teacher at al-Aziz University. Taking as his point of departure the Islamic doctrine of *tawhid*, Qutb argued that all worldly power belongs to the one and only Lord of the Worlds whose single, unchanging will is revealed in the Qur'an. Unconditional submission to His will entails the responsibility of every member of the umma to prevent the domination of humans over humans, which violates the absolute authority of Allah. According to Qutb, the highest purpose of human existence is "to establish the Sovereignty and Authority of God on earth, to establish the true system revealed by God for addressing the human life; to exterminate all the Satanic forces and their ways of life, to abolish the lordship of man over other human beings."[53]

Having failed to repel the corrupting influences of Islam's internal and external enemies, today's umma has fallen into the equivalent of the pre-Islamic pagan age of *jahiliyya* characterized by rampant materialism and the rebellion of unbelief against the sovereignty of God on earth. Qutb even suggests that with the disappearance of proper political governance according to shari'a, the umma itself had ceased to exist in its "true" form. If only ordinary Muslims somehow could be shown the seriousness of their predicament, they might renew their faith and cleanse Islamic culture of its debasing accretions. The final goal of such an Islamic revival would be the restoration of the umma to its original moral purity under a new *salaf* (righteous leadership). As Mary Habeck notes, Qutb's seemingly premodern inclinations actually contain strong modernist influences that turn political Islam into "a sort of liberation ideology, designed to end oppression by human institutions and man-made laws and to return God to his rightful place as unconditional ruler of the world."[54]

Qutb's version of political Islam greatly influenced al Qaeda's understanding of the umma as a single global community of believers united in their belief in the one and only God. As bin Laden emphasizes, "We are the children of an Islamic Nation, with the Prophet Muhammad as its leader; our Lord is one, our prophet is one, our direction of prayer is one, we are one *umma*, and our Book is one."[55] Expressing a populist yearning for strong leaders who set things right by fighting corrupt elites and returning power back to the "Muslim masses," al-Zawahiri shares his leader's vision of how to restore the umma to its earlier glory.[56] In their view, the process of regeneration must start with a small but dedicated vanguard willing to sacrifice their lives as martyrs to the holy cause of awakening the people to their religious duties—not just in traditionally Islamic countries but also wherever members of the umma yearn for the establishment of God's rule on earth. With a third of the world's Muslims living today as minorities in non-Islamic societies, bin Laden regards the restoration of the umma as no longer a local, national, or even regional event. Rather, it requires a concerted *global* effort spearheaded by a jihadist vanguard operating in various localities around the world. Al Qaeda's desired Islamization of modernity takes place in global space emancipated from the confining territoriality of "Egypt" or the "Middle East" that used to constitute the political framework of religious nationalists fighting modern secular regimes in the twentieth century. As Olivier Roy observes, "The Muslim *umma* (or community) no longer has anything to do with a territorial entity. It has to be thought of in abstract and imaginary terms."[57]

Although al Qaeda embraces the Manichaean dualism of a "clash of civilizations" between its imagined global umma and global *kufr* (unbelief), its globalism transcends clear-cut civilizational fault lines. Its desire for the restoration of a transnational umma attests to the globalization and westernization of the Muslim world just as much as it reflects the Islamization of the West. Constructed in the ideational interregnum between the national and the global, jihadist-globalist claims still retain potent metaphors that resonate with people's national or even tribal solidarities.[58] And yet, al Qaeda's focus is firmly on the global as its leaders successfully redirected militant Islamism's struggle from the traditional "Near Enemy" (secular-nationalist Middle Eastern regimes) to the "Far Enemy" (the globalizing West). This remarkable discursive and strategic shift reflects the destabilization of the national imaginary. By the early 1990s, nationally based Islamist groups were losing steam, partly as a result of their inability to mobilize their respective communities around national concerns and partly because they were subjected to more effective counterstrategies devised by secular-nationalist regimes.

Hence, bin Laden and al-Zawahiri urged their followers to take the war against Islam's enemies global. Al Qaeda's simple ideological imperative— rebuild a unified global umma through global jihad against global *kufr*— resonated with the dynamics of a globalizing world. It held a special appeal for Muslim youths between the ages of fifteen and twenty-five who lived for sustained periods of time in the individualized and deculturated environments of westernized Islam (or an Islamized West).[59] As Roy reminds us, this "second wave" of al Qaeda recruits, responsible for the most spectacular terrorist operations between 9/11 and the London bombings of July 7, 2005, were products of a westernized Islam. Most of them resided in Europe or North America and had few or no links to traditional Middle Eastern political parties. Their affinity for al Qaeda's transnational umma and its rigid religious code divorced from traditional cultural contexts made them prime candidates for recruitment. These young men followed in the footsteps of al Qaeda's first-wavers in Afghanistan who developed their ideological outlook among a multinational band of idealistic mujahideen.[60]

If the restored, purified umma—imagined to exist in a global space that transcended particular national or tribal identities—was the final goal of populist-jihadist globalism, then jihad surely served as its principal means. For our purposes, it is not necessary to engage in long scholastic debates about the many meanings and "correct" applications of jihad. Nor do we need to excavate its long history in the Islamic world. It suffices to note that jihadist globalists like bin Laden and al-Zawahiri endorse both "offensive" and "defensive" versions of jihad.[61] Their decontestation of this core concept draws heavily on interpretations offered by Azzam and Qutb, for whom jihad represents a divinely imposed *fard 'ayn* (individual obligation) on a par with the nonnegotiable duties of prayer and fasting. Likewise, bin Laden celebrates jihad as the "peak" or "pinnacle" of Islam, emphasizing time and again that armed struggle against global *kufr* is "obligatory today on our entire *umma*, for our *umma* will stand in sin until her sons, her money, and her energies provide what it takes to establish a *jihad* that repels the evil of the infidels from harming all the Muslims in Palestine and elsewhere."[62] For al Qaeda, jihad represents the sole path toward the noble goal of returning the umma to "her religion and correct beliefs"—not just because the venerable way of *da'wa* (preaching; admonishing) has failed to reform the treacherous Muslim elites or convert the hostile crusaders but, most importantly, because Islam is "the religion of *jihad* in the way of God so that God's word and religion reign supreme." Moreover, jihadist globalists are not choosy about the means of struggle: anything that might weaken the infidels—especially imperial globalists—suffices. Such tactics include large-scale terrorist attacks, suicide bombings, and the public killing of hostages: "To kill the Americans and their allies—civilians and military—is an individual duty incumbent upon every Muslim in all countries."[63]

For bin Laden, jihad and umma are important manifestations of the revealed truth of *tawhid*, the oneness of God and His creation. As we have seen, it demands that Islamic sovereignty be established on earth in the form of a caliphate without national borders or internal divisions. This totalistic vision of a divinely ordained world system of governance whose timeless legal code covers all aspects of social life has prompted many commentators to condemn "jihadist Islamism" as a particularly aggressive form of "totalitarianism" that poses a serious challenge to cultural pluralism and secular democracy.[64] Responding to this charge, the al Qaeda leadership has turned the tables on its critics. Pointing to the long legacy of Western aggression against the umma, bin Laden tends to portray his organization's attacks as retaliatory measures designed to respond in kind to the oppression and murder of thousands of Muslims by the "Judeo-Crusader Alliance." The leaders of al Qaeda never hesitate to include as legitimate targets of their strikes those Muslims deemed to be "apostates" and "handmaidens" of the infidel enemy. In their view, such actions of treachery have put Muslim "hypocrites" outside of the umma.[65] In the end, jihadist globalists fall back on a Manichaean dualism that divides the world into two antagonistic camps: "One side is the global Crusader alliance with the Zionist Jews, led by America, Britain, and Israel, and the other side is the Islamic world." For bin Laden and al-Zawahiri, reconciliation violates the Islamic imperatives of unconditional loyalty to the umma and absolute enmity to the non-Muslim world: "The Lord Almighty has commanded us to hate the infidels and reject their love. For they hate us and begrudge us our religion, wishing that we abandon it." Consequently, al Qaeda's message to Muslims all over the world is to nurture "this doctrine in their hearts" and release their hatred on Americans, Jews, and Christians: "This [hatred] is a part of our belief and our religion."[66] In an impassioned post-9/11 letter, bin Laden offers a detailed refutation of the notion that Islam should be a religion of "moderation" or "balance." In his view, "[I]t is, in fact, part of our religion to impose our particular beliefs on others. . . . And the West's notions that Islam is a religion of *jihad* and enmity toward the religions of the infidels and the infidels themselves is an accurate and true depiction." He also considers the UN-sponsored call for a "dialogue among civilizations" nothing but an "infidel notion" rooted in the "loathsome principles" of a secular West advocating an "un-Islamic" separation of religion and the state.[67]

His fierce rhetoric notwithstanding, bin Laden never loses sight of the fact that jihadist globalists are fighting a steep uphill battle against the forces of imperial globalism. For example, he discusses in much detail the ability of "American media imperialism" to "seduce the Muslim world" with its consumerist messages. He also makes frequent references to a "continuing and biased campaign" waged against jihadist globalism by the corporate media—"especially Hollywood"—for the purpose of misrepresenting Islam and hiding the "failures of the Western democratic system."[68] The al Qaeda leader leaves little doubt that what he considers to be the "worst civilization witnessed in the history of mankind" must be fought for its "debased materialism" and "immoral culture" as much as for its blatant "imperialism." He repeatedly accuses the United States of trying to "change the region's ideology" through the imposition of Western-style democracy and the "Americanization of our culture."[69] And yet, even against seemingly overwhelming odds, bin Laden and al-Zawahiri express their confidence in the ultimate triumph of jihad over "American Empire." The destruction of New York's "immense materialistic towers by nineteen young men" serves as an especially powerful symbol for the alleged "waning global appeal" of "Western civilization backed by America."[70] 9/11 assumes great significance in al Qaeda's jihad insofar as the successful terror attack offers the faithful clear proof that "this destructive, usurious global economy that America uses, together with its military force, to impose unbelief and humiliation on poor people, can easily collapse. Those blessed strikes in New York and other places forced it [America] to acknowledge the loss of more than a trillion dollars, by the grace of God Almighty."[71] Gloating over the staggering financial toll of the terrorist attacks on the global economy, bin Laden offers a chilling cost–benefit analysis of jihadist strategy:

> [A]l-Qaeda spent $500,000 on the September 11 attacks, while America lost more than $500 billion, at the lowest estimate, in the event and its aftermath. That makes a million American dollars for every al-Qaeda dollar, by the grace of God Almighty. This is in addition to the fact that it lost an enormous number of jobs—and as for the federal deficit, it made record losses, estimated over a trillion dollars. Still more serious for America was the fact that the *mujahideen* forced Bush to resort to an emergency budget in order to continue fighting in Afghanistan and Iraq. This shows the success of our plan to bleed America to the point of bankruptcy, with God's will.[72]

This passage is part of a videotaped address aired around the world only a few days before American voters went to the polls on November 3, 2004. Bin Laden ends his speech with a warning to the American people that their security is their own responsibility, not that of corrupt Democrat or Republican political elites. Thus, the sheikh managed to inject himself into a national electoral contest as the self-appointed leader of the global umma. Articulating the rising global imaginary as a set of political claims, jihadist globalism appeared on the TV screens of a global audience as the world's chief critic of American democracy. As Faisal Devji notes, bin Laden's brand of jihadism projected no national ambitions, for it was as global as the West itself, both being intertwined and even internal to each other: "This is why Bin Laden's calls for the United States to leave the Muslim world do not entail the return to a cold-war geopolitics of détente, but are conceived rather in terms of a global reciprocity on equal terms."[73]

Another videotaped message delivered by the al Qaeda leader in September 2007 unleashed further verbal broadsides against imperial globalism and the "corrupt American political system." He linked the Bush administration's involvement in Iraq to transnational corporate interests that held "the American people" hostage to their all-out scramble for war-related profits. Bin Laden's critique shows a remarkable resemblance to Pat Buchanan's populist tirades against corporate elites. Indeed, the sheikh charges "the capitalist system" with seeking "to turn the entire world into a fiefdom of the major corporations under the label of 'globalization.'"[74] However, unlike Buchanan's and Dobbs's defensive attempts to hold on to the weakening national imaginary, jihadist globalists project an ideological alternative that, despite its chilling content, imagines community in unambiguously global terms. Like justice globalists, they are not "antiglobalization" but "alter-globalization."

Thus, evaluating our rapidly changing ideological landscape, it appears that the stage is, indeed, set for what President Bush calls "the decisive ideological struggle of the twenty-first century." It involves the three major political belief systems of our age: market globalism (currently in its imperial garb), justice globalism, and jihadist globalism. What are the likely trajectories and outcomes of this "battle of ideas" over the meaning and direction of globalization?

# CHAPTER 6

## CONCLUSION: FUTURE PROSPECTS

As we have discussed in this book, the unfolding struggle between market globalism in its imperial garb and its two main ideological challengers constantly employs ideas, claims, slogans, metaphors, and symbols to win over the hearts and minds of a global audience. Will this epic contest lead to more extensive forms of international cooperation and interdependence, or will it stop the powerful momentum of globalization? In addressing this question, this conclusion offers a brief speculation on the future of globalization.

In the first edition of this book (published just a few weeks before 9/11), I introduced what I considered to be the three most likely future trajectories of the ideological confrontation over the direction and meaning of globalization. I called the first future scenario "market globalism with a human face." Having been confronted by their ideological challengers on the political Left with an effective strategy of resistance, market-globalist forces might make some moderate adjustments and pursue a less transparent road to their ultimate objective, the creation of a single global free market. Assuring people of their ability to "manage globalization better," market globalists would rely on their public-relations efforts to sell their milder version of corporate-driven globalization to the public. However, if implemented at all, their proposals would remain very modest, leaving the existing global economic architecture largely intact. Thus, without the implementation of serious reforms on a global level, national and international disparities in wealth and well-being would continue to widen even if top earners around the world continued to benefit from neoliberal measures.

In the past few years, this "moderate reformist scenario" has materialized to some extent. As we noted in previous chapters, former architects of market globalism like Joseph Stiglitz, Jeffrey Sachs, and George Soros admitted to the validity of "some concerns" raised by justice globalists. Conceding that globalization had been "mismanaged" in the 1990s, they nonetheless insisted that their original idea of liberalizing and globally integrating markets was still valid. Drawing together select experts from around the world, their mission was to explore neoliberal policy alternatives for developing and transition countries and to improve official decision making on economic issues. Criticizing the International-Monetary Fund (IMF) for its hypocrisy and dogmatic adherence to market globalism, these reformists endorsed the idea of changing the international economic institutions but rejected the "radical view" expressed by some justice globalists that the IMF and World Trade Organization ought to be abolished and replaced by more egalitarian organizations. The problem with such mild reformism is that it focuses only on certain institutions like the IMF and makes but vague assurances that it has become necessary to direct the process of globalization in a way that benefits all people. As James Mittelman has pointed out, Stiglitz and Co. reduced structural problems in the world's economic architecture to mere "management" issues: "Having criticized the market fundamentalists, Stiglitz then expresses his unshaken faith in the redeeming value of competition. At the end of the day, the agenda is to stabilize globalizing capitalism. It is to modify neoliberal globalization without tugging at the roots of its underlying structures."[1]

While insisting that "globalization is a fact of life," former UN Secretary-General Kofi Annan nonetheless warned global business leaders and politicians at several conferences at the World Economic Forum (WEF) in Davos that globalization had to be made to work for all, or else it would end up working for none. He asserted that "people do not wish to reverse globalization" but that they do aspire to a different and better kind than we have today. "The unequal distribution of benefits, and the imbalances in global rule-making," Annan emphasized, "inevitably will produce backlash and protectionism. And that, in turn, threatens to undermine and ultimately to unravel the open world economy that has been so painstakingly constructed over the course of the past half-century."[2] Throughout his long tenure, Annan sought to strengthen the Global Compact, an ongoing UN program designed to persuade transnational corporations to endorse a binding set of human rights, environmental, and labor principles and to allow private groups to monitor their compliance.

Unsurprisingly, market globalists arguing for moderate reform have embraced Annan's mild economic reformism to emphasize their unwavering commitment to "corporate responsibility." In a highly publicized 2007 speech, World Bank President Robert Zoellick eagerly seized on the UN Development Program's buzzword of "inclusive globalization" by asserting, "It is the vision of the World Bank Group to contribute to an inclusive and sustainable globalization—to overcome poverty, enhance growth with care for the environment, and create individual opportunity and hope." Pledging his support of the UN Millennium Development Goals—ambitious targets to halve poverty, fight hunger and disease, and deliver basic services to the world's poor by 2015—Zoellick made sure to emphasize that "sound social development" needed to be "combined with the requirements for sustainable growth, driven by the private sector, within a supportive framework of public policies."[3]

No question, these moderate reformists have learned to add some justice-globalist concepts to their neoliberal vision to make the resulting ideological stew more palatable to their global audiences. "Sustainability" is one such core concept torn from the ideological flanks of the political Left in order to be endowed with market-globalist meanings. Influential market-globalist codifiers like Klaus Schwab have gone to great lengths to link "sustainability" to new pet phrases such as "global corporate citizenship." In his much-cited 2008 *Foreign Affairs* article on the subject, the executive chair of the WEF suggests that companies have already taken a leading role in addressing sustainability issues "such as climate change, water shortages, infectious diseases, and terrorism. Other challenges include providing access to food, education, and information technology; extreme poverty; transnational crime; corruption; failed states; and disaster response and relief." "[F]or global corporate citizenship to be meaningful, effective, and sustainable," Schwab concludes, "it must align with a company's specific capabilites and with its business model and profit motive."[4] In short, one of the core concepts of justice globalism, once firmly associated with environmental and economic alternatives to the dominant paradigm, is now in danger of becoming subsumed in the discursive logic of market globalism.

Unfortunately, however, there is little empirical evidence that such rhetorical maneuvers have made much of a difference in how transnational corporations or the IMF are conducting business worldwide. The UN Millennium Development Goals appear to be receding into a future much further a way than 2015. Hence, the prospects for my second future scenario—a "global new deal"—are rather dim, to say the least. In the first edition of this book, I saw a slim possibility for the rise of political forces that would subject the global marketplace to greater democratic accountability by means of more effective global regulatory institutions. This would mean that most existing international political and economic institutions would undergo serious renovation and philosophical redirection or perhaps be dismantled altogether. Justice globalists who advocated this trajectory in the 1990s hoped that the countersystemic pressures generated by deteriorating social conditions would force market globalists to the bargaining table long before the world descended into a social or environmental catastrophe beyond repair. In their view, the implementation of their justice-globalist agenda represented the only chance for reversing the steady rise of global inequality and environmental degradation without surrendering to the parochial agenda of the national-populist camp. Indeed, serious attempts to build new global networks of solidarity lay at the very heart of the "global new deal" scenario.

Short of these profound changes, I argued, there was the very real possibility of a severe social backlash caused by the unbridled economic and cultural dynamics of neoliberal globalization. This backlash could unleash reactionary forces that dwarfed even those responsible for the suffering of millions during the 1930s and 1940s. The theoretical arguments underpinning such a "backlash scenario" are often associated with the work of the late political economist Karl Polanyi, who located the origins of the social crises that gripped the world during the first half of the twentieth century in ill-conceived efforts to liberalize markets. In his celebrated 1944 study *The Great Transformation*, he chronicled how commercial interests came to dominate society by means of a ruthless market logic that effectively disconnected people's economic activities from their social relations. The principles of the free market destroyed complex social relations of mutual obligation and undermined communal values such as civic engagement, reciprocity, and redistribution. As large segments of the population found themselves without an adequate system of social security and communal support, they resorted to radical measures to protect themselves against market globalization.

Extending his analysis to the workings of modern capitalism in general, Polanyi extrapolated that all modern capitalist societies contained two organizing principles that were fundamentally opposed to each other: one was the principle of economic liberalism, aiming at the establishment of a self-regulating market, relying on the support of the trading classes, and using largely laissez-faire and free trade as its method; the other was the principle of social protection aiming at the conservation of humans and nature as well as productive organizations, relying on the varying support of those most immediately affected by the deleterious actions of the market—primarily but not exclusively the working and the landed classes—and using protective legislation, restrictive associations, and instruments of intervention as its method.[5] Referring to these tendencies as a "double movement," Polanyi suggested that the stronger the liberal movement became, the more it would be able to dominate society by means of a market logic that effectively "disembedded" people's economic activity from their social relations. Hence, in their polished ideological formulation, the principles of economic liberalism provided a powerful justification for leaving large segments of the population to "fend for themselves." In a capitalist world organized around the notion of individual liberty—understood primarily as unrestrained economic entrepreneurship—the market ideal of competition trumped old social conceptions of cooperation and solidarity.[6]

It is important to remember the other half of Polanyi's theory of "double movement": the rapid advance of free-market principles also strengthened the resolve of working people to resist the liberal paradigm and struggle against its social effects. Polanyi noted that European workers' movements eventually gave birth to political parties that forced the passage of protective social legislation on the national level. After a prolonged period of severe economic dislocations following the end of World War I, the national-populist impulse experienced its most extreme manifestations in Italian fascism and German Nazism. In the end, the grand liberal dream of subordinating the nation to the requirements of the free market had generated an equally extreme countermovement that turned markets into mere appendices of totalitarian nation-states.[7]

Back in 2001, I did not envision that the backlash scenario would materialize so quickly, nor did I foresee the exact form it took. However, the applicability of Polanyi's analysis to our own global age seems obvious.

Like its nineteenth-century predecessor, the market globalism of the 1980s and 1990s represented an experiment in unleashing the utopia of the self-regulating market on society. This time, however, the acolytes of neoliberalism were prepared to turn the entire world into their laboratory. From the political Left, justice globalists challenged this project vigorously in the streets of the world's major cities, whereas from the political Right, the jihadist-globalist forces of radical Islamism launched a massive attack against what they considered to be a morally corrupt ideology of secular materialism that had engulfed the entire world. In response to the devastating al Qaeda strikes, the Bush administration switched from the soft-power strategy that prevailed in the 1990s to the hard-power model of imperial globalism that would reign supreme throughout the 2000s. As Jan Nederveen Pieterse has pointed out, "Neoliberal empire twins practices of empire with those of neoliberalism. The core of empire is the national security state and the military-industrial complex; neoliberalism is about business, financial operations, and marketing (including the marketing of neoliberalism itself)."[8]

Yet the militarization of market globalism highlights an embarrassing secret at the heart of the neoliberal project: from its earliest inception in the Thatcher and Reagan years, it required frequent and extensive use of state power in order to dismantle the old welfare structures and create new laissez-faire policies. As Polanyi noted, "free markets" did not appear on the historical stage ex nihilo. Rather, they were the deliberate products of concerted political action coordinated by modern states that found themselves captured by liberal interests. Similarly, the creation, expansion, and protection of global free markets demands massive infusions of central state power, hence the resulting ideological contradiction: market-globalist elites pushing for an ever-expanding mobility of capital must contend with the state's security logic that calls for inspection, surveillance, and other limitations on the free movement of people, goods, and information across national borders. With the emergence of imperial globalism, the embarrassing secret of neoliberalism is more easily exposed since the allegedly "invisible hand" of the market (claiming to operate best without interference from state power) must openly call on the iron fist of the state to save itself. In short, the coercive power of the state apparatus has been bought at the cost of bowing to empire. Thus, market-globalism's reliance on the forces of the old nation-state to battle its challengers has resulted in the dramatic disclosure of what during most of the 1990s remained hidden behind the ideological veil of the "self-regulating market": American Empire.

On first thought, it seems highly implausible that even a Global War on Terror expanding into Iran or other parts of the world could stop or slow down such a powerful set of social processes as globalization. Yet there are already some early warning signs. Intense border controls and security measures at the world's major airports and seaports have made travel and international trade more cumbersome. Laws have been passed in the democracies of the global North that curtail immigration, compromise civil liberties, and allow torture to be used on suspects during certain military interrogations. Belligerent patriotic sentiments are on display in many parts of the world, attesting to the severity of existing political and cultural divisions. A close look at modern history reveals that large-scale violent confrontations were capable of stopping and even reversing previous globalizing trends. As we noted in chapter 2, the period from 1860 to 1914 constituted a phase of internationalization characterized by the unprecedented development of transportation and communication networks, the rapid growth of international trade, and a huge flow of capital. But such "globalization" was capitalistic and imperialistic in character, involving the transfer of resources from the colonized global South in exchange for European manufactures. Great Britain, then the world's premier power, had spread its political system and cultural values across the globe. Its sustained efforts to engineer a global market under the auspices of the British Empire resulted in a severe backlash that culminated in the outbreak of World War I. The opponents of market globalism in the twenty-first century—especially jihadist globalists—have attracted thousands of followers and millions of sympathizers. Hence, as some commentators have recently suggested, it is quite conceivable that the backlash scenario reflected in a lasting global war on terror might put the brakes on market globalism and, in the long run, weaken the United States both economically and militarily while strengthening its chief competitors: China, India, and Russia. We could enter a period where "great powers" are once again competing for honor and influence. As Robert Kagan argued recently, such a world would remain unipolar, but America's international competitors would begin to catch up, thus raising new threats of regional or even global conflicts.[9]

On the other hand, as Fareed Zakaria suggests, it is also possible that the "rise of the Rest"—especially China and India—might actually increase international cooperation and encourage the forging of new global alliances and networks.[10] The prospects for such a "rosy scenario" would be enhanced with the possible electoral success of Barack Obama, an outspoken opponent of imperial globalism. A U.S. government led by President Obama would almost certainly pay more attention to combating both the social and the cultural causes of terrorism than the Bush administration. Moreover, Obama's family roots and his personal experiences of growing up in different parts of the world made him far more attuned to the grievances of the global South than any previous American or European political leader. However, it is highly unlikely that an Obama administration would go so far as to seriously consider replacing the dominant version of corporate-driven globalization with a substantive reform agenda. At best, moderate neoliberals like Stiglitz, Soros, or Warren Buffett would have the sympathetic ear of the new president. Thus, this more realistic version of our rosy scenario shows, regrettably, few signs of serious international cooperation toward a global new deal.

And yet, in the face of towering global problems like terrorism, nuclear weapons, climate change, poverty, and inequality, it seems that the world desperately needs fundamental change expressed in a fundamentally different vision of what our planet could look like. We have reached perhaps the most critical juncture in the history of our species. Lest we are willing to jeopardize our collective future, we must link the future course of globalization to a global new deal agenda. As we have emphasized throughout this book, there is nothing wrong with greater manifestations of social interdependence that emerge as a result of globalization as long as these transformative social processes address our global problems before it is too late. And we may have less time to act than we think.

The United States of America and rising powers like China, India, and Brazil carry a special responsibility to put their collective weight behind a form of globalization that is not defined by economic self-interest alone but, rather, is deeply infused with ethical concerns for humanity and our natural environment. In order to tackle our global problems, the people of the world need to pressure their political leaders for a global new deal that, in the cosmopolitan vision of British economist George Monbiot, would be sustained by novel global political and economic institutions such as a World Parliament, a Fair Trade Organization, and an International Clearing Union.[11] Monbiot's plea for the reconsideration of the role of ethics in global politics and economics has been echoed by many prominent spiritual and religious leaders, some of whom have explicitly called for a "global ethic" that would serve as the normative framework for a democratic global society.[12] For the Swiss theologian Hans Küng, for example, a global ethic contains four commitments: to a culture of nonviolence and respect of life, to a culture of solidarity and a just economic order, to a culture of tolerance and a life of truthfulness, and to a culture of equal rights, particularly racial and gender equality.[13] The Dalai Lama concurs, adding that imparting a critical mind and a sense of universal responsibility to the young is especially important. Ideals constitute the engine of progress; hence, it is imperative to introduce new generations to an ethical vision for a global society.[14]

For academics and educators, the most obvious step in this effort consists of developing a critical theory of globalization that contests both the script of market globalism and jihadist globalism while subjecting the claims of justice globalism to sustained scrutiny. Indeed, education and the media are key dimensions in any progressive strategy built around the idea that "another world is possible." Once harmful articulations of the global imaginary and their corresponding power bases in society begin to lose their grip on the construction of meaning, alternative interpretations of globalization can circulate more freely in public discourse. As a result, more and more people will realize that they have a stake in shaping the world they want to live in.

Thus, the three future scenarios laid out in this conclusion remain inextricably intertwined with matters of ideology: the kinds of ideas, values, and beliefs about globalization that shape our communities. It would be imprudent to expect that the great ideological struggle of the twenty-first century will end anytime soon, but it would be equally foolish to bank on humanity's inability to arrive at general principles that govern the world in a more peaceful, sustainable, and just manner.

# NOTES

## CHAPTER 1: THE ROOTS OF MARKET GLOBALISM

1. "Transcript of President Bush's Address to Nation on U.S. Policy in Iraq," *New York Times*, January 11, 2007; "President Bush Addresses American Legion Convention," August 31, 2006, <http://whitehouse.gov/news/releases/2006/08/print/20060831-1.html>; Condoleezza Rice, "Rethinking the National Interest: American Realism for a New World," *Foreign Affairs* 87, no. 4 (July/August 2008): 16.

2. For the main arguments of the debate, see Lyman Tower Sargent, *Contemporary Political Ideologies: A Comparative Analysis*, 11th ed. (Fort Worth, TX: Harcourt Brace College Publishers, 1999), 10–12; Mostafa Rejai, ed., *Decline of Ideology?* (Chicago: Aldine-Atherton, 1971); and Chaim I. Waxman, ed., *The End of Ideology Debate* (New York: Funk & Wagnalls, 1968).

3. Daniel Bell, *The End of Ideology: On the Exhaustion of Political Ideas in the Fifties* (Glencoe, IL: Free Press, 1960). See esp. 13–18, 369–75.

4. Francis Fukuyama, "The End of History?" *National Interest* 16 (Summer 1989): 4. See also Francis Fukuyama, *The End of History and the Last Man* (New York: Free Press, 1992).

5. Fukuyama, "The End of History?" 18.

6. Francis Fukuyama, "Economic Globalization and Culture: A Discussion with Dr. Francis Fukuyama," *Merrill Lynch Forum 2000*, online: <http://www.ml.com/woml/forum/global.html>; and Francis Fukuyama, "Second Thoughts: The Last Man in a Bottle," *National Affairs* 56 (Summer 1999): 16–44.

7. Fred Dallmayr, *Alternative Visions: Paths in the Global Village* (Lanham, MD: Rowman & Littlefield, 1998), 73.

8. Michael Freeden, *Ideologies and Political Theory: A Conceptual Approach* (Oxford: Clarendon Press, 1996), 77. For other definitions of ideology, see, for

example, Sargent, *Contemporary Political Ideologies*; Slavoj Zizek, ed., *Mapping Ideology* (London: Verso, 1994); Terry Eagleton, *Ideology: An Introduction* (London: Verso, 1991); Istvan Meszaros, *The Power of Ideology* (New York: New York University Press, 1989); David McLellan, *Ideology* (Milton Keynes: Open University Press, 1986); Paul Ricoeur, *Lectures on Ideology and Utopia*, edited by George H. Taylor (New York: Columbia University Press, 1986); Goran Therborn, *The Ideology of Power and the Power of Ideology* (London: New Left Books, 1980); Jorge Larrain, *The Concept of Ideology* (London: Hutchinson, 1979); and Karl Mannheim, *Ideology and Utopia: An Introduction to the Sociology of Knowledge* (1936; reprint, London: Routledge, 1991).

9. Terrell Carver, "Ideology: The Career of a Concept," in *Ideals and Ideologies: A Reader*, 3d ed., edited by Terrence Ball and Richard Dagger (New York: Longman, 1998), 9.

10. Robert J. Samuelson, "Why We're All Married to the Market," *Newsweek*, April 27, 1998, 47–50. I am grateful to Brian Michael Goss, who pointed these headlines out to me during his paper presentation at the 1998 Border Subjects 3 Conference at Illinois State University.

11. Ricoeur, *Lectures on Ideology and Utopia*. My summary of Ricoeur's discussion of ideology draws on George Taylor's "Editor's Introduction," in Ricoeur, *Lectures on Ideology and Utopia*, ix–xxxvi.

12. Ricoeur, *Lectures on Ideology and Utopia*, 266.

13. William I. Robinson, *Promoting Polyarchy: Globalization, U.S. Intervention, and Hegemony* (Cambridge: Cambridge University Press, 1996), 30. My explanation of Gramsci's notion of hegemony draws heavily on Robinson's excellent explication. A good selection of Gramsci's political writings is contained in Antonio Gramsci, *Selections from Prison Notebooks* (New York: International Publishers, 1971).

14. For a succinct explanation and critique of Ricardo's economic theories, see Theodore Cohn, *Global Political Economy: Theory and Practice* (New York: Longman, 2000), 200–203.

15. For a detailed exposition of Herbert Spencer's social and economic theories, see M. W. Taylor, *Men versus the State: Herbert Spencer and Late Victorian Individualism* (Oxford: Clarendon Press, 1992); and David Wiltshire, *The Social and Political Thought of Herbert Spencer* (Oxford: Oxford University Press, 1978). For a representative selection of Spencer's writings, see Herbert Spencer, *On Social Evolution*, edited by J. D. Y. Peel (Chicago: University of Chicago Press, 1972).

16. Jan Knippers Black, *Inequity in the Global Village: Recycled Rhetoric and Disposable People* (West Hartford, CT: Kumarian Press, 1999); Edward Luttwak, *Turbo-Capitalism: Winners and Losers in the Global Economy* (New York: HarperCollins, 1999). For a more detailed discussion of the rise of neoliberalism, see David Harvey, *A Brief History of Neoliberalism* (New York: Oxford University Press, 2007); Jeffry Frieden, *Global Capitalism: Its Fall and Rise in the Twentieth Century*

(New York: W. W. Norton, 2007); Peter Gowan, *The Global Gamble: Washington's Faustian Bid for World Dominance* (London: Verso, 1999); Daniel Yergin and Joseph Stanislaw, *The Commanding Heights: The Battle between Government and the Marketplace That Is Remaking the Modern World* (New York: Simon & Schuster, 1998); and John Gray, *False Dawn: The Delusions of Global Capitalism* (New York: New Press, 1998).

17. For a detailed description of this "transnational historic bloc of internationally oriented capitalists," see Mark Rupert, *Ideologies of Globalization: Contending Visions of a New World Order* (London: Routledge, 2000), 16–17, 154.

18. Joseph E. Stiglitz, *The Roaring Nineties: A New History of the World's Most Prosperous Decade* (New York: W. W. Norton, 2003).

19. See Manfred B. Steger, *The Rise of the Global Imaginary: Political Ideologies from the French Revolution to the Global War on Terror* (Oxford: Oxford University Press, 2008).

20. See Claire Turenne Sjolander, "The Rhetoric of Globalisation: What's in a Wor(l)d?" *International Journal* 51, no. 4 (1996): 603–16. For a critical discussion of such "market fundamentalism," see George Soros, *The Crisis of Global Capitalism: Open Society Endangered* (New York: Public Affairs, 1998), and *George Soros on Globalization* (New York: Public Affairs, 2002), and Joseph E. Stiglitz, *Globalization and Its Discontents* (New York: W. W. Norton, 2002), and *Making Globalization Work* (New York: W. W. Norton, 2007).

21. See Harvey Cox, "The Market as God: Living in the New Dispensation," *Atlantic Monthly*, March 1999, 18–23.

22. All citations are taken from Aaron Bernstein, "Backlash: Behind the Anxiety over Globalization," *BusinessWeek*, April 24, 2000, 44. This BusinessWeek–Harris poll on globalization was conducted by Harris Interactive from April 7 to 10, 2000. A total of 1,024 interviews were conducted. More recent polls seem to confirm these attitudes. A 2004 poll commissioned by the University of Maryland's Center on Policy Attitudes shows that slightly more than 50 percent of respondents saw globalization as "positive" or "somewhat positive." See <http://americans-world.org/digest/global_issues/globalization?gz_summary.cfm>.

23. Bernstein, "Backlash," 38–40.

24. For a discussion of how globalism has been modified in various parts of the world, see Manfred B. Steger, ed., *Rethinking Globalism* (Lanham, MD: Rowman & Littlefield, 2004).

25. Joseph Nye, *The Paradox of American Power* (Oxford: Oxford University Press, 2002), and *Soft Power: The Means to Success in World Politics* (New York: Public Affairs, 2005).

26. See, for example, James H. Mittelman, *The Globalization Syndrome: Transformation and Resistance* (Princeton, NJ: Princeton University Press, 2000), esp. chapter 9, 165–78; Ulrich Beck, *What Is Globalization?* (Cambridge: Polity Press, 2000); Barry K. Gills, ed., *Globalization and the Politics of Resistance* (New York: St.

Martin's Press, 2000); Richard Falk, *Predatory Globalization: A Critique* (Cambridge: Polity Press, 1999); Noam Chomsky, *Profit over People: Neoliberalism and Global Order* (New York: Seven Stories Press, 1999); and Pierre Bourdieu, *Acts of Resistance: Against the Tyranny of the Market* (New York: New Press, 1998).

27. For the importance of this distinction, see also Ankie Hoogvelt, *Globalization and the Postcolonial World: The New Political Economy of Development*, 2d ed. (Baltimore: Johns Hopkins University Press, 2001), 153–55.

28. For the metaphorical construction of globalization, see Markus Kornprobst, Vincent Pouliot, Nisha Shah, and Reuben Zaiotti, eds., *Metaphors of Globalization: Mirrors, Magicians, and Mutinies* (Houndsmill: Palgrave Macmillan, 2008).

29. For a general introduction to critical theory, see Stephen Eric Bronner and Douglas Kellner, eds., *Critical Theory and Society: A Reader* (London: Routledge, 1989); Stephen Eric Bronner, *Of Critical Theory and Its Theorists* (Malden, MA: Blackwell, 1994); and Rolf Wiggerhaus and Michael Robertson, *The Frankfurt School: Its History, Theories and Political Significance* (Boston: MIT Press, 1995). For various perspectives on developing a critical theory of globalization, see Steger, *Rethinking Globalism*, 10–11; Richard P. Appelbaum and William I. Robinson, eds., *Critical Globalization Studies* (New York: Routledge, 2005); James H. Mittelman, *Whither Globalization: The Vortex of Knowledge and Ideology* (New York: Routledge, 2005); Jan Aart Scholte, *Globalization: A Critical Introduction*, 2d ed. (Houndsmill: Palgrave Macmillan, 2005); and Douglas Kellner, "Theorizing Globalization," *Sociological Theory* (November 2002): 285–305.

30. See, for example, Heikki Patomaki and Teivo Teivanen, *A Possible World: Democratic Transformations of Global Institutions* (London: Zed Books, 2004); and Susan George, *Another World Is Possible, If . . .* (London: Verso, 2004).

## CHAPTER 2: THE ACADEMIC
## DEBATE OVER GLOBALIZATION

1. The parable of the "Blind Scholars and the Elephant" originated most likely in the Pali Buddhist *Udana*, which was apparently compiled in the second century BCE. Its many versions spread to other religions as well, most significantly Hinduism and Islam. For example, in his *Theology Revived*, Muhammad al-Ghazzali (1058–1128) refers to the tale in a discussion on the problem of human action in which the inadequacy of natural reason becomes evident. I am grateful to Ramdas Lamb in the Department of Religion at the University of Hawai'i at Manoa for explaining to me the origins of the parable.

2. Nayan Chanda, *Bound Together: How Traders, Preachers, Adventurers, and Warriors Shaped Globalization* (New Haven, CT: Yale University Press, 2007), 246.

3. James N. Rosenau, *Distant Proximities: Dynamics Beyond Globalization* (Princeton, NJ: Princeton University Press, 2003), 12.

4. Stephen J. Rosow, "Globalisation as Democratic Theory," *Millennium: Journal of International Studies* 29, no. 1 (2000): 31.

5. For various definitions of globalization, see, for example, Manfred B. Steger, *Globalization: A Very Short Introduction*, 2d ed. (Oxford: Oxford University Press, 2009); Frank J. Lechner and John Boli, eds., *The Globalization Reader*, 3d ed. (Oxford: Blackwell, 2007); David Held and Anthony McGrew, *Globalization/Antiglobalization* (Oxford: Polity Press, 2002); and Malcolm Waters, *Globalization*, 2d ed. (London: Routledge, 2001); Roland Robertson, *Globalization: Social Theory and Global Culture* (London: Sage, 1992); Anthony Giddens, *The Consequences of Modernity* (Stanford, CA: Stanford University Press, 1990); and David Harvey, *The Condition of Postmodernity* (Oxford: Blackwell, 1989).

6. For a fascinating genealogy of this term, see Michael Veseth, *Globaloney: Unraveling the Myths of Globalization* (Lanham, MD: Rowman & Littlefield, 2006). See also Richard J. Barnet and John Cavanagh, *Global Dreams: Imperial Corporations and the New World Order* (New York: Simon & Schuster, 1994); and Paul Krugman, *The Accidental Theorist* (New York: W. W. Norton, 1998), 73. For an excellent discussion of the skeptics' position, see Held and McGrew, *Globalization/Antiglobalization*.

7. Craig Calhoun, "Nationalism and Ethnicity," *Annual Review of Sociology* 19 (1993): 215–16.

8. Susan Strange, *The Retreat of the State: The Diffusion of Power in the World Economy* (Cambridge: Cambridge University Press, 1996), xii–xiii. My discussion of this aspect of the globalization debate has greatly benefited from Ian Clark's excellent exposition in his *Globalization and International Relations Theory* (Oxford: Oxford University Press, 1999), 34–40.

9. Linda Weiss, *The Myth of the Powerless State: Governing the Economy in a Global Era* (Ithaca, NY: Cornell University Press, 1998), 212.

10. Robert Holton, *Globalization and the Nation-State* (New York: St. Martin's Press, 1998), 196.

11. Robert Wade, "Globalization and Its Limits: Reports on the Death of the National Economy Are Greatly Exaggerated," in *National Diversity and Global Capitalism*, edited by Suzanne Berger and Ronald Dore (Ithaca, NY: Cornell University Press, 1996), 60–88; Paul Hirst and Graham Thompson, *Globalization in Question: The International Economy and the Possibilities of Governance*, 2d ed. (Cambridge: Polity Press, 1999). See also Alan Rugman, *The End of Globalization* (New York: Random House, 2001).

12. Hirst and Thompson, *Globalization in Question*, 2. For a similar conclusion, see Michael Veseth, *Selling Globalization: The Myth of the Global Economy* (Boulder, CO: Lynne Rienner, 1998); Paul N. Doremus, William W. Keller, Louis W. Pauly, and Simon Reich, *The Myth of the Global Corporation* (Princeton, NJ: Princeton University Press, 1998); and John Zysman, "The Myth of a 'Global'

Economy: Enduring National Foundations and Emerging Regional Realities," *New Political Economy* 1, no. 2 (1996): 157–84.

13. See, for example, David Held, Anthony McGrew, David Goldblatt, and Jonathan Perraton, *Global Transformations: Politics, Economics, and Culture* (Stanford, CA: Stanford University Press, 1999).

14. Robert Gilpin, *The Challenge of Global Capitalism: The World Economy in the 21st Century* (Princeton, NJ: Princeton University Press, 2000), 294–95. For a similar assessment, see Dani Rodrik, *Has Globalization Gone Too Far?* (Washington, DC: Institute for International Economics, 1997), 7–8, and Gary Burtless, Robert Z. Lawrence, Robert E. Litan, and Robert J. Shapiro, *Globaphobia: Confronting Fears about Open Trade* (Washington, DC: Brookings Institution Press, 1998), 6–7.

15. Immanuel Wallerstein, *The Capitalist World Economy* (Cambridge: Cambridge University Press, 1979), and *The Politics of the World Economy* (Cambridge: Cambridge University Press, 1984); Andre Gunder Frank, *ReORIENT: Global Economy in the Asian Age* (Berkeley: University of California Press, 1998). See also Christopher Chase-Dunn, *Global Formation: Structures of the World Economy* (Lanham, MD: Rowman & Littlefield, 1998). For a Gramscian neo-Marxist perspective, see Mark Rupert and Hazel Smith, eds., *Historical Materialism and Globalization* (London: Routledge, 2002).

16. Immanuel Wallerstein, "Culture as the Ideological Battleground of the Modern World System," in *Global Culture*, edited by Mike Featherstone (London: Sage, 1990), 38.

17. William I. Robinson, *A Theory of Global Capitalism: Production, Class, and the State in a Transnational World* (Baltimore: Johns Hopkins University Press, 2004); William Carroll, Radhika Desai, and Warren Magnusson, *Globalization, Social Justice and Social Movements: A Reader* (Victoria, ON: University of Victoria, 1996), 21, 107; Samir Amin, "The Challenge of Globalization," *Review of International Political Economy* 3, no. 2 (1996): 244–45.

18. Ash Amin, "Placing Globalization," *Theory, Culture and Society* 14, no. 2 (1997): 123–38.

19. Gills, *Globalization and the Politics of Resistance*.

20. Leslie Sklair, *Globalization: Capitalism and Its Alternatives*, 3d ed. (Oxford: Oxford University Press, 2002).

21. For various accounts of economic globalization, see, for example, Dani Rodrik, *One Economics, Many Recipes: Globalization, Institutions, and Economic Growth* (Princeton, NJ: Princeton University Press, 2007); Daniel Cohen, *Globalization and Its Enemies* (Cambridge, MA: MIT Press, 2006); Held and McGrew, *Globalization/Antiglobalization*, 38–57; Hoogvelt, *Globalization and the Postcolonial World*; Lechner and Boli, *The Globalization Reader*; Hugo Radice, "Taking Globalisation Seriously," in *Global Capitalism versus Democracy: The Socialist Register 1999*, edited by Leo Panitch and Colin Leys (New York: Monthly Review Press,

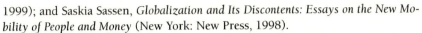

1999); and Saskia Sassen, *Globalization and Its Discontents: Essays on the New Mobility of People and Money* (New York: New Press, 1998).

22. The most comprehensive treatment of this nature is Robert O. Keohane, *After Hegemony* (Princeton, NJ: Princeton University Press, 1984). For a more recent update of Keohane's position on globalization, see Robert O. Keohane and Joseph S. Nye Jr., "Globalization: What's New? What's Not? (And So What)?" *Foreign Policy* 118 (Spring 2000): 104–19; Robert O. Keohane, "Governance in a Partially Globalized World," *American Political Science Review* 95, no. 1 (March 2001): 1–13; and Robert O. Keohane, "Moral Commitment and Liberal Approaches to World Politics," in *The Globalization of Liberalism*, edited by Eivind Hovden and Edward Keene (New York: Palgrave, 2002), 11–35.

23. Gilpin, *The Challenge of Global Capitalism*, 299.

24. Gilpin, *The Challenge of Global Capitalism*, 19.

25. Perhaps the most accessible example of this genre is Robert K. Schaeffer's very readable study, *Understanding Globalization*, 3d ed. (Lanham, MD: Rowman & Littlefield, 2005).

26. Luttwak, *Turbo-Capitalism*, xii, 27.

27. See Gilpin, *The Challenge of Global Capitalism*, 65–75, and Beth A. Simmons and Zachary Elkins, "Globalization of Liberalization: Policy Diffusion in the International Political Economy," *American Political Science Review* 98, no. 1 (February 2004): 171–89.

28. Manuel Castells, "Information Technology and Global Capitalism," in *Global Capitalism*, edited by Will Hutton and Anthony Giddens (New York: The New Press, 2000), 53.

29. Gilpin, *The Challenge of Global Capitalism*, 20.

30. Ameet Sachdev, "Law Firms Slow to Outsource," *Chicago Tribune*, January 19, 2004, sec. 4, 1.

31. See David Ashley, *History without a Subject: The Postmodern Condition* (Boulder, CO: Westview Press, 1997), 109; Gary Gereffi, "The Elusive Last Lap in the Quest for Developed-Country Status," in Mittelman, *The Globalization Syndrome*, 64–69; and Gary Gereffi and Miguel Korzeniewicz, eds., *Commodity Chains and Global Capitalism* (Westport, CT: Greenwood Press, 1993).

32. Gilpin, *The Challenge of Global Capitalism*, 24.

33. Steger, *Globalization*, 51.

34. See, for example, Robert T. Kurdle, "The Three Types of Globalization: Communication, Market, and Direct," in *Globalization and Global Governance*, edited by Raimo Väyrynen (Lanham, MD: Rowman & Littlefield, 1999), 3–23; C. P. Rao, ed., *Globalization, Privatization and Free Market Economy* (Westport, CT: Quorum Books, 1998); and Lowell Bryan and Diana Farrell, *Market Unbound: Unleashing Global Capitalism* (New York: Wiley, 1996).

35. Richard Langhorne, *The Coming of Globalization: Its Evolution and Contemporary Consequences* (New York: Palgrave, 2001), 2.

36. Bryan and Farrell, *Market Unbound*, 187.

37. Kenichi Ohmae, *The End of the Nation-State: The Rise of Regional Economies* (New York: Free Press, 1995), *The Borderless World: Power and Strategy in the Interlinked World Economy* (New York: Harper Business, 1990), and *Next Global Stage: Challenges and Opportunities in Our Borderless World* (Philadelphia: Wharton School Publishing, 2005). For a more recent example of the "end of the nation-state thesis" from the opposite end of the ideological spectrum, see Prem Shankar Jha, *The Twilight of the Nation-State: Globalisation, Chaos and War* (London: Pluto Press, 2006).

38. Caroline Thomas, "Globalization and the South," in *Globalization and the South*, edited by Caroline Thomas and Peter Wilkin (New York: St. Martin's Press, 1997), 6. See also Roger Burbach, Orlando Nunez, and Boris Kagarlitsky, *Globalization and Its Discontents: The Rise of Postmodern Socialisms* (London: Pluto Press, 1997). A more popular version of this argument can be found in William Greider, *One World, Ready or Not: The Manic Logic of Global Capitalism* (New York: Simon & Schuster, 1997).

39. See, for example, Ethan B. Kapstein, *Sharing the Wealth: Workers and the World Economy* (New York: W. W. Norton, 1999); Gowan, *The Global Gamble*; Luttwak, *Turbo-Capitalism*; David C. Korten, *When Corporations Rule the World*, 2d ed. (West Hartford, CT: Kumarian Press, 2001).

40. Daniel Singer, *Whose Millennium? Theirs or Ours?* (New York: Monthly Review Press, 1999), 186–87.

41. Saskia Sassen's work emphasizes the key role played by global cities in the organization and control of globally oriented economic and social processes. See Saskia Sassen, *The Global City: New York, London, Tokyo* (Princeton, NJ: Princeton University Press, 1991), *A Sociology of Globalization* (New York: W. W. Norton, 2007), and *Territory, Authority, Rights: From Medieval to Global Assemblages* (Princeton, NJ: Princeton University Press, 2008). See also Neil Brenner, ed., *The Global Cities Reader* (London: Routledge, 2006), and Mark Amen, Kevin Archer, and Martin Bosman, eds., *Relocating Global Cities: From the Center to the Margins* (Lanham, MD: Rowman & Littlefield, 2006).

42. Jan Aart Scholte, *Globalization: A Critical Introduction*, 2d ed. (New York: St. Martin's Press, 2005).

43. For an excellent exposition of this argument, see Edward S. Cohen, *The Politics of Globalization in the United States* (Washington, DC: Georgetown University Press, 2001). See also Geoffrey Garrett, *Partisan Politics in the Global Economy* (Cambridge: Cambridge University Press, 1998); Leo Panitch, "Rethinking the Role of the State," in Mittelman, *Globalization*, 83–113; Eric Helleiner, "Post-Globalisation: Is the Financial Liberalisation Trend Likely to Be Reversed?" in *States against Markets: The Limits of Globalisation*, edited by Robert Boyer and Daniel Drache (London: Routledge, 1996); and Eric Helleiner, *States and the Reemergence of Global Finance* (Ithaca, NY: Cornell University Press, 1994).

44. John Gray, *False Dawn: The Delusions of Global Capitalism* (New York: New Press, 1998), 23.

45. Gray, *False Dawn*, 218.

46. Manuel Castells, *The Information Age: Economy, Society, and Culture*, 3 vols. (Oxford: Blackwell, 1996–1998), vol. 3, 356.

47. Castells, *The Information Age*, vol. 3, 368.

48. Castells, *The Information Age*, vol. 3, 379.

49. See, for example, the various essays collected in Rorden Wilkinson, ed., *The Global Governance Reader* (London: Routledge, 2005).

50. See, for example, the essays collected in Alison Brysk, ed., *Globalization and Human Rights* (Berkeley: University of California Press, 2002).

51. Martin Shaw, *Theory of the Global State: Globality as an Unfinished Revolution* (Cambridge: Cambridge University Press, 2000), 16.

52. John Keane, *Global Civil Society?* (Cambridge: Cambridge University Press, 2003), 98.

53. Falk, *Predatory Globalization*.

54. David Held, "Democracy and the New International Order," in *Cosmopolitan Democracy: An Agenda for a New World Order*, edited by Daniele Archibugi and David Held (Cambridge: Polity Press, 1995), 96–120. For a more detailed elaboration of Held's vision, see David Held, *Democracy and the Global Order* (Stanford, CA: Stanford University Press, 1995), and *Models of Democracy*, 3d ed. (Stanford, CA: Stanford University Press, 2006).

55. Held and McGrew, *Globalization/Antiglobalization*, 131.

56. Falk, *Predatory Globalization*, 7. See also Richard Falk, *Human Rights Horizons: The Pursuit of Justice in a Globalizing World* (New York: Routledge, 2000).

57. Richard Falk, *The Great Terror War* (New York: Olive Branch Press, 2003), 186.

58. See, for example, Rodney Bruce Hall and Thomas J. Biersteker, eds., *The Emergence of Private Authority in Global Governance* (Cambridge: Cambridge University Press, 2002).

59. See Holton, *Globalization and the Nation-State*, 202–203.

60. John Tomlinson, *Globalization and Culture* (Chicago: University of Chicago Press, 1999), 1.

61. Tomlinson, *Globalization and Culture*, 28.

62. George Ritzer, *The McDonaldization of Society: An Investigation into the Changing Character of Contemporary Social Life* (Thousand Oaks, CA: Pine Forge Press, 1993).

63. Benjamin R. Barber, *Jihad vs. McWorld* (New York: Ballantine Books, 1996), 17. For a more skeptical assessment of the supposed "Americanness" of globalization, see William H. Marling, *How "American" Is Globalization?* (Baltimore: Johns Hopkins University Press, 2006).

64. Barber, *Jihad vs. McWorld*, 19. For a neo-Marxist perspective on the rise

of a global capitalist monoculture, see Herbert Schiller, "The Global Information Highway: Project for an Ungovernable World," in *Resisting the Virtual Life*, edited by James Brook and Iain A. Boal (San Francisco: City Lights, 1995), 17–33.

65. Samuel P. Huntington, *The Clash of Civilizations and the Remaking of World Order* (New York: Touchstone, 1997), 26–27, 45–48.

66. Amy Chua, *World on Fire: How Exporting Free Market Democracy Breeds Ethnic Hatred and Global Instability* (New York: Doubleday, 2003), 9; Roger Scruton, *The West and the Rest: Globalization and the Terrorist Threat* (Wilmington, DE: ISI Books, 2002), 157–58.

67. Scruton, *The West and the Rest*, 159.

68. Serge Latouche, *The Westernization of the World* (Cambridge: Polity Press, 1996), 3.

69. See Steger, *Globalization*, 82–85.

70. Selma K. Sonntag, *The Local Politics of Global English: Case Studies in Linguistic Globalization* (Lanham, MD: Lexington Books, 2003), 123.

71. See, for example, Arjun Appadurai, *Modernity at Large: Cultural Dimensions of Globalization* (Minneapolis: University of Minnesota Press, 1996), and Ulf Hannerz, *Cultural Complexity: Studies in the Social Organization of Meaning* (New York: Columbia University Press, 1992), and *Transnational Connections: Cultures, People, Places* (London: Routledge, 1996). Peter Berger and Samuel Huntington offer a highly unusual version of this "pluralism thesis." Emphasizing that cultural globalization is "American in origin and content," they nonetheless allow for "many variations and sub-globalizations" on the dominant U.S. cultural theme in various parts of the world. See Peter L. Berger and Samuel P. Huntington, eds., *Many Globalizations: Cultural Diversity in the Contemporary World* (Oxford: Oxford University Press, 2002).

72. Roland Robertson, *Globalization*, and "Glocalization: Time–Space and Homogeneity–Heterogeneity," in *Global Modernities*, edited by Mike Featherstone, Scott Lash, and Roland Robertson (London: Sage, 1995), 25–44.

73. Jan Nederveen Pieterse, *Globalization and Culture: Global Melange* (Lanham, MD: Rowman & Littlefield, 2003), 117.

74. Hannerz, *Cultural Complexity*, 96. See also Eduardo Mendieta, *Global Fragments: Latinamericanisms, Globalizations, and Critical Theory* (Albany: State University of New York Press, 2007).

75. Ulrich Beck, *What Is Globalization?* (Cambridge: Polity Press, 2000), 102.

76. Appadurai, *Modernity at Large*, 33.

77. Martin Albrow, *The Global Age: State and Society beyond Modernity* (Cambridge: Polity Press, 1996), 192.

78. For a more detailed account of this debate, see Scholte, *Globalization*; Tomlinson, *Globalization and Culture*, 32–70; and Kate Nash, *Contemporary Political Sociology: Globalization, Politics, and Power* (Malden, MA: Blackwell, 2000), 71–88.

79. Franz J. Broswimmer, *Ecocide: A History of Mass Extinction of Species* (London: Pluto Press, 2002). For a comprehensive overview of facts and data related to global climate change, see S. George Philander, ed., *Encyclopedia of Global Warming and Climate Change* (London: Sage, 2008). For a more readable account, see Al Gore, *An Inconvenient Truth* (New York: Rodale Books, 2006).

80. Nicholas Stern, *The Economics of Climate Change: The Stern Review* (Cambridge: Cambridge University Press, 2007).

81. One of the most comprehensive surveys of the subject can be found in Held et al., *Global Transformations*.

82. Alan Golacinski, cited in Barbara Lochbihler, "Militarism a Facilitator for Globalization," undated paper, online: <http://www.wilpf.int.ch/~wilpf/globalization/paper1.htm>.

83. Fredric Jameson, "Preface," in *The Cultures of Globalization*, edited by Fredric Jameson and Masao Miyoshi (Durham, NC: Duke University Press, 1998), xi–xii.

84. For a discussion of five emerging points of agreement, see Manfred B. Steger, ed., *Rethinking Globalism* (Lanham, MD: Rowman & Littlefield, 2004), 1–4.

85. Clark, *Globalization and International Relations Theory*, 39.

86. See Claus Offe, *Modernity and the State: East, West* (Cambridge: Polity Press, 1996), 5.

87. See Mauro F. Guillen, "Is Globalization Civilizing, Destructive or Feeble? A Critique of Five Key Debates in the Social Science Literature," *Annual Review of Sociology* 27, no. 1 (2001): 237.

88. Hans-Georg Gadamer, *Truth and Method* (New York: Seabury Press, 1975).

89. Robert W. Cox, "A Perspective on Globalization," in Mittelman, *Globalization*, 21–30; Stephen Gill, "Globalization, Democratization, and the Politics of Indifference," in Mittelman, *Globalization*, 205–28, and "Globalisation, Market Civilisation, and Disciplinary Neoliberalism," *Millennium: Journal of International Studies* 24, no. 2 (1995): 399–423. For a discussion of the ideological dimensions of globalization with scholarly contributions from all five continents, see Steger, *Rethinking Globalism*.

90. Alan Scott, "Introduction: Globalization: Social Process or Political Rhetoric?" in *The Limits of Globalization: Cases and Arguments*, edited by Alan Scott (London: Routledge, 1997), 2.

## CHAPTER 3: FROM MARKET GLOBALISM TO IMPERIAL GLOBALISM

1. George Lichtheim, *Imperialism* (New York: Praeger, 1971), 13, 25.

2. See Robert Folz, *The Concept of Empire in Western Europe: From the Fifth to the Fourteenth Century* (London: Edward Arnold, 1969), 4–5.

3. Michael W. Doyle, *Empires* (Ithaca, NY: Cornell University Press, 1986),

19. See also Herfried Munkler, *Empires: The Logic of World Domination from Ancient Rome to the United States* (Cambridge: Polity Press, 2007).

4. Lichtheim, *Imperialism*, 9.

5. Ronald Robinson and John Gallagher, "The Imperialism of Free Trade," *Economic History Review* 6 (1953): 1–15. For excellent discussions of informal imperialism and an evaluation of Robinson and Gallagher's theory, see Wolfgang J. Mommsen, *Theories of Imperialism* (New York: Random House, 1980), 86–93, and Doyle, *Empires*, 32–34.

6. The post-9/11 literature on "American Empire" is vast and rapidly growing. See, for example, Chalmers Johnson, *The Sorrows of Empire: Militarism, Secrecy, and the End of the Republic* (New York: Metropolitan Books, 2004), and *Nemesis: The Last Days of the American Republic* (New York: Holt, 2008); David Ray Griffin and Peter Dale Scott, eds., *9/11 and American Empire: Intellectuals Speak Out* (New York: Olive Branch Press, 2006); Carl Boggs, *The New Militarism: U.S. Empire and Endless War* (Lanham, MD: Rowman & Littlefield, 2004); Emmanuel Todd, *After Empire: The Breakdown of the American Order* (New York: Columbia University Press, 2003); Michael Mann, *Incoherent Empire* (London: Verso, 2003); Ellen Meiksins Wood, *Empire of Capital* (London: Verso, 2003); and David Harvey, *The New Imperialism* (Oxford: Oxford University Press, 2003). Michael Walzer, for example, suggests that the post-9/11 American Empire constitutes a "new beast" characterized by "a looser form of rule, less authoritarian than empire is or was, more dependent on the agreement of others." At the same time, Walzer concedes that "George W. Bush's unilateralism is a bid for hegemony without compromise; perhaps he sees America playing an imperial—perhaps also messianic—role in the world." See Michael Walzer, "Is There an American Empire?" *Dissent* (Fall 2003): 27–31.

7. Walter LaFeber, *The New Empire: An Interpretation of American Expansion 1860–1898* (Ithaca, NY: Cornell University Press, 1963); William A. Williams, *The Contours of American History* (Chicago: Quadrangle Books, 1966). For an insightful discussion of the role of the Spanish-American War in the formation of a global American Empire, see Thomas Schoonover, *Uncle Sam's War of 1898 and the Origins of Globalization* (Lexington: University Press of Kentucky, 2003).

8. Albert J. Beveridge, cited in Tristram Coffin, *The Passion of the Hawks: Militarism in Modern America* (New York: Macmillan, 1964), 1–2.

9. Joseph S. Nye, *The Paradox of American Power* (Oxford: Oxford University Press, 2002), and *Soft Power: The Means to Success in World Politics* (New York: Public Affairs, 2005).

10. All direct quotes are taken from Stiglitz, *The Roaring Nineties*, chapter 9, 202–40.

11. Adam Wolfson, "Conservatives and Neoconservatives," *The Public Interest* (Winter 2004), online: <http://www.thepublicinterest.com/current/article2

.html?>. See also Michael Lind, "A Tragedy of Errors," *The Nation*, February 23, 2004, 23–32.

12. Cited in Mann, *Incoherent Empire*, 2.

13. George W. Bush, "Remarks," National Cathedral, September 14, 2002, online: <http://www.whitehouse.gov/news/releases/2001/09.html>. The entire 2002 National Security Strategy document is available online at <http://www.white house.gov/nsc/nss.html>. For an enlightening philosophical analysis of Bush's moralistic language, see Peter Singer, *The President of Good and Evil: Questioning the Ethics of George W. Bush* (New York: Dutton, 2004).

14. Tom Barry and Jim Lobe, "The People," in *Power Trip: U.S. Unilateralism and Global Strategy after September 11*, edited by John Feffer (New York: Seven Stories Press, 2003), 39–49.

15. Harvey, *The New Imperialism*, chapter 1.

16. George W. Bush, "Securing Freedom's Triumph," *New York Times*, September 11, 2002, A33. For an enlightening discussion on the ideological and religious components of the new U.S. imperialism, see Claes G. Ryn, "The Ideology of American Empire," *Orbis* (Summer 2003): 383–97.

17. Colin Powell cited in Naomi Klein, "Failure to Brand USA," *In These Times* (2002), online: <http://www.inthesetimes.com>.

18. Beers cited in Robert Satloff, "Battling for the Hearts and Minds in the Middle East: A Critique of U.S. Public Diplomacy Post–September 11," *Policywatch* 657 (September 17, 2002), online: <http://www.washingtoninstitute.org/watch/Policy watch/policywatch2002/657.htm>.

19. Jan Nederveen Pieterse, *Globalization or Empire?* (New York: Routledge, 2004), 45.

20. Charlotte Beers, interviewed by Alexandra Starr in "Building Brand America," *BusinessWeek online* (December 10, 2001).

21. Pew Research Center for the People and the Press poll (March 16, 2004), <http://www.people-press.org/reports>.

22. These numbers are taken from the 2007 BBC World Service/Age Global Poll. See Michael Gordon, "Global Backlash against America," *The Age* (January 23, 2007). For a balanced critique of American public diplomacy initatives under the three undersecretaries appointed during the Bush administration, see Carnes Lord, *Losing Hearts and Minds? Public Diplomacy and Strategic Influence in the Age of Terror* (Westport, CT: Praeger, 2006).

23. Michael Freeden, *Ideology: A Very Short Introduction* (Oxford: Oxford University Press, 2003), 103.

24. Andrew Chadwick, "Studying Political Ideas: A Public Political Discourse Approach," *Political Studies* 48 (2000): 283–301. For accessible introductions to the methods of critical discourse analysis, see Norman Fairclough, *Analyzing Discourse: Textual Analysis for Social Research* (New York: Routledge, 2003); Jan Blommaert, *Discourse: A Critical Introduction* (Cambridge: Cambridge University Press,

2005); Gilbert Weiss and Ruth Wodak, eds., *Critical Discourse Analysis: Theory and Interdisciplinarity* (Houndsmill: Palgrave Macmillan, 2007); and Teun van Dijk, *Discourse and Power* (Houndsmill: Palgrave Macmillan, 2008).

25. Freeden, *Ideology*, 109.

26. See Chadwick, "Studying Political Ideas," 290–92.

27. Michael Veseth, *Selling Globalization: The Myth of the Global Economy* (Boulder, CO: Lynne Rienner, 1998), 16–18.

28. Friedrich Hayek, *Law, Legislation, and Liberty*, 3 vols. (London: Routledge & Kegan Paul, 1979), vol. 1, 55.

29. Isaiah Berlin, "Two Concepts of Liberty," in *Four Essays on Liberty* (Oxford: Oxford University Press, 1969), 121–22.

30. Milton Friedman, *Capitalism and Freedom* (Chicago: University of Chicago Press, 1962), 9.

31. Editorial, *BusinessWeek*, December 13, 1999, 212.

32. Martin Wolf, "Why This Hatred of the Market?," 9–11, and Peter Martin, "The Moral Case for Globalization," 12–13, both in *The Globalization Reader*, 3d ed., edited by Frank J. Lechner and John Boli (Oxford: Blackwell, 2007).

33. George W. Bush, *The National Security Strategy of the United States*, 2002/2006 (*NSSUS*), online: <http://www.whitehouse.gov/nsc/nss/2006/>.

34. Charlene Barshefsky, cited in Mark Levinson, "Who's in Charge Here?" *Dissent* (Fall 1999): 22.

35. Michael Camdessus, cited in Levinson, "Who's in Charge Here?"; Michael Camdessus, "Globalization and Asia: The Challenges for Regional Cooperation and Implications for Hong Kong" (address to Hong Kong Monetary Authority, Hong Kong, March 7, 1997), online: <http://www.imf.org/external/np/speeches/1997/MDS9703.html>.

36. See, for example, William Bole, "Tales of Globalization," *America* 181, no. 18 (December 4, 1999): 14–16.

37. Thomas L. Friedman, *The Lexus and the Olive Tree: Understanding Globalization* (New York: Farrar, Straus & Giroux, 1999), xii, 23–24.

38. Friedman, *The Lexus and the Olive Tree*, 9.

39. Friedman, *The Lexus and the Olive Tree*, 104, 152.

40. Friedman, *The Lexus and the Olive Tree*, 105.

41. Friedman, *The Lexus and the Olive Tree*, 109–10.

42. Arundhati Roy, "The New American Century," *The Nation* (February 9, 2004): 11.

43. Thomas L. Friedman, *Longitudes and Attitudes: The World in the Age of Terrorism* (New York: Anchor Books, 2003), 222–23; see also Thomas L. Friedman, *The World Is Flat 3.0: A Brief History of the Twenty-First Century* (New York: Picador, 2007), esp. chapter 10.

44. Friedman, *Longitudes and Attitudes*, 78.

45. Bush at the Republican debate in West Columbia, SC, January 7, 2000, online: <http://www.issues2002.org/Background_Free_Trade.htm>.

46. *NSSUS*, <http://www.whitehouse.gov/nsc/nss/2006/>.

47. Ben Bernanke, cited in Edmund L. Andrews, "Fed Chief Sees Faster Pace for Globalization," *New York Times,* August 25, 2006.

48. Goh Chok Tong, cited in Jennifer Lien, "Open Trade Doors in East Asia," *Business Times Singapore*, May 9, 2003. For similar assessments by African political leaders, see Eric E. Otenyo, "Local Governments Connecting to the Global Economy: Globalization as Catalyst in Governance of East African Cities," *Public Organization Review* 4 (2004): 339–60.

49. *NSSUS*, <http://www.whitehouse.gov/nsc/nss/2006/>.

50. For a detailed discussion of these neoliberal policy initiatives, see John Micklethwait and Adrian Woolridge, *A Future Perfect: The Challenge and Hidden Promise of Globalization* (New York: Crown Publishers, 2000), 22–54, and John Ralston Saul, *The Collapse of Globalism: And the Reinvention of the World* (London: Penguin, 2005).

51. Edward Luttwak, *Turbo-Capitalism: Winners and Losers in the Global Economy* (New York: HarperCollins, 1999), 152.

52. Ulrich Beck, *What Is Globalization?* (Cambridge: Polity Press, 2000), 122.

53. See Robert W. McChesney, "Global Media, Neoliberalism, and Imperialism," *Monthly Review* (March 2001), online: <http://www.monthlyreview.org/301rwm.html>.

54. For a critical assessment of Thatcher's experiment, see John Gray, *False Dawn: The Delusions of Global Capitalism* (New York: New Press, 1998), 24–34.

55. Bill Clinton, "Remarks by the President on Foreign Policy" (San Francisco, February 26, 1999), online: <http://www.pub.whitehouse.gov/urires/12R?urn:pdi://oma.eop.gove.us/1999/3/1 /3.text.1.html>.

56. President Clinton, cited in Sonya Ross, "Clinton Talks of Better Living," *Associated Press*, October 15, 1997, online: <http://more.abcnews.go.com/sections/world/brazil1014/index.html>.

57. Stuart Eizenstat, "Remarks to Democratic Leadership Council" (January 19, 1999), online: <http://www.usinfo.org/wf/990120/epf305.html>.

58. Economic Strategy Institute Editorial, "International Finance Experts Preview Upcoming Global Economic Forum," April 1, 1999, online: <http://www.econstrat.org/pctranscript.html>.

59. Friedman, *The Lexus and the Olive Tree*, 407.

60. Rahul Bajaj, "Interview with the Rediff Business Interview," February 2, 1999, online: <http://rediff.com/business/1999/feb/02bajaj.html>. See also <http://www.ascihyd.org/asci701.html>.

61. Manuel Villar Jr., "High-Level Dialogue on the Theme of the Social and Economic Impact of Globalization and Interdependence and Their Policy Implica-

tions," speech delivered at the United Nations, New York, September 17, 1998, online: <http://www.un.int/philippines/villar.html>.

62. Masaru Hayami, "Globalization and Regional Cooperation in Asia," Tokyo, March 17, 2000, online: <http://www.boj.or.jp/en/press/koen049.html>.

63. John R. Malott, "Globalization, Competitiveness, and Asia's Economic Future," speech delivered in Kuala Lumpur, Malaysia, March 13, 1998, online: <http://www.csis.org/pacfor/pac1198.html>.

64. Alain Lipietz, *Towards a New Economic Order* (Oxford: Oxford University Press, 1993), x.

65. David Smith, "Putting a Human Face on the Global Economy: Seeking Common Ground on Trade" (1999 DLC Annual Conference, Washington, DC, October 14, 1999), online: <http://www.dlcppi.org/speeches/99conference/99conf_panel1.html>.

66. Harvey Cox, "The Market as God: Living in the New Dispensation," *Atlantic Monthly*, March 1999, 18–23. See also Thomas Frank, *One Market under God: Extreme Capitalism, Market Populism, and the End of Economic Democracy* (New York: Doubleday, 2000).

67. Lorenzo Zambrano, "Putting the Global Market in Order," online: <http://www.globalprogress.org/ingles/Mexico/Zambrano.html>.

68. Merrill Lynch Forum, "Economic Globalization and Culture: A Discussion with Dr. Francis Fukuyama," online: <http://www.ml.com/woml/forum/global2.html>.

69. Friedman, *The Lexus and the Olive Tree*, 474–75. See also Friedman's remark on page 294: "Today, for better or worse, globalization is a means for spreading the fantasy of America around the world. . . . Globalization is Americanization."

70. Gray, *False Dawn*, 131.

71. Steven Kline, "The Play of the Market: On the Internationalization of Children's Culture," *Theory, Culture and Society* 12 (1995): 110.

72. See Benjamin R. Barber, *Jihad vs. McWorld* (New York: Ballantine Books, 1996), 119–51. For Barber's more recent analysis of consumerism, see his *Consumed: How Markets Corrupt Children, Infantilize Adults, and Swallow Citizens Whole* (New York: W. W. Norton, 2008).

73. Robert J. Samuelson, "Globalization Goes to War," *Newsweek*, February 24, 2003, 41.

74. Transcript of George W. Bush's speech in London on Iraq and the Middle East printed in the *New York Times*, November 19, 2003.

75. Christopher Shays, "Free Markets and Fighting Terrorism," *Washington Times*, June 10, 2003.

76. Robert Hormats, "PBS Interview with Danny Schechter," February 1998, online: <http://pbs.org/globalization/hormats1.html>.

77. Friedman, *The Lexus and the Olive Tree*, 112–13.

78. Steward Brand, "Financial Markets," Global Business Network Book Club, December 1998, online: <http://www.gbn.org/public/services/bookclub/reviews/ex_8812.html>.

79. Michael Hardt and Antonio Negri, *Empire* (Cambridge, MA: Harvard University Press, 2000), 3.

80. Cited in Richard Gott, *In the Shadow of the Liberator: Hugo Chávez and the Transformation of Venezuela* (London: Verso, 2000), 52–53.

81. Will Hutton, "Anthony Giddens and Will Hutton in Conversation," in *Global Capitalism*, edited by Will Hutton and Anthony Giddens (New York: Free Press, 2000), 41.

82. Friedman, *The Lexus and the Olive Tree*, 381.

83. Friedman, *The Lexus and the Olive Tree*, 464.

84. Statement of Joseph Gorman before the Subcommittee on Trade of the Committee on Ways and Means, March 18, 1997, online: <http://fasttrack.org/track/congress/gorman.html>.

85. Robert Kagan, "The U.S.–Europe Divide," *Washington Post*, May 26, 2002.

86. *NSSUS.*

87. Ryn, "The Ideology of American Empire," 384–85.

88. Economic Communiqué, Lyon G-7 Summit, June 28, 1996, online: <http:// library.utoronto.ca/www/g7/96ecopre.html>.

89. Robert Rubin, "Reform of the International Financial Architecture," *Vital Speeches* 65, no. 15 (1999): 455.

90. Denise Froning, "Why Spurn Free Trade?" *Washington Times*, September 15, 2000.

91. Alan Greenspan, "The Globalization of Finance," October 14, 1997, online: <http://cato.org/pubs/journal/cj17n3–1.html>.

92. George W. Bush, cited in Elisabeth Bumiller, "Bush, in High-Tech Center, Urges Americans to Welcome Competition from India," *New York Times*, March 4, 2006.

93. See, for example, the data collected in Christian E. Weller and Adam Hersh, "Free Markets and Poverty," *The American Prospect* (Winter 2002): A13–15.

94. See Laura Secor, "Mind the Gap," *Boston Globe*, January 5, 2003.

95. Jay Mazur, "Labor's New Internationalism," *Foreign Affairs* (January/February 2000): 80–81.

96. "Tropical Disease Drugs Withdrawn," *BBC News*, October 31, 2000.

97. John J. Meehan, Chairman of the Public Securities Association, "Globalization and Technology at Work in the Bond Markets" (speech given in Phoenix, AZ, March 1, 1997), online: <http://www.bondmarkets.com/news/Meehanspeech final.shtml>.

98. Newt Gingrich, interview with Danny Schechter at the 1998 World Economic Forum in Davos, Switzerland, <http://www.pbs.org/globalization/newt .html>.

99. See Barber, *Jihad vs. McWorld*, 77–87.

100. Friedman, *The Lexus and the Olive Tree*, 364.

101. Jagdish Bhagwati, *In Defense of Globalization* (New York: Oxford University Press, 2004), 30.

102. *NSSUS.*

103. Merrill Lynch Forum, "Economic Globalization and Culture: A Discussion with Dr. Francis Fukuyama," online: <http://www.ml.com/woml/forum/global2.html>.

104. William I. Robinson, *Promoting Polyarchy: Globalization, U.S. Intervention, and Hegemony* (Cambridge: Cambridge University Press, 1996), 56–62.

105. Friedman, *The Lexus and the Olive Tree*, 187.

106. George W. Bush, "Securing Freedom's Triumph," *New York Times*, September 11, 2002.

107. Transcript of George W. Bush's Inaugural Address, *New York Times*, January 20, 2005.

108. Bush, cited in David Stout, "Bush Calls for World Bank to Increase Grants," *New York Times*, July 17, 2001. Bush's "Three Pillar speech" is taken from a transcript of his address in London on Iraq and the Middle East, *New York Times*, November 19, 2003.

109. Richard Falk, "Will the Empire Be Fascist?" *The Transnational Foundation for Peace and Future Research Forum*, March 24, 2003, online: <http://www.transnational.org/forum/meet/2003/Falk_FascistEmpire.html>.

110. William H. Thornton, *New World Empire: Civil Islam, Terrorism, and the Making of Neoglobalism* (Lanham, MD: Rowman & Littlefield, 2005), 19.

111. Ryn, "The Ideology of American Empire," 384. In his article "Will the Empire Be Fascist?" Richard Falk, too, argues that the "American response to September 11 has greatly accelerated the drive for global dominance, although it has been masked beneath the banners of anti-terrorism."

112. Chalmers Johnson, *The Sorrows of Empire: Militarism, Secrecy, and the End of the Republic* (New York: Metropolitan Books, 2004), 24, 288.

113. Robert McFarlane and Michael Bleyzer, "Taking Iraq Private," *Wall Street Journal*, March 27, 2003.

114. Robert D. Kaplan, *Warrior Politcs: Why Leadership Demands a Pagan Ethos* (New York: Vintage, 2003).

115. Robert D. Kaplan, "Supremacy by Stealth," *Atlantic Monthly* (July/August 2003), <http://www.theatlantic.com/issues/2003/07/kaplan.htm>.

116. Kaplan, "Supremacy by Stealth."

117. Norman Podhoretz, *World War IV: The Long Struggle against Islamofascism* (New York: Doubleday, 2007).

118. Thomas P. M. Barnett, *The Pentagon's New Map: War and Peace in the Twenty-First Century* (New York: G. P. Putnam's Sons, 2004). The sequel to this

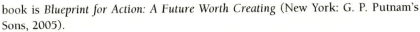

book is *Blueprint for Action: A Future Worth Creating* (New York: G. P. Putnam's Sons, 2005).

119. A milder version of this argument can be found in Walter Russell Mead's advocacy of an "American project—a grand strategic vision of what it is that the United States seeks to build in the World." See *Power, Terror, Peace, and War: America's Grand Strategy in a World of Risk* (New York: Knopf, 2004), 7.

120. Barnett, *The Pentagon's New Map*, 31–32, 294–302.

121. Barnett, *The Pentagon's New Map*, chapters 3 and 4.

122. Barnett, *Blueprint for Action*, xvii.

123. Barnett, *The Pentagon's New Map*, 245.

124. Robert D. Kaplan, "The Hard Edge of American Values," *Atlantic Monthly Online*, June 18, 2003, <http://www.theatlantic.com/unbound/interviews/int2003-06-18.htm>.

## CHAPTER 4: CHALLENGES FROM THE POLITICAL LEFT

1. Anthony Giddens, *Beyond Left and Right: The Future of Radical Politics* (Stanford, CA: Stanford University Press, 1994), 251.

2. Norberto Bobbio, *Left and Right: The Significance of a Political Distinction* (Chicago: University of Chicago Press, 1996), 60–71.

3. Bobbio, *Left and Right*, 90.

4. Alain Noel and Jean-Phillipe Therien, *Left and Right in Global Politics* (Cambridge: Cambridge University Press, 2008), esp. chapter 2.

5. Sidney Tarrow, *The New Transnational Activism* (Cambridge: Cambridge University Press, 2005), 40–60.

6. Subcomandante Marcos, "First Declaration of La Realidad," August 3, 1996, <http://www.apostate.com/politics/realidad2.html>.

7. Mary Kaldor, *Global Civil Society: An Answer to War* (Cambridge: Polity Press, 2003), 78. Other notable recent examples of this burgeoning literature on global civil society and transnational activism include, for example, Kevin McDonald, *Global Movements: Action and Culture* (Oxford: Blackwell, 2006); Donatella della Porta, Massimiliano Andretta, Lorenzo Mosca, and Herbert Reiter, *Globalization from Below: Transnational Activists and Protest Networks* (Minneapolis: University of Minnesota Press, 2006); and Donatella della Porta and Sidney Tarrow, eds., *Transnational Protest and Global Activism* (Lanham, MD: Rowman & Littlefield, 2005).

8. See Alexander Cockburn, Jeffrey St. Clair, and Allan Sekula, *Five Days That Shook the World: Seattle and Beyond* (London: Verso, 2000); Martin Khor, "Seattle Debacle: Revolt of the Developing Nations," in Danaher and Burbach, *Globalize This!* 48; and Mary Kaldor, "'Civilising' Globalisation? The Implications of the 'Battle in Seattle,'" *Millennium: Journal of International Studies* 29, no. 1 (2000):

105–15. For a useful collection of leftist positions taken by various antiglobalist groups, see Eddie Yuen, George Katsiaficas, and Daniel Burton Rose, eds., *The Battle of Seattle: The New Challenge to Capitalist Globalization* (New York: Soft Skull Press, 2002), and Robin Broad, ed., *Global Backlash: Citizen Initiatives for a Just World Economy* (Lanham, MD: Rowman & Littlefield, 2002).

9. Danaher and Burbach, *Globalize This!*, 24–25.

10. Cockburn et al., *Five Days That Shook the World*, 39, 101.

11. Danaher and Burbach, *Globalize This!* 23; Cockburn et al., *Five Days That Shook the World*, 51.

12. Cockburn et al., *Five Days That Shook the World*, 34.

13. Cockburn et al., *Five Days That Shook the World*, 51–52.

14. Cockburn et al., *Five Days That Shook the World*, 38. Jeffrey St. Clair asserts that at the very moment President Clinton was publicly expressing some sympathy with the demonstrators, his aides were ordering Seattle Mayor Shell to use all available force to clear the streets (see Cockburn et al., *Five Days That Shook the World*, 39).

15. Charlene Barshefsky, cited in Martin Khor, "Seattle Debacle: Revolt of the Developing Nations," in Danaher and Burbach, *Globalize This!* 51.

16. Cockburn et al., *Five Days That Shook the World*, 8.

17. See Mazur, "Labor's New Internationalism," 79–93. See also Dimitris Stevis and Terry Boswell, *Globalization and Labor: Democratizing Global Governance* (Lanham, MD: Rowman & Littlefield, 2007).

18. Cockburn et al., *Five Days That Shook the World*, 70–71.

19. Anthony Williams, cited in John Kifner and David E. Sanger, "Financial Leaders Meet as Protests Clog Washington," *New York Times*, April 17, 2000.

20. Desko Vladic, cited in Joseph Kahn, "Protesters Assemble, Hoping for a Rerun of Seattle's Show," *New York Times*, September 23, 2000.

21. Stefan Theil, "Taking It to the Streets," *Newsweek* (Atlantic edition), September 25, 2000, 40.

22. Theil, "Taking It to the Streets," 40.

23. Joseph Kahn, "Protests Diminish at Conference in Prague on Worldwide Aid," *New York Times*, September 28, 2000.

24. For a description of the demonstrations in Nice, see Suzanne Daley, "Europeans, and Protesters, Meet on the Riviera," *New York Times*, December 8, 2000.

25. "Police Quell Davos Protests," BBC News, January 28, 2001, online: <http://www.bbc.co.uk>; Onna Coray, "Swiss Police Catch Heat for Anti-Global Melee," *Chicago Tribune*, January 30, 2001.

26. David Greising, "Free Speech Not on Agenda of Global Leaders," *Chicago Tribune*, January 28, 2001.

27. Oona Coray, "Swiss Police Catch Heat for Anti-Global Melee."

28. Associated Press, "Police and Protesters Clash as Economic Summit Opens," *New York Times*, July 20, 2001; David E. Sanger and Alessandra Stanley,

"Skirmishes Mark Big Protest March at Talks in Italy," *New York Times*, July 22, 2001.

29. Walden Bello's report was made available on the website of *The Nation*, <http://www.thenation.com>.

30. Stefania Milan, "Globalization: Protests Return to Haunt Italy," *Inter Press Service*, March 11, 2004, online: <http://www.commondreams.org/headlines04/0311–01.htm>.

31. Melinda Henneberger, "Italians Hold Large Protest Rally after Parliament Clears Police," *New York Times*, September 23, 2001. For an excellent discussion of the significance of Genoa for the GJM, see Massimiliano Andretta, Donatella della Porta, Lorenzo Mosca, and Herbert Reiter, *No Global—New Global: Identitaet und Strategien der Antiglobalisierungsbewegung* (Frankfurt: Campus, 2002), esp. chapters 1–3.

32. Naomi Klein, "Signs of the Times," *The Nation*, October 22, 2001, 15–20.

33. Duncan Green and Matthew Griffith, "Globalization and Its Discontents," *International Affairs* 78 (2002): 66.

34. Dan Barry, "A Little Violence and Lots of Police Equal 150 Arrests Far from Forum," *New York Times*, February 4, 2002.

35. R. C. Longworth, "After the Mainstream Has Stolen Your Agenda," *Chicago Tribune*, February 4, 2002.

36. Stephen Labaton, "Many Thousands in Washington March in Support of Palestinians," *New York Times*, April 21, 2002.

37. Hugh Dellios, "Anti-WTO Protests Erupt," *Chicago Tribune*, September 11, 2003.

38. Elizabeth Becker, "African Nations Press for an End to Cotton Subsidies in the West," *New York Times*, September 12, 2003.

39. Elizabeth Becker, "Western Farmers Fear Third-World Challenge to Subsidies," *New York Times*, September 9, 2003.

40. Robert Zoellick, cited in Andrew Martin and Hugh Dellios, "WTO Talks Fail as Poor Nations Balk," *Chicago Tribune*, September 15, 2003.

41. David Greising and Andrew Martin, "U.S. to Pursue Regional, Individual Trade Talks," *Chicago Tribune*, September 15, 2003.

42. Jagdish Bhagwati, cited in William Greider, "The Real Cancún: WTO Heads Nowhere," *The Nation*, September 22, 2003.

43. Reuters, "Doha Round Trade Deal Still Possible, Bush Says," March 29, 2008, <http://www.nytimes.com>.

44. Ralph Nader, "Statement of Ralph Nader, Announcing His Candidacy for the Green Party's Nomination for President" (statement delivered February 21, 2000, Washington, DC), online: <http://www.votenader.org/press/000221/press-announce.html>.

45. Green Party Platform, as ratified at the National Convention, June 25, 2000, online: <http://www.gp.org>.

46. Ralph Nader, "Acceptance Statement for the Association of State Green Parties Nomination for President of the United States" (June 25, 2000, Denver, CO), online: <http://votenader.org/press/000625acceptance_speech.html>.

47. Time.com online interview with Patrick Buchanan and Ralph Nader, November 28, 1999, online: <http://www.time.com/community/transcripts/1999/112899buchanan-nader.html> .

48. Ralph Nader, "Global Trade Concentrates Power and Homogenizes the Globe," *Public Interest*, December 7, 1999, online: <http://www.issues2000.org/Ralph_Nader_Free ...Trade_&_Immigration.html>.

49. Ralph Nader, "Introduction," in *The WTO: Five Years of Reasons to Resist Corporate Globalization*, by Lori Wallach and Michelle Sforza (New York: Seven Stories Press, 1999), 7.

50. Nader, cited in Harold Meyerson, "Nader Speaks," *LA Weekly*, June 30–July 6, 2000, online: <http://www.laweekly.com/ink/00/32/cover-meyerson2.shtml>.

51. PBS interview with Ralph Nader, March 1998, online: <http://www.pbs.org/globalization/nader.html>.

52. Nader, "Acceptance Statement for the Association of State Green Parties Nomination for President of the United States."

53. See the 2000 UN Human Development Report and 1999 UN Human Development Report, online: <http://www.undp.org/hdr2000> and <http://www.undp.org/hdr1999>. See also Thomas W. Pogge, "The Moral Demands of Global Justice," *Dissent* (Fall 2000): 37–43.

54. Nader, "Introduction," in Wallach and Sforza, *The WTO*, 12.

55. Ralph Nader, "The Concord Principles: An Agenda for a New Initiatory Democracy," February 1, 1992, online: <http://petra.greens.org/~cls/nader/concord.html>.

56. Nader, "Acceptance Statement for the Association of State Green Parties Nomination for President of the United States."

57. Dennis Kucinich, 2004 Platform, <http://www.kucinich.us/issues/world_hunger.php>.

58. Dennis Kucinich, 2004 Platform, <http://www.kucinich.us/issues/departmentpeace.php>.

59. Candido Grzybowski, "Civil Societies Responses to Globalization," Rio de Janeiro, November 8, 1995, <http://www.corpwatch.org/trac/feature/planet/gr_twn.html>.

60. The two most accessible introductions to the WSF and its policy positions are José Correa Leite, *The World Social Forum: Strategies of Resistance* (Chicago: Haymarket Books, 2005), and Jackie Smith, Marina Karides, Marc Becker, Dorval Brunelle, Christopher Chase-Dunn, Donatella della Porta, Rosalba Icaza Garza, Jeffrey S. Juris, Lorenzo Mosca, Ellen Reese, Peter (Jay) Smith, and Rolando Vasquez, *Global Democracy and the World Social Forums* (Boulder, CO: Paradigm Publishers, 2008).

19. Patrick J. Buchanan, "Address to the Chicago Council on Foreign Relations," speech in Chicago, November 18, 1998, <http://www.chuckbaldwin live.com/read.freetrade.html>.

20. Buchanan, "Address to the Chicago Council on Foreign Relations."

21. Buchanan, "The Second Battle of NAFTA."

22. Patrick J. Buchanan, *Day of Reckoning: How Hubris, Ideology and Greed Are Tearing America Apart* (New York: Thomas Dunne Books, 2007), 1.

23. Buchanan, "The Second Battle of NAFTA," and "Subprime Nation," January 15, 2008, <http://buchanan.org/blog/2008/01/pjb-subprime-nation/>.

24. Patrick J. Buchanan, "The Global-Warming Hucksters," October 23, 2007, <http://buchanan.org/blog/2007/10/pjb-the-global-warming-hucksters>.

25. Patrick J. Buchanan, "The Decline of the Anglos," September 18, 2007, <http://buchanan.org/blog/2007/09/pjb-stopping-the-next-war-2/>.

26. Patrick Buchanan, press release, July 2, 1999, <http://www.issues2000. org/Pat_Buchanan_Free_Trade_&_Immigration.html>; Patrick J. Buchanan, *State of Emergency: The Third World Invasion and Conquest of America* (New York: Thomas Dunne Books, 2007).

27. Speech by Patrick Buchanan (May 28, 1999), <http://www.gopatgo2000 .com/000-immigration.html>.

28. Buchanan, "The Decline of the Anglos," and "The Way Our World Ends," May 2, 2008, <http://buchanan.org/blog/2008/05/pjb-the-way-our-world-ends/>.

29. Pat Robertson, *The New World Order* (Dallas: Word Publishing, 1991), 37. For a broader discussion of the political and ideological agenda of such groups, see Lane Crothers, *Rage on the Right: The American Militia Movement from Ruby Ridge to Homeland Security* (Lanham, MD: Rowman & Littlefield, 2003).

30. Peter King, quoted in Bill Carter and Jacques Steinberg, "Anchor-Advocate on Immigration Wins Viewers," *New York Times*, March 29, 2006.

31. David Leonhardt, "Truth, Fiction and Lou Dobbs," *New York Times*, May 30, 2007. Lou Dobbs's recent best sellers are *War on the Middle Class: How Government, Big Business, and Special Interest Groups Are Waging War on the American Dream and How to Fight Back* (New York: Penguin, 2007) and *Independents Day: Awakening the American Spirit* (New York: Viking, 2007).

32. James K. Glassman, "Two Faces of Lou Dobbs," *Capitalism Magazine*, March 4, 2004, online: <http://capmag.com>.

33. Selections from a transcript of the February 26, 2004, *Lou Dobbs Tonight Show*, online: <http://edition.cnn.com/CNN/Programs/lou.dobbs.tonight>.

34. Dobbs, cited in Matt Drudge, "CNN Dobbs on Hot Seat after Call for War on 'Islamists,'" *Drudge Report*, June 6, 2002, online: <http://www.drudgereport .com/lou.htm>.

35. Leonhardt, "Truth, Fiction and Lou Dobbs."

36. Minxin Pei, "The Paradoxes of American Nationalism," *Foreign Policy* (May/June 2003), online: <http://www.foreignpolicy.com>.

37. Buchanan, cited in Thomas Friedman, "America's Labor Pains," *New York Times*, May 9, 2000, online: <http://www.nytimes.com>; Leonhardt, "Truth, Fiction and Lou Dobbs."

38. See, for example, Mark P. Worrell, "The Veil of Peculiar Subjectivity: Buchananism and the New World Order," *Electronic Journal of Sociology* 4, no. 3 (1999), <http://www.sociology.org/content/vol004.003/buchanan.html>.

39. Worrell, "The Veil of Peculiar Subjectivity."

40. Patrick J. Buchanan, "Speech to the Daughters of the American Revolution" (Washington, DC, April 22, 1992), cited in Frederick W. Mayer, *Interpreting NAFTA: The Science and Art of Political Analysis* (New York: Columbia University Press, 1998), 232.

41. For more on the nature and role of the corporations mentioned, see <http://www.timex.com> and <http://kalashnikov.guns.ru>. See also Manfred B. Steger, *Globalization: A Very Short Introduction*, 2d ed. (Oxford: Oxford University Press, 2009).

42. See, for example, Mehdi Mozaffari, "What Is Islamism? History and Definition of a Concept," *Totalitarian Movements and Political Religions* 8, no. 1 (March 2007): 17–33; Greg Barton, *Jemaah Islamiyah: Radical Islamism in Indonesia* (Singapore: Ridge Books, 2005); Khaled Abou El Fadl, *The Great Theft: Wrestling Islam from the Extremists* (New York: HarperCollins, 2005); Olivier Roy, *Globalized Islam: The Search for a New Ummah* (New York: Columbia University Press, 2004); Azza Karam, ed., *Transnational Political Islam: Religion, Ideology and Power* (London: Pluto Press, 2004); Thomas W. Simons, *Islam in a Globalizing World* (Stanford, CA: Stanford University Press, 2003); Gilles Kepel, *The War for Muslim Minds* (Cambridge, MA: Belknap Press, 2004), and *Jihad: On the Trail of Political Islam* (London: I. B. Tauris, 2002); and Malise Ruthven, *A Fury for God: The Islamist Attack on America* (London: Granta Books, 2002).

43. Bruce Lawrence, "Introduction," in Osama bin Laden, *Messages to the World: The Statements of Osama Bin Laden*, edited by Bruce Lawrence and translated by James Howarth (London: Verso, 2005), xvii; xi. See also Bernard Lewis, "License to Kill," *Foreign Affairs* (November–December 1998).

44. Osama bin Laden, "Under Mullah Omar" (April 9, 2001), in Bin Laden, *Messages to the World*, 96, and "The Winds of Faith" (7 October 2001), 104–105.

45. Ayman al-Zawahiri, "Loyalty and Enmity" (n.d.), in Raymond Ibrahim, ed. and trans., *The Al Qaeda Reader* (New York: Broadway Books, 2007), 102.

46. Osama bin Laden, "From Somalia to Afghanistan" (March 1997), in *Messages to the World*, 50–51.

47. Osama bin Laden, "The Saudi Regime" (November 1996), in *Messages to the World*, 39.

48. Osama bin Laden, "The Invasion of Arabia" (c. 1995/1996), in *Messages to the World*, 15. See also Osama bin Laden, "The Betrayal of Palestine" (December 29, 1994), in *Messages to the World*, 3–14.

49. See, for example, bin Laden, "The Saudi Regime," 32–33.

50. Mohammed Bamyeh, "Global Order and the Historical Structures of *dar al-Islam*," in Manfred B. Steger, ed., *Rethinking Globalism* (Lanham, MD: Rowman & Littlefield, 2004), 225.

51. Bin Laden, "The Betrayal of Palestine," in *Messages to the World*, 9.

52. Osama bin Laden, "A Muslim Bomb" (December 1998), in bin Laden, *Messages to the World*, 88.

53. Sayyid Qutb, "War, Peace, and Islamic Jihad," in *Modernist and Fundamentalist Debates in Islam: A Reader*, edited by Mansoor Moaddel and Kamran Talattof (New York: Palgrave Macmillan, 2002), 240.

54. Mary R. Habeck, *Knowing the Enemy: Jihadist Ideology and the War on Terror* (New Haven, CT: Yale University Press, 2006), 62.

55. Osama bin Laden, "Terror for Terror" (21 October 2001), in bin Laden, *Messages to the World*, 119.

56. Ayman al-Zawahiri, "I Am among the Muslim Masses" (2006), in *The Al Qaeda Reader*, 227–28.

57. Roy, *Globalized Islam*, 19.

58. For an insightful analysis of the tribal, national, and global dimensions in bin Laden's discourse, see Denis McAuley, "The Ideology of Osama Bin Laden: Nation, Tribe and World Economy," *Journal of Political Ideologies* 10, no. 3 (October 2005): 269–87. For a brilliant discussion of globalizing dynamics involving tribal identities, see Paul James, *Globalism Nationalism Tribalism: Bringing the State Back In* (London: Sage, 2006).

59. Bin Laden, "A Muslim Bomb," in *Messages to the World*, 91.

60. Roy, *Globalized Islam*, chapter 7.

61. Osama bin Laden, "Moderate Islam Is a Prostration to the West" (2003), in Ibrahim, *The Al Qaeda Reader*, 22–62. For a readable overview of the history and meanings of jihad, see David Cook, *Understanding Jihad* (Berkeley: University of California Press, 2005).

62. Osama bin Laden, "Among a Band of Knights" (February 14, 2003), in bin Laden, *Messages to the World*, 202; "Resist the New Rome" (January 4, 2004), in *Messages to the World*, 218; and "A Muslim Bomb," in *Messages to the World*, 69.

63. Osama bin Laden, "The World Islamic Front" (February 23, 1998), in *Messages to the World*, 61; "To the Americans" (October 6, 2002), 166; "The World Islamic Front" (February 23, 1998), in *Messages to the World*, 61; "To the Americans" (October 6, 2002), 166.

64. See, for example, Bassam Tibi, "The Totalitarianism of Jihadist Islamism and Its Challenge to Europe and to Islam," *Totalitarian Movements and Political Religion* 8, no. 1 (March 2007): 35–54, and Hendrik Hansen and Peter Kainz, "Radical Islamism and Totalitarian Ideology: A Comparison of Sayyid Qutb's Islamism with Marxism and National Socialism," *Totalitarian Movements and Political Religion* 8, no. 1 (March 2007): 55–76.

65. Osama Bin Laden, "Depose the Tyrants" (December 16, 2004), in *Messages to the World*, 245–75; Ayman al-Zawahiri, "*Jihad*, Martyrdom, and the Killing of Innocents" (n.d.), in Ibrahim, *The Al Qaeda Reader*, 141–71.

66. Bin Laden, "A Muslim Bomb," 73, 87; and "The Winds of Faith," in *Messages to the World*, 105.

67. Bin Laden, "Moderate Islam Is a Prostration to the West," in Ibrahim, *The Al Qaeda Reader*, 51–52, 30–31.

68. Osama bin Laden, untitled transcript of the videotaped message (September 6, 2007), <http://www.msnbcmedia.msn.com/i/msnbc/sections/news/070907_bin_laden_transcript.pdf>.

69. Bin Laden, "To the Americans," 167–68, and "Resist the New Rome," in *Messages to the World*, 214.

70. Osama bin Laden, "Nineteen Students" (December 26, 2001), in *Messages to the World*, 150, and untitled transcript of a videotaped message to the American people (September 6, 2007).

71. Bin Laden, "Terror for Terror," in *Messages to the World*, 112.

72. Osama bin Laden, "The Towers of Lebanon" (October 29, 2004), in *Messages to the World*, 242.

73. Faisal Devji, "Osama Bin Laden's Message to the World," *Open Democracy* (December 21, 2005), 2. See also Faisal Devji, *Landscapes of Jihad: Militancy, Morality, Modernity* (Ithaca, NY: Cornell University Press, 2005), 144.

74. Bin Laden, untitled transcript of a videotaped message to the American people (September 6, 2007).

## CHAPTER 6: CONCLUSION

1. James H. Mittelman, "Ideologies and the Globalization Agenda," in Manfred B. Steger, ed., *Rethinking Globalism* (Lanham, MD: Rowman & Littlefield, 2004), 22.

2. Kofi Annan, address to the World Economic Forum in Davos, Switzerland, January 28, 2001, online: <http://www.un.org/News/dh/latest/address_2001.html>.

3. Robert B. Zoellick, "Catalyzing the Future: An Inclusive and Sustainable Globalization," remarks at the annual meeting of the Board of Governors of the World Bank Group, October 22, 2007, <http://web.worldbank.org/wbsite/external/news>, and "Inclusive Globalization," *2007 Annual Report of the United Nations Development Programme*, <http://www.undp.org/publications/annualreport2007/inclusive_globalization.shtml>.

4. Klaus Schwab, "Global Corporate Citizenship: Working with Governments and Civil Society," *Foreign Affairs* (January/February 2008), <http://www.foreignaffairs.org/20080101faessay87108/klaus-schwab/global-corporate-citizenship>.

5. Karl Polanyi, *The Great Transformation: The Political and Economic Origins of Our Time* (1944; reprint, Boston: Beacon Press, 1957), 132.

6. For a concise explication of Polanyi's ethical theory, see Gregory Baum, *Karl Polanyi on Ethics and Economics* (Montreal: McGill-Queen's University Press, 1996).

7. Polanyi, *The Great Transformation*, 237.

8. Jan Nederveen Pieterse, *Globalization or Empire?* (New York: Routledge, 2004), 45.

9. Robert Kagan, *The Return of History and the End of Dreams* (New York: Knopf, 2008).

10. Fareed Zakaria, *The Post-American World* (New York: W. W. Norton, 2008).

11. For a detailed blueprint of these new institutions and their functions, see George Monbiot, *Manifesto for a New World Order* (New York: New Press, 2006). For Monbiot's ecological vision, see *Heat: How to Stop the Planet from Burning* (Boston: South End Press, 2007).

12. See, for example, Dalai Lama, *Ethics for the New Millennium* (New York: Riverhead Books, 1999), and Pope John Paul II, *Crossing the Threshold of Hope*, edited by Vittorio Messori (New York: Knopf, 1994).

13. Hans Küng, *A Global Ethic for Global Politics and Economics* (New York: Oxford University Press, 1998), 111.

14. Dalai Lama, *Ethics for the New Millennium*, 197.

# SELECTED BIBLIOGRAPHY

Albertazzi, Daniele, and Duncan McDonnell. *Twenty-First-Century Populism: The Spectre of Western European Democracy.* Basingstoke: Palgrave Macmillan, 2007.

Albrow, Martin. *Globalization.* London: Routledge, 1995.

————. *The Global Age: State and Society beyond Modernity.* Cambridge: Polity Press, 1996.

Altman, Dennis. *Global Sex.* Chicago: University of Chicago Press, 2001.

Amen, Mark, Kevin Archer, and Martin Bosman, eds. *Relocating Global Cities: From the Center to the Margins.* Lanham, MD: Rowman & Littlefield, 2006.

Amin, Samir. *Capitalism in the Age of Globalization: The Management of Contemporary Society.* London: Zed Books, 1997.

Anderson, Sarah, ed. *Views from the South: The Effects of Globalization and the WTO on Third World Countries.* Chicago: Food First Books, 2000.

Anderson, Sarah, and John Cavanagh, with Thea Lee. *Field Guide to the Global Economy.* New York: New Press, 2000.

Andretta, Massimiliano, Donatella della Porta, Lorenzo Mosca, and Herbert Reiter. *No Global—New Global: Identitaet und Strategien der Antiglobalisierungsbewegung.* Frankfurt: Campus, 2002.

Appadurai, Arjun. *Modernity at Large: Cultural Dimensions of Globalization.* Minneapolis: University of Minnesota Press, 1996.

Appelbaum, Richard P., and William I. Robinson, eds. *Critical Globalization Studies.* New York: Routledge, 2005.

Arendt, Hannah. *On Violence.* New York: Harcourt Brace Jovanovich, 1970.

Axtmann, Roland, ed. *Globalization in Europe: Theoretical and Empirical Investigations.* Washington, DC: Pinter, 1998.

Bamyeh, Mohammed A. *The Ends of Globalization.* Minneapolis: University of Minnesota Press, 2000.

Barber, Benjamin R. *Jihad vs. McWorld.* New York: Ballantine Books, 1996.

———. *Consumed: How Markets Corrupt Children, Infantilize Adults, and Swallow Citizens Whole.* New York: W. W. Norton, 2008.

Barker, Chris. *Television, Globalization and Cultural Identities.* Buckingham: Open University Press, 1999.

Barnet, Richard J., and John Cavanagh. *Global Dreams: Imperial Corporations and the New World Order.* New York: Simon & Schuster, 1994.

Barnett, Thomas P. M. *The Pentagon's New Map: War and Peace in the Twenty-First Century.* New York: G. P. Putnam's Sons, 2004.

———. *Blueprint for Action: A Future Worth Creating.* New York: G. P. Putnam's Sons, 2005.

Barton, Greg. *Jemaah Islamiyah: Radical Islamism in Indonesia.* Singapore: Ridge Books, 2005.

Bauman, Zygmunt. *Globalization: The Human Consequences.* New York: Columbia University Press, 1998.

Beck, Ulrich. *What Is Globalization?* Cambridge: Polity Press, 2000.

Bell, Daniel. *The End of Ideology: On the Exhaustion of Political Ideas in the Fifties.* Glencoe, IL: Free Press, 1960.

Berger, Peter L., and Samuel P. Huntington, eds. *Many Globalizations: Cultural Diversity in the Contemporary World.* Oxford: Oxford University Press, 2002.

Berlet, Chip, and Matthew N. Lyons. *Right-Wing Populism in America: Too Close for Comfort.* New York: Guilford Press, 2000.

Betz, Hans-Georg, and Stefan Immerfall, eds. *The New Politics of the Right: Neo-Populist Parties and Movements in Established Democracies.* New York: St. Martin's Press, 1998.

Bhagwati, Jagdish. *The Wind of the Hundred Days: How Washington Mismanaged Globalization.* Cambridge, MA: MIT Press, 2000.

———. *In Defense of Globalization: With a New Afterword.* Oxford: Oxford University Press, 2007.

Bin Laden, Osama. *Messages to the World: The Statements of Osama Bin Laden.* Edited by Bruce Lawrence and translated by James Howarth. London: Verso, 2005.

Black, Jan Knippers. *Inequity in the Global Village: Recycled Rhetoric and Disposable People.* West Hartford, CT: Kumarian Press, 1999.

Blommaert, Jan. *Discourse: A Critical Introduction.* Cambridge: Cambridge University Press, 2005.

Bobbio, Norberto. *Left and Right: The Significance of a Political Distinction.* Chicago: University of Chicago Press, 1996.

Bodansky, Yossef. *Bin Laden: The Man Who Declared War on America.* New York: Forum/Random House, 2001.

Boggs, Carl, ed. *The End of Politics: Corporate Power and the Decline of the Public Sphere.* New York: Guilford Press, 2000.

———. *Masters of War: Militarism and Blowback in the Era of American Empire.* New York: Routledge, 2003.

———. *The New Militarism: U.S. Empire and Endless War.* Lanham, MD: Rowman & Littlefield, 2004.

Bourdieu, Pierre. *Acts of Resistance: Against the Tyranny of the Market.* New York: New Press, 1998.

Boyer, Robert, and Daniel Drache, eds. *States against Markets: The Limits of Globalisation.* London: Routledge, 1996.

Brecher, Jeremy, and Tim Costello. *Global Village or Global Pillage? Economic Reconstruction from the Bottom Up.* 2d ed. Cambridge, MA: South End Press, 1998.

Brecher, Jeremy, Tim Costello, and Brendan Smith. *Globalization from Below: The Power of Solidarity.* Cambridge, MA: South End Press, 2000.

Brenner, Neil, ed. *The Global Cities Reader.* London: Routledge, 2006.

Broad, Robin, ed. *Global Backlash: Citizen Initiatives for a Just World Economy.* Lanham, MD: Rowman & Littlefield, 2002.

Bronner, Stephen Eric. *Of Critical Theory and Its Theorists.* Malden, MA: Blackwell, 1994.

Broswimmer, Franz J. *Ecocide: A History of Mass Extinction of Species.* London: Pluto Press, 2002.

Bryan, Lowell, and Diana Farrell. *Market Unbound: Unleashing Global Capitalism.* New York: Wiley, 1996.

Brysk, Alison, ed. *Globalization and Human Rights.* Berkeley: University of California Press, 2002.

Buchanan, Patrick J. *The Great Betrayal: How American Sovereignty and Social Justice Are Being Sacrificed to the Gods of the Global Economy.* Boston: Little, Brown, 1998.

———. *A Republic, Not an Empire: Reclaiming America's Destiny.* Washington, DC: Regnery Publishing, 1999.

———. *State of Emergency: The Third World Invasion and Conquest of America.* New York: Thomas Dunne Books, 2006.

———. *Day of Reckoning: How Hubris, Ideology and Greed Are Tearing America Apart.* New York: Thomas Dunne Books, 2007.

Buelens, Frans. *Globalisation and the Nation-State.* Northampton, MA: Edward Elgar Publishing, 2000.

Burbach, Roger. *Globalization and Postmodern Politics: From Zapatistas to High-Tech Robber Barons.* London: Pluto Press, 2001.

Burbach, Roger, Orlando Nunez, and Boris Kagarlitsky. *Globalization and Its Discontents: The Rise of Postmodern Socialisms.* London: Pluto Press, 1997.

Burtless, Gary, Robert Z. Lawrence, Robert E. Litan, and Robert J. Shapiro. *Globaphobia: Confronting Fears about Open Trade.* Washington, DC: Brookings Institution Press, 1998.

Cable, Vincent. *Globalization and Global Governance*. London: Royal Institute of International Affairs, 1999.

Canovan, Margaret. *Populism*. New York: Harcourt Brace Jovanovich, 1981.

Carnoy, Martin, Manuel Castells, and Stephen S. Cohen., eds. *The Global Economy in the Information Age*. University Park: Pennsylvania State University Press, 1993.

Carroll, William, Radhika Desai, and Warren Magnusson. *Globalization, Social Justice and Social Movements: A Reader*. Victoria, ON: University of Victoria, 1996.

Castells, Manuel. *The Information Age: Economy, Society and Culture*. 3 vols. Oxford: Blackwell, 1996–1998.

Chanda, Nayan. *Bound Together: How Traders, Preachers, Adventurers, and Warriors Shaped Globalization*. New Haven, CT: Yale University Press, 2007.

Chase-Dunn, Christopher. *Global Formation: Structures of the World Economy*. Lanham, MD: Rowman & Littlefield, 1998.

Chomsky, Noam. *Profit over People: Neoliberalism and Global Order*. New York: Seven Stories Press, 1999.

Chua, Amy. *World on Fire: How Exporting Free Market Democracy Breeds Ethnic Hatred and Global Instability*. New York: Doubleday, 2003.

Clark, Ian. *Globalization and International Relations Theory*. Oxford: Oxford University Press, 1999.

Cockburn, Alexander, Jeffrey St. Clair, and Allan Sekula. *Five Days That Shook the World: Seattle and Beyond*. London: Verso, 2000.

Cohen, Daniel. *Globalization and Its Enemies*. Cambridge, MA: MIT Press, 2006.

Cohen, Edward S. *The Politics of Globalization in the United States*. Washington, DC: Georgetown University Press, 2001.

Cohn, Theodore H. *Global Political Economy: Theory and Practice*. New York: Longman, 2000.

Cook, David. *Understanding Jihad*. Berkeley: University of California Press, 2005.

Cox, K. R., ed. *Spaces of Globalization: Reasserting the Power of the Local*. New York: Guilford Press, 1997.

Cox, Robert W. *Production, Power, and World Order: Social Forces in the Making of History*. New York: Columbia University Press, 1987.

Crothers, Lane. *Rage on the Right: The American Militia Movement from Ruby Ridge to Homeland Security*. Lanham, MD: Rowman & Littlefield, 2003.

———. *Globalization and American Popular Culture*. Lanham, MD: Rowman & Littlefield, 2006.

Cvetkovich, Ann, and Douglas Kellner. *Articulating the Global and the Local: Globalization and Cultural Studies*. Boulder, CO: Westview Press, 1996.

Danaher, Kevin, and Roger Burbach, eds. *Globalize This! The Battle against the World Trade Organization and Corporate Rule*. Monroe, ME: Common Courage Press, 2000.

———. *Democratizing the Global Economy: The Battle Against the World Bank and the IMF.* Monroe, ME: Common Courage Press, 2001.

Della Porta, Donatella, Massimiliano Andretta, Lorenzo Mosca, and Herbert Reiter. *Globalization from Below: Transnational Activists and Protest Networks.* Minneapolis: University of Minnesota Press, 2006.

Della Porta, Donatella, and Sidney Tarrow, eds. *Transnational Protest and Global Activism.* Lanham, MD: Rowman & Littlefield, 2005.

DeMartino, George F. *Global Economy, Global Justice: Theoretical Objections and Policy Alternatives to Neoliberalism.* London: Routledge, 2000.

Derber, Charles. *Corporation Nation.* New York: St. Martin's Press, 1998.

Devji, Faisal. *Landscapes of Jihad: Militancy, Morality, Modernity.* Ithaca, NY: Cornell University Press, 2005.

Dirlif, Arif. *Postcolonial Aura: Third World Criticism in the Age of Global Capitalism.* Boulder, CO: Westview Press, 1997.

Dobbs, Lou. *Independents Day: Awakening the American Spirit.* New York: Viking, 2007.

———. *War on the Middle Class: How Government, Big Business, and Special Interest Groups Are Waging War on the American Dream and How to Fight Back.* New York: Penguin, 2007.

Doremus, Paul, William W. Keller, Louis W. Pauly, and Simon Reich. *The Myth of the Global Corporation.* Princeton, NJ: Princeton University Press, 1998.

Dunkerley, David, and John Beynon. *The Globalisation Reader.* London: Athlone, 1999.

Eagleton, Terry. *Ideology: An Introduction.* London: Verso, 1991.

El Fadl, Khaled Abou. *The Great Theft: Wrestling Islam from the Extremists.* New York: HarperCollins, 2005.

Eschle, Catherine. *Feminism, Social Movements, and the Globalization of Democracy.* Boulder, CO: Westview Press, 2001.

Fairclough, Norman. *Analyzing Discourse: Textual Analysis for Social Research.* New York: Routledge, 2003.

Falk, Richard. *Predatory Globalization: A Critique.* Cambridge: Polity Press, 1999.

———. *Human Rights Horizons: The Pursuit of Justice in a Globalizing World.* New York: Routledge, 2000.

———. *The Great Terror War.* New York: Olive Branch Press, 2003.

Featherstone, Mike. *Consumer Culture and Postmodernism.* London: Sage, 1991.

———. *Undoing Culture: Globalization, Postmodernism and Identity.* London: Sage, 1995.

———, ed. *Global Culture.* London: Sage, 1990.

Featherstone, Mike, Scott Lash, and Roland Robertson, eds. *Global Modernities.* London: Sage, 1995.

Feffer, John, ed. *Power Trip: U.S. Unilateralism and Global Strategy after September 11.* New York: Seven Stories Press, 2003.

Ferleger, Lou, and Jay Mandle. *Dimensions of Globalization.* Thousand Oaks, CA: Sage, 2000.

Fishlow, Albert, and Karen Parker, eds. *Growing Apart: The Causes and Consequences of Global Wage Inequality.* New York: Council of Foreign Relations Press, 1999.

Frank, Andre Gunder. *ReORIENT: Global Economy in the Asian Age.* Berkeley: University of California Press, 1998.

Frank, Thomas. *One Market under God: Extreme Capitalism, Market Populism, and the End of Economic Democracy.* New York: Doubleday, 2000.

Freeden, Michael. *Ideologies and Political Theory: A Conceptual Approach.* Oxford: Clarendon Press, 1996.

———. *Ideology: A Very Short Introduction.* Oxford: Oxford University Press, 2003.

French, Hilary. *Vanishing Borders: Protecting the Planet in the Age of Globalization.* New York: W. W. Norton, 2000.

Frieden, Jeffry. *Global Capitalism: Its Fall and Rise in the Twentieth Century.* New York: W. W. Norton, 2007.

Friedman, Milton. *Capitalism and Freedom.* Chicago: University of Chicago Press, 1962.

Friedman, Thomas L. *The Lexus and the Olive Tree: Understanding Globalization.* New York: Farrar, Straus & Giroux, 1999.

———. *Longitudes and Attitudes: The World in the Age of Terrorism.* New York: Anchor Books, 2003.

———. *The World Is Flat 3.0: A Brief History of the Twenty-First Century.* New York: Picador, 2007.

Fukuyama, Francis. *The End of History and the Last Man.* New York: Free Press, 1992.

———. *The Great Disruption: Human Nature and the Reconstitution of Social Order.* New York: Free Press, 1999.

Gardels, Nathan, ed. *The Changing Global Order.* London: Blackwell, 1997.

George, Susan. *Another World Is Possible, If . . .* London: Verso, 2004.

Gereffi, Gary, and Miguel Korzeniewicz, eds. *Commodity Chains and Global Capitalism.* Westport, CT: Greenwood Press, 1993.

Germain, Randall D. *Globalization and Its Critics: Perspectives from Political Economy.* New York: St. Martin's Press, 2000.

Giddens, Anthony. *The Consequences of Modernity.* Stanford, CA: Stanford University Press, 1990.

———. *Beyond Left and Right: The Future of Radical Politics.* Stanford, CA: Stanford University Press, 1994.

———. *Runaway World.* London: Routledge, 2000.

Gills, Barry K., ed. *Globalization and the Politics of Resistance.* New York: St. Martin's Press, 2000.

Gilpin, Robert. *The Challenge of Global Capitalism: The World Economy in the 21st Century*. Princeton, NJ: Princeton University Press, 2000.

Gore, Al. *An Inconvenient Truth*. New York: Rodale Books, 2006.

Gott, Richard. *In the Shadow of the Liberator: Hugo Chávez and the Transformation of Venezuela*. London: Verso, 2000.

Gowan, Peter. *The Global Gamble: Washington's Faustian Bid for World Dominance*. London: Verso, 1999.

Gramsci, Antonio. *Selections from Prison Notebooks*. New York: International Publishers, 1971.

Gray, John. *False Dawn: The Delusions of Global Capitalism*. New York: New Press, 1998.

Grefe, Christiane, Mathias Greffrath, and Harald Schumann. *ATTAC: Was wollen die Globalisierungskritiker?* Hamburg: Rowohlt, 2002.

Greider, William. *One World, Ready or Not: The Manic Logic of Global Capitalism*. New York: Simon & Schuster, 1997.

Griffin, David Ray, and Peter Dale Scott, eds. *9/11 and American Empire: Intellectuals Speak Out*. New York: Olive Branch Press, 2006.

Gunn, Geoffrey C. *First Globalizations: The Eurasian Exchange 1500–1800*. Lanham, MD: Rowman & Littlefield, 2003.

Habeck, Mary R. *Knowing the Enemy: Jihadist Ideology and the War on Terror*. New Haven, CT: Yale University Press, 2006.

Hall, Rodney Bruce, and Thomas J. Biersteker, eds. *The Emergence of Private Authority in Global Governance*. Cambridge: Cambridge University Press, 2002.

Hannerz, Ulf. *Cultural Complexity: Studies in the Social Organization of Meaning*. New York: Columbia University Press, 1992.

———. *Transnational Connections: Cultures, People, Places*. London: Routledge, 1996.

Hardt, Michael, and Antonio Negri. *Empire*. Cambridge, MA: Harvard University Press, 2000.

Hart, Jeffrey A., and Aseem Prakash. *Coping with Globalization*. London: Routledge, 2000.

———. *Responding to Globalization*. London: Routledge, 2000.

Harvey, David. *The Condition of Postmodernity*. Oxford: Blackwell, 1989.

———. *The New Imperialism*. Oxford: Oxford University Press, 2003.

———. *A Brief History of Neoliberalism*. New York: Oxford University Press, 2007.

Hayek, Friedrich. *Law, Legislation, and Liberty*. 3 vols. London: Routledge & Kegan Paul, 1979.

Held, David. *Democracy and the Global Order*. Stanford, CA: Stanford University Press, 1995.

———. *Models of Democracy*. 3d ed. Stanford, CA: Stanford University Press, 2006.

Held, David, and Anthony McGrew. *The Global Transformations Reader: An Introduction to the Globalization Debate*. Cambridge: Polity Press, 2000.

———. *Globalization/Antiglobalization*. Oxford: Polity Press, 2002.

Held, David, Anthony McGrew, David Goldblatt, and Jonathan Perraton. *Global Transformations: Politics, Economics, and Culture*. Stanford, CA: Stanford University Press, 1999.

Helleiner, Eric. *States and the Reemergence of Global Finance*. Ithaca, NY: Cornell University Press, 1994.

Henderson, Hazel. *Beyond Globalization: Shaping a Sustainable Global Economy*. West Hartford, CT: Kumarian Press, 1999.

Herman, Edward S., and Robert W. McChesney. *The Global Media: The New Missionaries of Corporate Capitalism*. London: Cassell, 1997.

Hirst, Paul, and Graham Thompson. *Globalization in Question: The International Economy and the Possibilities of Governance*. 2d ed. Cambridge: Polity Press, 1999.

Hodges, Michael R., John J. Kirton, and Joseph P. Daniels, eds. *The G8's Role in the New Millennium*. Aldershot: Ashgate, 1999.

Holton, Robert J. *Globalization and the Nation-State*. New York: St. Martin's Press, 1998.

Hovden, Eivind, and Edward Keene, eds. *The Globalization of Liberalism*. New York: Palgrave, 2002.

Huntington, Samuel P. *The Clash of Civilizations: Remaking of World Order*. New York: Touchstone, 1997.

Hurrell, Andrew, and Ngaire Woods, eds. *Inequality, Globalization, and World Politics*. Oxford: Oxford University Press, 1999.

Hutton, Will, and Anthony Giddens, eds. *Global Capitalism*. New York: Free Press, 2000.

Ibrahim, Raymond, ed. and trans. *The Al Qaeda Reader*. New York: Broadway Books, 2007.

James, Paul. *Globalism Nationalism Tribalism: Bringing the State Back In*. London: Sage, 2006.

Jameson, Fredric, and Masao Miyoshi, eds. *The Cultures of Globalization*. Durham, NC: Duke University Press, 1998.

Jha, Prem Shankar. *The Twilight of the Nation-State: Globalisation, Chaos and War*. London: Pluto Press, 2006.

Johnson, Chalmers. *The Sorrows of Empire: Militarism, Secrecy, and the End of the Republic*. New York: Metropolitan Books, 2004.

———. *Nemesis: The Last Days of the American Republic*. New York: Holt, 2008.

Juergensmeyer, Mark. *Terror in the Mind of God: The Global Rise of Religious Violence*. 3d ed. Berkeley: University of California Press, 2003.

———. *Global Revolt: Religious Challenges to the Secular State, from Christian Militias to al Qaeda*. Berkeley: University of California Press, 2008.

Kagan, Robert. *The Return of History and the End of Dreams*. New York: Knopf, 2008.

Kagarlitsky, Boris. *The Twilight of Globalization: Property, State and Capitalism.* London: Pluto Press, 2000.

Kalb, Don, Marco van der Land, Richard Staring, Bart van Steenbergen, and Nico Wilterding, eds. *The Ends of Globalization: Bringing Society Back In.* Lanham, MD: Rowman & Littlefield, 2000.

Kaplan, Robert D. *Warrior Politcs: Why Leadership Demands a Pagan Ethos.* New York: Vintage, 2003.

Kapstein, Ethan B. *Sharing the Wealth: Workers and the World Economy.* New York: W. W. Norton, 1999.

Karam, Azzam, ed. *Transnational Political Islam: Religion, Ideology and Power.* London: Pluto Press, 2004.

Karliner, Joshua. *The Corporate Planet: Ecology and Politics in the Age of Globalization.* San Francisco: Sierra Club Books, 1997.

Kazin, Michael. *The Populist Persuasion: An American History.* Rev. ed. Ithaca, NY: Cornell University Press, 1998.

Keane, John. *Global Civil Society?* Cambridge: Cambridge University Press, 2003.

Kelly, Rita Mae, Jane H. Bayes, Mary E. Hawkesworth, and Brigitte Young, eds. *Gender, Globalization, and Democratization.* Lanham, MD: Rowman & Littlefield, 2001.

Keohane, Robert O. *After Hegemony.* Princeton, NJ: Princeton University Press, 1984.

Kepel, Gilles. *Jihad: On the Trail of Political Islam.* London: I. B. Tauris, 2002.

———. *The War for Muslim Minds.* Cambridge, MA: Belknap Press, 2004.

Klak, Thomas. *Globalization and Neoliberalism: The Caribbean Context.* Lanham, MD: Rowman & Littlefield, 1998.

Klein, Naomi. *Fences and Windows: Dispatches from the Frontline of the Globalization Debate.* New York: Picador, 2002.

Kornprobst, Markus, Vincent Pouliot, Nisha Shah, and Reuben Zaiotti, eds. *Metaphors of Globalization: Mirrors, Magicians, and Mutinies.* Houndsmill: Palgrave Macmillan, 2008.

Korten, David C. *The Post-Corporate World.* West Hartford, CT: Kumarian Press, 1999.

———. *When Corporations Rule the World.* 2nd ed. West Hartford, CT: Kumarian Press, 2001.

Kozloff, Nikolas. *Hugo Chavez: Oil, Politics, and the Challenge to the US.* Basingstoke: Palgrave Macmillan, 2007.

Krugman, Paul. *The Accidental Theorist.* New York: W. W. Norton, 1998.

Küng, Hans. *A Global Ethic for Global Politics and Economics.* New York: Oxford University Press, 1998.

Laclau, Ernesto. *On Populist Reason.* London: Verso, 2006.

Laclau, Ernesto, and Chantal Mouffe. *Hegemony and Socialist Practice: Towards a Radical Democratic Politics.* London: Verso, 1985.

LaFeber, Walter. *Michael Jordan and Global Capitalism*. New York: W. W. Norton, 1999.

Langhorne, Richard. *The Coming of Globalization: Its Evolution and Contemporary Consequences*. New York: Palgrave, 2001.

Latouche, Serge. *The Westernization of the World*. Cambridge: Polity Press, 1996.

Lechner, Frank J., and John Boli, eds. *The Globalization Reader*. 2d ed. Oxford: Blackwell, 2007.

Leggewiese, Claus. *Die Globalisierung und ihre Gegner*. Munich: Beck, 2003.

Leite, José Correa. *The World Social Forum: Strategies of Resistance*. Chicago: Haymarket Books, 2005.

Lipietz, Alain. *Towards a New Economic Order*. Oxford: Oxford University Press, 1993.

Lord, Carnes. *Losing Hearts and Minds? Public Diplomacy and Strategic Influence in the Age of Terror*. Westport, CT: Praeger, 2006.

Lukacs, John. *Democracy and Populism: Fear and Hatred*. New Haven, CT: Yale University Press, 2005.

Luttwak, Edward. *Turbo-Capitalism: Winners and Losers in the Global Economy*. New York: HarperCollins, 1999.

Mander, Jerry, and Edward Goldsmith, eds. *The Case against the Global Economy*. New York: Random House (Sierra Club), 1999.

Mann, Michael. *Incoherent Empire*. London: Verso, 2003.

Mannheim, Karl. *Ideology and Utopia: An Introduction to the Sociology of Knowledge*. 1936. Reprint, London: Routledge, 1991.

Marcuse, Peter, and Ronald van Kempen. *Globalizing Cities: A New Spatial Order?* Malden, MA: Blackwell, 2000.

Marling, William H. *How "American" Is Globalization?* Baltimore: Johns Hopkins University Press, 2006.

Mayer, Frederick W. *Interpreting NAFTA: The Science and Art of Political Analysis*. New York: Columbia University Press, 1998.

Mazzoleni, Gianpietro, Julianne Stewart, and Bruce Horsfield, eds. *The Media and Neo-Populism: A Contemporary Comparative Analysis*. Westport, CT: Praeger, 2003.

McBride, Stephen Kenneth, and John Richard Wiseman. *Globalization and Its Discontents*. New York: St. Martin's Press, 2000.

McDonald, Kevin. *Global Movements: Action and Culture*. Oxford: Blackwell, 2006.

McLellan, David. *Ideology*. Milton Keynes: Open University Press, 1986.

McNeill, J. R. *Something New under the Sun: An Environmental History of the Twentieth-Century World*. New York: W. W. Norton, 2000.

Mead, Walter Russell. *Power, Terror, Peace, and War: America's Grand Strategy in a World of Risk*. New York: Knopf, 2004.

Mendieta, Eduardo. *Global Fragments: Latinamericanisms, Globalizations, and Critical Theory*. Albany: State University of New York Press, 2007.

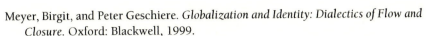

Meyer, Birgit, and Peter Geschiere. *Globalization and Identity: Dialectics of Flow and Closure*. Oxford: Blackwell, 1999.

Micklethwait, John, and Adrian Woolridge. *A Future Perfect: The Challenge and Hidden Promise of Globalization*. New York: Crown Publishers, 2000.

Mishra, Ramesh. *Globalization and the Welfare State*. Cheltenham: Elgar, 1999.

Mittelman, James H., ed. *Globalization: Critical Reflections*. Boulder, CO: Lynne Rienner, 1996.

———. *The Globalization Syndrome: Transformation and Resistance*. Princeton, NJ: Princeton University Press, 2000.

———. *Whither Globalization: The Vortex of Knowledge and Ideology*. New York: Routledge, 2005.

Moaddel, Mansoor, and Kamran Talattof, eds. *Modernist and Fundamentalist Debates in Islam: A Reader*. New York: Palgrave Macmillan, 2002.

Mokhiber, Russell, and Robert Weissman. *Global Predators: The Hunt for Mega-Profits and the Attack on Democracy*. Monroe, ME: Common Courage Press, 1999.

Monbiot, George. *Manifesto for a New World Order*. New York: New Press, 2006.

———. *Heat: How to Stop the Planet from Burning*. Boston: South End Press, 2007.

Mooney, Harold A. *The Globalization of Ecological Thought*. Oldendorf, Germany: Ecology Institute, 1998.

Mosler, David, and Robert Catley. *Global America: Imposing Liberalism on a Recalcitrant World*. Westport, CT: Praeger, 2000.

Munck, Ronaldo, and Peter Waterman, eds. *Labour Worldwide in the Era of Globalisation: Alternative Union Models in the New World Order*. New York: St. Martin's Press, 1999.

Munkler, Herfried. *Empires: The Logic of World Domination from Ancient Rome to the United States*. Cambridge: Polity Press, 2007.

Nash, Kate. *Contemporary Political Sociology: Globalization, Politics, and Power*. Malden, MA: Blackwell, 2000.

Nassar, Jamal. *Globalization and Terrorism: The Migration of Dreams and Nightmares*. Lanham, MD: Rowman & Littlefield, 2004.

Nederveen Pieterse, Jan, ed. *Global Futures: Shaping Globalization*. London: Zed Books, 2000.

———. *Globalization and Culture: Global Melange*. Lanham, MD: Rowman & Littlefield, 2003.

———. *Globalization or Empire?* New York: Routledge, 2004.

Noel, Alain, and Jean-Phillipe Therien. *Left and Right in Global Politics*. Cambridge: Cambridge University Press, 2008.

Nye, Joseph. *The Paradox of American Power*. Oxford: Oxford University Press, 2002.

———. *Soft Power: The Means to Success in World Politics*. New York: Public Affairs, 2005.

Offe, Claus. *Modernity and the State: East, West*. Cambridge: Polity Press, 1996.

Ohmae, Kenichi. *The Borderless World: Power and Strategy in the Interlinked World Economy*. New York: Harper Business, 1990.

——. *The End of the Nation-State: The Rise of Regional Economies*. New York: Free Press, 1995.

——. *Next Global Stage: Challenges and Opportunities in Our Borderless World*. Philadelphia: Wharton School Publishing, 2005.

O'Meara, Patrick, Howard M. Mehlinger, and Matthew Krain, eds. *Globalization and the Challenges of a New Century: A Reader*. Bloomington: Indiana University Press, 2000.

O'Rourke, Kevin H., and Jeffrey G. Williamson. *Globalization and History: The Evolution of a Nineteenth-Century Atlantic Economy*. Cambridge, MA: MIT Press, 1999.

Panitch, Leo, and Colin Leys, eds. *Global Capitalism versus Democracy: The Socialist Register 1999*. New York: Monthly Review Press, 1999.

Panizza, Francisco, ed. *Populism and the Mirror of Democracy*. London: Verso, 2005.

Patomaki, Heikki, and Teivo Teivanen. *A Possible World: Democratic Transformations of Global Institutions*. London: Zed Books, 2004.

Petras, James. *The Left Strikes Back: Class Conflict in the Age of Neoliberalism*. Boulder, CO: Westview Press, 1998.

Philander, S. George, ed. *Encyclopedia of Global Warming and Climate Change*. London: Sage, 2008.

Podhoretz, Norman. *World War IV: The Long Struggle against Islamofascism*. New York: Doubleday, 2007.

Polyani, Karl. *The Great Transformation: The Political and Economic Origins of Our Time*. 1944. Reprint, Boston: Beacon Press, 1957.

Rajaee, Farhang. *Globalization on Trial: The Human Condition and the Information Civilization*. West Hartford, CT: Kumarian Press, 2000.

Rangan, Subramanian, and Robert Z. Lawrence. *A Prism on Globalization: Corporate Responses to the Dollar*. Washington, DC: Brookings Institution Press, 1999.

Rao, C. P., ed. *Globalization, Privatization and Free Market Economy*. Westport, CT: Quorum Books, 1998.

Rejai, Mostafa, ed. *Decline of Ideology?* Chicago: Aldine-Atherton, 1971.

Ricoeur, Paul. *Lectures on Ideology and Utopia*. Edited by George H. Taylor. New York: Columbia University Press, 1986.

Ritzer, George. *The McDonaldization of Society: An Investigation into the Changing Character of Contemporary Social Life*. Thousand Oaks, CA: Pine Forge Press, 1993.

——. *The McDonaldization Thesis: Explorations and Extensions*. Thousand Oaks, CA: Pine Forge Press, 1997.

————, ed. *The Blackwell Companion to Globalization*. Malden, MA: Wiley-Black-well, 2007.

————. *The Globalization of Nothing 2*. Thousand Oaks, CA: Pine Forge Press, 2007.

Robbins, Bruce. *Feeling Global*. New York: New York University Press, 1999.

Roberts, J. Timmons, and Amy Hite, eds. *From Modernization to Globalization*. Oxford: Blackwell, 2000.

Robertson, Roland. *Globalization: Social Theory and Global Culture*. London: Sage, 1992.

Robinson, William I. *Promoting Polyarchy: Globalization, U.S. Intervention, and Hegemony*. Cambridge: Cambridge University Press, 1996.

————. *A Theory of Global Capitalism: Production, Class, and the State in a Transnational World*. Baltimore: Johns Hopkins University Press, 2004.

Rodrik, Dani. *Has Globalization Gone Too Far?* Washington, DC: Institute for International Economics, 1997.

————. *One Economics, Many Recipes: Globalization, Institutions, and Economic Growth*. Princeton, NJ: Princeton University Press, 2007.

Rosenau, James N. *Distant Proximities: Dynamics beyond Globalization*. Princeton, NJ: Princeton University Press, 2003.

Roy, Olivier. *Globalized Islam: The Search for a New Ummah*. New York: Columbia University Press, 2004.

Rugman, A. *The End of Globalization*. New York: Random House, 2001.

Rupert, Mark. *Ideologies of Globalization: Contending Visions of a New World Order*. London: Routledge, 2000.

Rupert, Mark, and Hazel Smith, eds. *Historical Materialism and Globalization*. London: Routledge, 2002.

Ruthven, Malise. *A Fury for God: The Islamist Attack on America*. London: Granta, 2002.

Rydgren, Jens, ed. *Movements of Exclusion: Radical Right-Wing Populism in the Western World*. New York: Nova Science Publishers, 2005.

Sargent, Lyman Tower. *Contemporary Political Ideologies: A Comparative Analysis*. 11th ed. Fort Worth, TX: Harcourt Brace College Publishers, 1999.

Sassen, Saskia. *The Global City: New York, London, Tokyo*. Princeton, NJ: Princeton University Press, 1991.

————. *Globalization and Its Discontents: Essays on the New Mobility of People and Money*. New York: New Press, 1998.

————. *A Sociology of Globalization*. New York: W. W. Norton, 2007.

————. *Territory, Authority, Rights: From Medieval to Global Assemblages*. Princeton, NJ: Princeton University Press, 2008.

Saul, John Ralston. *The Collapse of Globalism: And the Reinvention of the World*. London: Penguin, 2005.

Schaeffer, Robert K. *Understanding Globalization*. 3d ed. Lanham, MD: Rowman & Littlefield, 2005.

Scholte, Jan Aart. *Globalization: A Critical Introduction*. 2d ed. Houndsmill: Palgrave Macmillan, 2005.

Schoonover, Thomas. *Uncle Sam's War of 1898 and the Origins of Globalization*. Lexington: University Press of Kentucky, 2003.

Scott, Alan, ed. *The Limits of Globalization: Cases and Arguments*. London: Routledge, 1997.

Scruton, Roger. *The West and the Rest: Globalization and the Terrorist Threat*. Wilmington, DE: ISI Books, 2002.

Sen, Amartya. *Development as Freedom*. New York: Knopf, 1999.

Sernau, Scott. *Bound: Living in the Globalized World*. West Hartford, CT: Kumarian Press, 2000.

Shaw, Martin. *Theory of the Global State: Globality as an Unfinished Revolution*. Cambridge: Cambridge University Press, 2000.

Simons, Thomas W. *Islam in a Globalizing World*. Stanford, CA: Stanford University Press, 2003.

Singer, Daniel. *Whose Millennium? Theirs or Ours?* New York: Monthly Review Press, 1999.

Singer, Peter. *The President of Good and Evil: Questioning the Ethics of George W. Bush*. New York: Dutton, 2004.

Sklair, Leslie. *Globalization: Capitalism and Its Alternatives*. 3d ed. Oxford: Oxford University Press, 2002.

Smith, Jackie. *Social Movements for Global Democracy*. Baltimore: Johns Hopkins University Press, 2007.

Smith, Jackie, and Hank Johnston, eds. *Globalization and Resistance: Transnational Dimensions of Social Movements*. Lanham, MD: Rowman & Littlefield, 2002.

Smith, Jackie, and Marina Karides, Marc Becker, Dorval Brunelle, Christopher Chase-Dunn, Donatella della Porta, Rosalba Icaza Garza, Jeffrey S. Juris, Lorenzo Mosca, Ellen Reese, Peter (Jay) Smith, and Rolando Vasquez. *Global Democracy and the World Social Forums*. Boulder, CO: Paradigm Publishers, 2008.

Sonntag, Selma K. *The Local Politics of Global English: Case Studies in Linguistic Globalization*. Lanham, MD: Lexington Books, 2003.

Soros, George. *The Crisis of Global Capitalism: Open Society Endangered*. New York: Public Affairs, 1998.

———. *George Soros on Globalization*. New York: Public Affairs, 2002.

Spencer, Herbert. *On Social Evolution*. Edited by J. D. Y. Peel. Chicago: University of Chicago Press, 1972.

Steger, Manfred B., ed. *Rethinking Globalism*. Lanham, MD: Rowman & Littlefield, 2004.

———. *The Rise of the Global Imaginary: Political Ideologies from the French Revolution to the Global War on Terror*. Oxford: Oxford University Press, 2008.

————. *Globalization: A Very Short Introduction.* 2nd ed. Oxford: Oxford University Press, 2009.

Stern, Nicholas. *The Economics of Climate Change: The Stern Review.* Cambridge: Cambridge University Press, 2007.

Stevis, Dimitris, and Terry Boswell. *Globalization and Labor: Democratizing Global Governance.* Lanham, MD: Rowman & Littlefield, 2007.

Stiglitz, Joseph E. *Globalization and Its Discontents.* New York: W. W. Norton, 2002.

————. *Making Globalization Work.* New York: W. W. Norton, 2007.

Strange, Susan. *The Retreat of the State: The Diffusion of Power in the World Economy.* Cambridge: Cambridge University Press, 1996.

————. *Mad Money: When Markets Outgrow Governments.* Ann Arbor: University of Michigan Press, 1997.

Tabb, William K. *The Amoral Elephant: Globalization and the Struggle for Social Justice in the Twenty-First Century.* New York: Monthly Review Press, 2001.

Taggart, Paul. *Populism.* Buckingham: Open University Press, 2000.

Taguieff, Pierre-Andre. *L'illusion populiste.* Paris: Berg International, 2002.

Tarrow, Sidney. *The New Transnational Activism.* Cambridge: Cambridge University Press, 2005.

Thomas, Caroline, and Peter Wilkin, eds. *Globalization and the South.* New York: St. Martin's Press, 1997.

Thornton, William H. *New World Empire: Civil Islam, Terrorism, and the Making of Neoglobalism.* Lanham, MD: Rowman & Littlefield, 2005.

Todd, Emmanuel. *After Empire: The Breakdown of the American Order.* New York: Columbia University Press, 2003.

Tomlinson, John. *Globalization and Culture.* Chicago: University of Chicago Press, 1999.

Van Dijk, Teun. *Discourse and Power.* Houndsmill: Palgrave Macmillan, 2008.

Väyrynen, Raimo, ed. *Globalization and Global Governance.* Lanham, MD: Rowman & Littlefield, 1999.

Veseth, Michael. *Selling Globalization: The Myth of the Global Economy.* Boulder, CO: Lynne Rienner, 1998.

————. *Globaloney: Unraveling the Myths of Globalization.* Lanham, MD: Rowman & Littlefield, 2006.

Wallach, Lori, and Michelle Sforza. *The WTO: Five Years of Reasons to Resist Corporate Globalization.* New York: Seven Stories Press, 1999.

Wallerstein, Immanuel. *The Politics of the World Economy.* Cambridge: Cambridge University Press, 1984.

Waters, Malcolm. *Globalization.* 2d ed. London: Routledge, 2001.

Waxman, Chaim I., ed. *The End of Ideology Debate.* New York: Funk & Wagnalls, 1968.

Weiss, Gilbert, and Ruth Wodak, eds. *Critical Discourse Analysis: Theory and Interdisciplinarity.* Houndsmill: Palgrave Macmillan, 2007.

Weiss, Linda. *The Myth of the Powerless State: Governing the Economy in a Global Era*. Ithaca, NY: Cornell University Press, 1998.

Went, Robert. *Globalization: Neoliberal Challenge, Radical Responses*. London: Pluto Press, 2000.

Wiggerhaus, Rolf, and Michael Robertson. *The Frankfurt School: Its History, Theories and Political Significance*. Boston: MIT Press, 1995.

Wilkinson, Rorden, ed. *The Global Governance Reader*. London: Routledge, 2005.

Wiltshire, David. *The Social and Political Thought of Herbert Spencer*. Oxford: Oxford University Press, 1978.

Wood, Ellen Meiksins. *Empire of Capital*. London: Verso, 2003.

Woods, Ngaire, ed. *The Political Economy of Globalization*. Basingstoke: Macmillan, 2000.

Yergin, Daniel, and Joseph Stanislaw. *The Commanding Heights: The Battle between Government and the Marketplace That Is Remaking the Modern World*. New York: Simon & Schuster, 1998.

Yuen, Eddie, George Katsiaficas, and Daniel Burton Rose, eds. *The Battle of Seattle: The New Challenge to Capitalist Globalization*. New York: Soft Skull Press, 2002.

Zakaria, Fareed. *The Post-American World*. New York: W. W. Norton, 2008.

Zizek, Slavoj, ed. *Mapping Ideology*. London: Verso, 1994.

# INDEX

# ABOUT THE AUTHOR

**Manfred B. Steger** is professor of global studies and director of the Globalism Research Centre at the Royal Melbourne Institute of Technology. He is also a senior research fellow at the Globalization Research Centre and affiliated faculty member in the Department of Political Science at the University of Hawaiʻi at Mānoa. He has served as an academic consultant on globalization for the U.S. State Department and as an adviser to the PBS television series *Heaven on Earth: The Rise and Fall of Socialism*. He is the author of fifteen books on globalization and the history of political ideas, including *The Rise of the Global Imaginary: Political Ideologies from the French Revolution to the Global War on Terror* (2008) and the best-selling *Globalization: A Very Short Introduction* (2003).